AFRICAN LAW: ADAPTATION AND DEVELOPMENT

Published under the auspices of the African Studies Center
University of California, Los Angeles

AFRICAN LAW: ADAPTATION AND DEVELOPMENT

Edited by HILDA KUPER
and LEO KUPER

UNIVERSITY OF CALIFORNIA PRESS
BERKELEY AND LOS ANGELES

1965

University of California Press
Berkeley and Los Angeles, California

Cambridge University Press
London, England

Library of Congress Catalog Card Number: 65-24589

Printed in the United States of America

PREFACE

The second interdisciplinary seminar arranged by the African Studies Center of the University of California, Los Angeles, was held in the spring of 1963. Its subject, "The Adaptation and Development of Law in Africa," poses theoretical problems for jurists, political scientists, sociologists and anthropologists; the practical implications for governments of the new African states are obviously crucial. The contributors of the essays that follow include social scientists concerned primarily with analysis of data, and legal experts more or less directly involved in drawing up statutes and framing constitutions.

We acknowledge contributions made to the discussions by the following participants: Ukpabi Asika, John Ballard, Ernst Benjamin, Edouard Bustin, Saul Cohen, James Coleman, Roberta Dunbar, Akin Euba, John Galbraith, Walter Goldschmidt, Bayo Kuku, Frank Kuntz, Ernest Landauer, Wyatt McGaffey, Paul Proehl, Kenneth Rothman, Murray Schwartz, Foster Sherwood, Inez Smith, Leonard Thompson, Gustave von Grunebaum, Cyril S. Whitaker, and Edgar Winans.

We are grateful to Professor Hassan Nouty of the University of California, Los Angeles, for editorial suggestions.

H. K. *and* L. K.

CONTRIBUTORS

ALLOTT, ANTONY N. Professor of African Law, School of Oriental and African Studies, University of London. Field experience in West Africa. Publications include *Essays in African Law with Special Reference to the Law of Ghana*; *Judicial and Legal Systems in Africa* (ed.); Managing Editor, *Journal of African Law*.

ANDERSON, J. N. D. Director, Institute of Advanced Legal Studies, and Dean, Faculty of Law, University of London. Field experience in North, East, and West Africa. Publications include *Islamic Law in Africa*; *Islamic Law in the Modern World*; "Islamic Law in Africa: Problems of Today and Tomorrow," in *Changing Law in Developing Countries*.

D'ARBOUSSIER, GABRIEL. Undersecretary of the Senegal Mission to the United Nations and Executive Director, United Nations Institute for Training and Research. Field experience in West Africa. Publications include "La Sénégal: exemple d'organisation judiciaire," *Recueil Penant* (April-May, 1961); "La Législation du Sénégal: législation de développement," in *Communication au Colloque des Facultés de Droit*, Dakar (May, 1962); "Le Fondement du socialisme africain," in *Cahiers: Documents pour l'action*, Léopoldville (1963).

ELIAS, T. O. Minister of Justice, Federal Government of Nigeria. Field experience in West Africa. Publications include *Groundwork of Nigerian Law; The Impact of English Law upon Nigerian Law; British Colonial Law.*

FORDE, DARYLL. Professor of Anthropology, University College, University of London, and Director of the International African Institute. Field experience in West Africa. Publications include *The Ibo and Ibibio-speaking Peoples of South-eastern Nigeria* (with G. I. Jones); *African System of Kinship and Marriage; Context of Belief; The Yakö.*

GLUCKMAN, MAX. Professor of Anthropology, University of Manchester, England. Field experience in South and Central Africa. Publications include *The Judicial Process among the Barotse of Northern Rhodesia; The Ideas in Barotse Jurisprudence; Politics, Law, and Ritual in Tribal Society.*

KUPER, HILDA. Professor of Anthropology, University of California, Los Angeles. Field experience in South Africa. Publications include *An African Aristocracy; The Uniform of Color; Indian People of Natal.*

KUPER, LEO. Professor of Sociology, University of California, Los Angeles. Field experience in South Africa. Publications include *Durban: A Study in Racial Ecology* (with Hilstan Watts and Ronald Davies); *Passive Resistance in South Africa; An African Bourgeoisie.*

MAYER, PHILIP. Professor of Anthropology, University of Witwatersrand, Johannesburg, Republic of South Africa. Field experience in South and East Africa. Publications include *The Lineage Principle in Gusii Society; Gusii Bridewealth Law and Custom; Townsmen or Tribesmen.*

RUBIN, LESLIE. Professor of Comparative Government and Acting Director, Program of African Studies, Howard University. Field experience in South and West Africa. Publications include *The Law of Costs in South Africa; Unauthorized Administration in South Africa; The Constitution and Government of Ghana* (with Pauli Murray).

SMITH, M. G. Professor of Anthropology, University of California, Los Angeles. Field experience in West Africa and West Indies. Publications include *Government in Zazzau, 1800-1950; The Plural Society in the British West Indies; Stratification in Grenada.*

VANSINA, JAN. Professor of History and Anthropology, University of Wisconsin. Field experience in Central Africa. Publications include "Histoire du Rwanda des origines à 1900," in *Académie royale des sciences d'outremer* (Brussels, 1962); "Le Royaume Kuba," in *Annales du Musée Tervuren* (1964); *Oral traditions.*

CONTENTS

PART I.

THEORETICAL INTRODUCTION

1.

INTRODUCTION*

by Hilda Kuper and Leo Kuper

The Concept of Law

Law is a word in such common usage that most people in Western societies are not likely to seek its meaning in a dictionary. They think they know what "law" means, even though they admit ignorance of specific laws. They accept law, together with government and religion, as part of their social equipment; in their dealings with their fellowmen they equate law with order, politics with government, religion with God.

But for jurists and sociologists who designate their disciplines as social sciences the matter is less simple. They are confronted with problems of comparison and generalization. A wide range of ethnographic data has led them to question familiar concepts and probe beyond current verbal symbols to deeper cultural meaning. Are politics, religion, and law conventional ethnocentric categories of Western intellectual development, rather than analytic constructs of general validity? Are they reflections, not of any universal reality, but of our pragmatic, culture-bound methods of organizing thought and behavior? Do they provide any units for systematic comparison?

Sociological studies of legal systems, based on research in preliterate societies, are indeed few,[1] partly because jurisprudence is not an area in which many anthropologists have specialized training, and partly because of limitations to sociological theory. There has been much controversy over definition in terms of the relative emphasis to be placed on function, structure, or ideation. The functional emphasis served to distinguish among general principles of social control; functionalists analyzed the operation of sanctions (moral and ritual as well as "legal") behind rules of conduct, rather than the structured units through which they were effected.[2] Structurally, the legal system was conceived as em-

*We are grateful to Professors James Coleman, Max Gluckman, Murray Schwartz, and Michael Smith for criticism of an earlier draft of this paper.

[1] For notes to chapter 1, see page 243.

bedded in corporate groups, whose boundaries might be deduced by regulation of membership; the alignment of these groups vis-à-vis one another provided the broad framework for social behavior. The ideational dimension was derived from interpretations of justice, rights, wrongs, and obligations of people toward one another and toward those selected meaningful things that become the property constituents of their society.[3]

Law has been considered an inclusive rubric for all rules of conduct, or has been narrowly defined as rules enforced by a specific and limiting procedure. If defined in narrow legalistic terms as that which is "recognized by the courts," or as "social control through the systematic application of force by politically organized society," the existence of "law" is denied many societies. This denial of law does not deny the maintenance of order by other mechanisms. As Radcliffe-Brown states, "some simple societies have no law, although all have customs which are supported by sanctions."[4]

Studies of people in different parts of the world indicate that there are many societies that have no separate lawmaking body, no courts, and no specific legal machinery for enforcing rules, yet they carry on a regulated existence and are able to cope with disputes without self-annihilation.[5] Such societies apparently continue to operate effectively through other types of organization and control. In societies that are relatively undifferentiated the component units of the structure are multifunctional in that they serve purposes we commonly define as religious, political, and legal. Multifunctional units are also more frequently based on the limiting principles of status—descent, locality, and age—than on contracted relationships established on the basis of individual training or interests. Even when their structures are consciously separated, they may operate within a single, conceptual frame of reference, so that the ideology of religious activity may act as a legal code or a political dogma.

The essays in this volume deal with societies different in many respects from those of America or Europe, and from one another. The range includes segmentary African societies (the Gusii and the Ibo), a partly centralized African kingdom (the Kuba), English and French colonies, the white settler–dominated state of South Africa, and independent African states. The societies vary also in the extent to which they differentiate legal structures and functions, and in the manner in which they deal with rights and obligations.

Whether or not their legal systems can be translated into mutually comprehensible, let alone comparable, concepts is recognized as being a controversial issue. In this volume, Jan Vansina, following Paul Bohannan's approach to law,[6] raises the question when he writes (p. 117):

"Kuba law is thus very different from any European legal system, and to try to define it in terms of European legal concepts is like trying to fit a Bantu grammar into a Latin model of grammatical categories, something that actually was done until descriptive linguistics taught us better." Vansina contrasts Kuba society, in which there are no legal norms but in which social norms function as legal norms, with "our society," in which "every institution" has been given a legal definition and all our social norms have been translated into legally defined norms.

The social scientist must, however, attempt both to interpret single, historically unique societies and to relate and classify them in more general categories. To refuse to speak of law, politics, or religion because nothing quite like them is to be found in other societies would be to refuse recognition of the study of "society" as something common to all forms of human existence.[7] In fact, Vansina is able to describe the Kuba system in terms of the concepts of Western jurisprudence. The difficulty arises in part from an implicit conception of law as a rational, systematic, codified body of rules (exemplified in the Code Napoléon) applied by the courts. But both Kuba and Western systems of law could be embraced in a more flexible concept of law, as, for example, that developed by H. L. A. Hart, professor of jurisprudence in the University of Oxford, who finds the core of a legal system in the union of primary rules of obligation, with secondary rules of recognition, change, and adjudication.[8]

A flexible and eclectic approach, rather than a firm semantic commitment, seems necessary. A comparative sociology of law requires the use of a wide range of terms to distinguish different legal processes in the context of the social relationships within which they occur,[9] and the analysis of legal systems in terms of the three dimensions of structure, function, and ideation. These dimensions appear in later sections of the introduction: the structural dimension is used in the distinction between homogeneous and plural societies; the functional, in the relations between law and society; and the ideational, in the role of theories of law in plural societies.

The Structural Context: Traditional, Homogeneous, and Colonial Plural Societies

If the analysis of law in its broad social and historical framework is to yield theoretically meaningful results, and not simply an assembly of unique and discrete items of knowledge, it is necessary that the observations be related within a theoretical system. A widely used approach is provided by comparative and developmental morphology: Thus Max Gluckman writes that

To understand a particular tribe's law we must see it in a comparative frame; and the main outlines of that frame have been drawn by Maine and many other jurists. When we contrast any tribal society with modern society we are also working with a distinction whose implications have been elaborated by many sociologists and anthropologists; the difference between Durkheim's mechanical and organic solidarities, Tönnies' gemeinschaft and gesellschaft, von Wiese's sacred and secular societies, Weber's traditional and bureaucratic societies, Stalin's patriarchal and industrial societies, Redfield's folk-society and urban civilization.[10]

These theories, as they are being refined by continuing research, offer a primary, theoretical orientation to the problem of the adaptation of African traditional systems of law to Western industrial society, represented by the colonial powers, and in the contemporary processes of modernization. They provide a classification of types of society, and a description of their characteristic elements, to which different systems of law may be related. But they are mainly concerned with change from societies in which social relations based on status predominate, to societies in which social relationships rest increasingly on contract; or from societies with a simple division of labor and bonds of similarity among their members, to societies with a complex division of labor and bonds of differentiation and interdependence; and so on. Or the theories deal with sharply contrasted pure or ideal types.

The essential characteristic of the colonies and the white-settler states of Africa was precisely the combination of sharply contrasted societal types within one political society at one historical moment in time, and the confrontation between different systems of law and government, and different theories of law and government, rooted in different structures of social relationships and organized in profoundly different institutional patterns. They are "plural" societies, and not "homogeneous" societies differentiating by evolutionary or internal process of change. But they are a special type of plural society, because of the nature of the contrast in social characteristics among their component parts. Africans may move directly from their communities, in which most of their rights and duties are defined by status, to social situations governed largely by contract, even without corresponding changes or progressive differentiation in their own communities. There are in consequence abrupt transitions by individuals from gemeinschaft to gesellschaft, and sharp discontinuities between groups. Elements derived from both the polar societal types are combined in unique constellations.

The plural society of colonialism, characterized by the simultaneous existence of often conflicting institutions of sharply contrasted types of society, was kept together at different levels of organization and was invested with legal (constitutional) validity by the politically dominant colonial power. It was necessary to incorporate an increasing range of situations—the multiple contingencies that fell outside the framework of both societies but resulted from their interaction.

We suggest that it clarifies concepts to distinguish the plural society as a special type of society with its own characteristic mechanisms of change and modes of social control, rather than to subsume it as a variant of one of the polar types in the developmental theories. This approach is taken by Smith in the first paper of this colloquium, "The Sociological Framework of Law." In the homogeneous society, members share the same basic institutions—political, economic, religious, familial, and educational. In plural societies, there is a combination of structural pluralism and cultural pluralism, the former term describing cleavage between groups, and the latter term, their use of different institutions.[11]

The traditional [12] African societies of the Gusii, the Ibo, and the Kuba, considered in abstraction from the colonial setting, are examples of relatively homogeneous societies. Although they are characterized by varied types of structural differentiation—lineage or clan segmentation among the Gusii, territorial grouping among the Ibo, and more or less independent chiefdoms in the Kuba Kingdom—members of each society nevertheless share the same basic institutions. The colonial societies, the newly independent African states, and the Republic of South Africa are all plural societies, characterized by the diversity of their peoples and cultures, and, in varying measure, by the cleavages between culturally distinctive racial and ethnic groups.

The Structural Dimension of Law in Traditional Societies

The legal systems of "traditional" African societies are extremely diverse. In some there are no units or offices that coincide with the Western concept of a judiciary. In others, only the religious aspect of power is institutionalized, and it provides the main sanction for public activities. Yet in others there are elaborately conceptualized and verbally defined distinctions, a separation of legal from other institutions. The differentiation of jural components within the total social structure provides a possible, albeit limited, starting point for comparative analysis of these different legal systems.

The traditional systems in this volume are primarily those of the Gusii, the Ibo, and the Kuba. The Gusii, described by the Mayers, are East African agriculturalists and pastoralists. In the indigenous society they were organized into a number of clans, with no central authority and no clan hierarchy; the clans were autonomous, discrete units, characterized by equality in structure. The Gusii identified the land they used with clan membership, and, in clan land, agnates formed the core of corporate neighborhood communities. Conduct toward clansmen and outsiders was regulated by the fact that "every Gusii accepted in principle certain codes of law, usage, and convention." Political and legal relations were scarcely differentiated. Competition was considered inherent in the nature of man: clans competed for territory and power; families and individuals, for cattle and personal influence. There were no recognized agents for peaceful settlement of disputes between clans. Within the clan the most specific procedure for dealing with conflict, and lessening recourse to violence, was provided by appeal to individual men who were sufficiently recognized to be specifically designated, *etureti*. Their position was based on personality, knowledge, and ability, but was not rigidly defined nor attached to any corporate group, and carried no executive authority. Yet their opinion was taken as expressing a general consensus, which, if not accepted by a disputant, permitted the other party to seize his due with the approval of the community. Paradoxically, in a society emphasizing the principle of descent, the main position of legal significance was not hereditary.

The Ibo society of West Africa, described by Forde, has certain structural similarities with the Gusii, though in many aspects of culture they are strikingly dissimilar. Like the Gusii, the Ibo were acephalous and organized on the basis of descent. But the Ibo descent units were lineages of unequal size and power, associated with local villages, which might incorporate unrelated people. Legal functions were more clearly delineated than among the Gusii. Although no single individual was recognized as chief, there were well-defined councils corresponding to different levels of lineage structure, and ritual and moral (not executive) authority was vested in the *okpara,* senior representative of the lineage. The Ibo council was a corporation of important elders with formal office and distinctive insignia, who relied in matters of common concern on other members of the lineage. Distinct from the genealogical validation of positions of influence was the recognition of achieved power by the personal qualities of an ambitious individual, a "big man" (*onye uku*). These "big men" were men of wealth or ability who, like the Gusii etureti, could stand outside lineage alignment. But whereas the etureti were essentially arbitrators required to express what they considered to be the general consensus, the Ibo big men were able to manipulate the system and influence decisions. Restraining them from behaving in too arbitrary a fashion was the fact that they themselves were vulnerable to the local opinion that had brought them into prominence and operated within the community of descent. Enforcement of decisions varied with the nature of the offense, the span of the group involved, and the roles assigned to age-grades and other associations.

Superficially, the acephalous societies of Gusii and Ibo stand in sharp contrast to the centralized Kuba Kingdom in the former Kasai Province of the Republic of Congo, described by Vansina. Formed by eighteen tribes of some cultural diversity, their political unity was symbolized by the chief of the tribe that had won its position by force. The other tribes, each with its own representatives, constituted local and relatively autonomous chiefdoms. Lineage ties were effective, but within narrow local boundaries; there is nothing intrinsically incompatible between a lineage system and a centralized monarchy. A developed interregional market complex underpinned the political structure, and the chiefdoms were linked to the kingdom by economic tribute,[13] diplomatic marriages, and representation on councils of titleholders in an elaborate system of graded political and administrative offices. Each chiefdom included a number of villages, inhabited by people of several clans. Within the village (the smallest political unit), disputes were dealt with by "moots," informal gatherings of neighbors and kinsmen; within the chiefdom judgment was dispensed by formal courts with well-defined procedure; within the kingdom, conflicts between chiefdoms led either to war or to arbitration by an outsider, not necessarily the king.

The two principles of candidature for office which were kept distinct among the Ibo—birth and personality—were combined in the office of Kuba chiefs. Chieftaincy was restricted to certain clans, but the chief, himself, was elected by a council of other clans which also had the power to depose. Although the office was held to exist by divine right, the person was not divine, and there was no genealogical precedence of lineages from which a chief or a king was drawn. In one sense, the king was only the leading prince, but, once appointed, he was invested with a sacred aura which bestowed authority in various public situations.

Among the Lozi of Northern Rhodesia, in whose judicial procedures Gluckman has analyzed the concept of the "reasonable man" discussed by him in this volume, there was a yet more structured hierarchy of courts and a more definite legal procedure.[14] Like the Kuba, the Lozi represent a conquest state built of culturally heterogeneous groups. They adapted their mode of life to seasonal floods which forced a large proportion of the population, including the king and his royal household, to move from the villages on the mounds, permanent loci of social organization, to more temporary residences on the margins of the plain. Through historical circumstances combined with these unusual ecological conditions, the Lozi developed a highly complex political network revolving around two pivotal, but politically unequal, regions, each associated with the concept of kingship. Within the kingdom the villages, which vary considerably in their composition, are the basic political units. The Lozi have no segmentary lineages, and some of the villages, attached to offices of state, are under headmen whose position is not hereditary. Other villages are groupings of kin, with hereditary headmanship. Disputes are contained within a well-defined hierarchy of *kuta* (councils which are also courts), each with its officials, titles, and ordered process of investigation and judgment. Theoretically, the total body of law is known and certain, but each contestant is involved in a range of interacting and varied interests and the court is concerned with elements of reconciliation as well as blame. The courts established by the king are able to enforce judgment, and all verdicts are ultimately given in the king's name.

The religious context of the legal system in these societies is as varied as the political. There is a general assumption that in traditional societies "religion" is widely diffused and sanctions conduct in all situations. But, in fact, religion influences a larger or smaller field of social life according to the total conceptual structure of particular societies, and sanctions are associated with different sources of religious authority. The Gusii have no distinctive priesthood; but a well-defined ancestral cult, which does not exclude recognition of other deities, sanctions behavior between clansmen. The Ibo also have "right" kinship behavior emphasized by lineage elders who intercede with their own ancestors, but in addition there are local priests who officiate in the cult of the earth or other tutelary deity of the community. The techniques of the priests include invocation and ordeal, and the cults exert strong moral pressure against violence, incest, adultery, and "other abominations."

The Kuba have a different conceptual particularization in their legal system. Cases of murder and witchcraft (but no others) are referred to the poison ordeal, control of which is vested in the king, because, Vansina argues, matters of life and death are matters of kingship derived from the same supernatural source. Among the Lozi, disputes between kinsmen may provoke ancestral spirits to inflict punishment. In addition to priests of the ancestral cult, who occupy their offices by virtue of their positions in kinship groups, the Lozi have ritual specialists who act for the state. In the past, the Lozi manipulated "extrajudicial" methods, particularly in charges of sorcery; cases involving the spilling of blood, an accusation of sorcery, or treason, had to be referred to the capital *kuta*.[15] The use of the ordeal by Kuba, Ibo, and Lozi indicates that it may buttress different types of authority and moral order.

Descriptions of empirical association between different elements in the various legal systems and their structural contexts are not causal explanations, nor do they indicate necessary correlations. There is no logical *necessity* for the coherence of particular cultural elements in any social structure; there is only a probability. Jural obligations may be articulated by persons other than judges. Formal legal procedures are not necessarily absent from societies organized only in corporate lineages; conversely, councils of kinsmen may have legal functions in centralized kingdoms with a hierarchy of courts. A council of elders is only one of several possible types of legal corporation which could be linked with an earth cult. The ordeal, which may assume a wide variety of forms, is not restricted to societies with kingship, and the position of king may receive different types of "supernatural" as well as mundane validation.

Justice is structured in many situations outside the legal system. The laws, the standards of right and wrong behavior, are contingent on such principles as kinship, status, and office. Action and counteraction reflect the evaluation of particular social relations. Among the Kuba, the king is above the law. Among the Ibo, there is a tacit right of notables, guilty of recognized major offenses, to offer their less fortunate fellows as substitutes for punishment. Intention or nonintention is relative; in cases of homicide where killer and victim are of the same lineage, expiation is the dominant principle, but when the killer is of another lineage, the circumstances—whether the killing was murderous or unintended—affect the redress.

The obligation to settle disputes and the manner of settlement are also relative to the structure of the social relationship between the parties. Certain general principles may be involved. The closer the relationship, the greater the danger of antagonism and the stronger the control over destructive retaliation. Hence the type of weapon among the Gusii is regulated by the social distance between disputants. When kinsmen dispute, the ancestors are likely to intervene; between unrelated people other mechanisms are necessary.

Social life implies not only order, but continuity. Every society provides for future contingencies; thus rules of descent, succession, and inheritance project into the future the intimate relationship between man and woman and the probability of children, and every office involves modes of dealing with foreseeable emergencies. But the contingencies provided for in a traditional society are largely within the established framework and within the range of expectations of its members. A different situation arises when traditional autonomous communities are brought within the confines of a new political unit, created by an alien power with its own externally defined policies of social change and its own legal concepts and apparatus.

Inevitably the social context of law in the traditional societies was changed under colonial rule, and the legal systems were modified even where policy was directed to the maintenance of indigenous institutions. These changes, which are referred to in the papers that follow, vary with the different characteristics of the traditional systems. The principles governing the variation are still a problem for research. Some contribution may be made to the understanding of these principles by examining the reactions of different traditional legal systems to the same colonial policy, and of similar legal systems to different policies.

Theory of Law in Plural Societies: An Ideational Analysis

Apart from the internal differences indicated in the discussion of traditional societies, which are relevant to an understanding of adaptation of legal systems in modern Africa, the varied policies of the colonial powers are of major significance. These policies are based on different theoretical premises.

Smith, in his paper, seeks an explanation for variations among French, British, and Islamic policies in different theories of law, historically rooted in the dominant societies. French civil law, he argues, most perfectly expresses the dominant rational Western theory of law, logically coherent, complete and closed; it assumes a primary, sovereign corporation, the state, and regards the imperium of the French state as the sole and ultimate source of law. It could not admit the logical or historical existence of native corporations independent of or antecedent to the colonial regime; hence the French theory of law denied recognition, and the French practice of law found difficulty in according recognition, to African polities and customs. British common law derives from a secular empiricist tradition, in which corporations emerged as independent juridical personalities with relative autonomy and rule-making functions. The sources of law include not only custom, precedent, judicial decision, legislation, and equity, but also the rules made by these corporations; hence the British theory of law accorded recognition to African polities and customs, and the practice of law permitted flexible accommodation to African societies. By contrast, Muslim law is based on a tradition of theocratic pragmatism; law is sacred, its source being the Koran and the Sunna. In practice it is supplemented by regulations derived from custom or the discretion of the ruler, who is free to recognize the corporate organization of his subjects; hence, in both theory and practice, recognition may readily be accorded to African polities and customs.

Many different elements enter into this thesis, both as causal factors and as consequences. The theory of law in the above discussion is primarily a theory relating to sources of law: the imperium of the French state, British tradition, divine ordinance in Islam. A theory of the sources of law is presumably at the same time a theory of the legitimation of law. In the present context, the theory includes a distinction between the sacred and the secular nature of law, which may be related in turn to the range of behavior regulated by law. Anderson comments in his paper on the greatly extended range of regulated behavior under Islamic law, a concept that may be valid for other systems of sacred law. The theory of law, as Smith shows, also includes differences in the style of legal thought, such as the extent of logical closure and formal completeness, or in emphasis on specific rule as against general principle.

These causal elements may be expected to affect the adaptation of law by their influence on government and administration, by the nature of the social differentiations or cleavages they make legally relevant, by the problems they raise in regard to the legitimation of law, and by the processes of legal and social change they encourage. The theory and practice of government are related to the theory of law, as the recognition accorded corporations has relevance for policies of direct or indirect rule. The administration of law is affected, the common-law tradition having a greater affinity for a dual system of African and English law than the more highly rationalized civil-law system, with its emphasis on imperium. The content of law is also affected, though clearly there is no simple correlation between the French theory of law and tendencies toward the unification of law in the colonies, on the one hand, and, on the other hand, the British theory of law and trends toward diversification of law.

From the point of view of social differentiation, the plural society itself may be organized in different ways, and may emphasize different lines of cleavage, in some relationship to the theory of law. Law deriving from divine revelation may tend to emphasize divisions between believers and nonbelievers; British common-law tradition, and recognition of African authority and custom, encourage distinction by race and division between whites and Africans; French civil-law tradition and the policy of assimilation substitute culture for race, in theory, and distinguish French and *évolué* from *indigène*. Reflecting the cleavages in plural societies, the different bases for the legitimation of law are likely to be a source of conflict. For the French colonial rulers, for example, the law of the colonial society derives legitimacy from the authority of the French state; for its subject peoples, this law can have legitimacy only insofar as they recognize the French imperium as legitimate. Conversely, the legitimacy of African law may rest on tradition or divine ordinance in African society, but may depend for legitimacy in the colonial society on explicit statutory recognition under the imperium of the colonial power.

With respect to processes of change, theories of law may be associated with conservative or liberal tendencies; presumably secular law is more easily changed than sacred law, and a common-law system may be more flexible than a civil-law system. Perhaps different theories of law affect the approach to the relations between law and society, and the choice of techniques of social change. Emphasis on imperium and the primacy of the state would tend to emphasize the role of law in shaping society, and to encourage the use of legislation for directed social change. Emphasis on tradition and recognition of corporate autonomy would tend to emphasize law as derivative from society, and to diminish the role of legislation in directed change.[16] The theory of law in the colonial society may also be related to the attitude to lawmaking on independence. Thus Elias, in "The Evolution of Law and Government in Modern Africa," contrasts the eclecticism of legislators and jurists in the former British territories with the commitment to the Code Napoléon and the indifference to the study of indigenous customary law and comparative law in the former French territories.

The papers collected in this volume offer much material bearing on the relations between theories of law and the adaptation of legal systems, but any precise testing of these relationships is a matter of great complexity. A theory of law is not without ambiguity; or, at any rate, schools of jurisprudents may differ in regard to their interpretation of the theory of law embodied in a particular system of law, or in the relative emphasis given to component elements of the theory of law. Hence very different practices may be explained by reference to the same theory of law.

Even if a theory of law should be quite unambiguous, it operates in a context of other ideas, religious or political. The recognition of African authority and custom which Smith relates to the theories of law in the civil- and common-law systems is usually ascribed, in the present conventions of African studies, to the different political theories of assimilation (identity) or differentiation (association). Save in such specifically legal situations as judicial decision, it becomes difficult to extricate the theory of law from its wider context, and to assess its relative significance. This raises the question as to whether the theory of law is essentially an aspect or an expression of political theory, or whether it has a broad independent sphere of influence.

Further difficulties in assessing the consequences of a theory of law arise from the complex relations between a theory of law and its practice. According to Anderson, it is impossible to discuss Islamic law, in any context, with clarity or precision without making a clear-cut distinction between jurisprudential theory of the law and its theological concepts, on the one hand, and the realities of that law, as it has evolved in history and is administered in practice, on the other: "The theory is rigid, monolithic, uncompromising; the facts are often much more flexible, syncretic, and equivocal" (p. 151).

There may be sharp divergence between the rationally anticipated and the actually observed consequences of a theory. Discussing the French policy of assimilation,[17] d'Arboussier points out that the legislators in the newly independent state of Senegal had anticipated that the foundations of custom would have disappeared, whereas in fact the great mass of the population had continued to live "absolument selon la coutume." Here there was a divergence between theory and practice, assimilation being directed, according to d'Arboussier, only toward those who were useful to the colonial power under a system of laws serving French economic interests and certain public functions.

Colonial practice is full of contradictions. Delavignette writes that "France, supposedly assimilationist, has given votes to certain Senegalese and made them eligible for election to her Parliament; but has she not at the same time respected the principle of association in safeguarding their Moslem status? . . . Assimilation *or* Association? In fact one does not have to make an unconditional choice. Assimilation *and* Association. The two formulas are often combined; the dosage of each varies with the practitioner's dexterity and the temperature of events."[18] Leslie Rubin, in "The Adaptation of Customary Family Law in South Africa," points to similar inconsistencies. The Cape Colony in the nineteenth century did not formally recognize African customary law, but in the Transkei, on the contrary, from the date of its incorporation into the Cape Colony, customary law was recognized. Natal, under the same system of Roman-Dutch law, modified and amplified by English law, followed a policy of differentiation toward the Zulu, with codification of their laws and customs; and yet at the same time it provided the means for exemption from customary law on proof of ability to read and write, an exemption more consistent with policies of assimilation.

Policy may change over time, with or without corresponding changes in the theory of law. Hoebel and Schiller[19] describe the fluctuations between legal dualism and unification in the policy of the Netherlands toward Indonesia. Crowder[20] shows changes in the attitude toward assimilation and its implementation in Senegal, while the French theory of law presumably remained unchanged. In South Africa there has been an increasing emphasis on a policy of thoroughgoing differentiation, accompanied—paradoxically, in terms of the thesis we are discussing—by an increasing emphasis on the imperium of the state as the source and the legitimation of law.

Adding to the complexity of the relations between the theory of law and the practice of law is the fact that the theory may actually provide for deviation in practice, or, in a sense, may legitimize deviation. This is the tenor of Smith's argument regarding Islam. The duty of obedience to the ruler enjoined in the Koran, and the overriding religious obligation of the ruler to maintain and expand Islam, serve to legitimate expedient deviations. Anderson gives a slightly different interpretation; instead of a conception of the ruler as in some measure authorized to deviate from the *sharī'a*, he suggests rather the possibility of a plausible ex post facto justification of deviation as a legitimate manifestation of the ruler's right, under the *sharī'a* itself, to confine and define the jurisdiction of his courts. In either event, whether the process is interpreted as a legitimation or as a rationalization, the theory of law provides a mechanism for the recognition of systems of law in conflict with the *sharī'a*.

Many rationalizations or legal fictions or ways of defining a situation may be used to reconcile theory and practice. Anderson shows that rules actually derived from custom may nevertheless be regarded as owing their authority to one or another of the four formal sources of Islamic law. A flexible device for adjusting divine law to practical necessity, and indeed for making new laws without sacrifice of orthodoxy, may be found in the variety of opinions held by schools of jurists. New codes of law may be perceived as additions to divine law, rather than as contraventions; the divine law may be set aside, and in this way be preserved intact and inviolate. Where customary law is unwritten, conflict with the divine law is less manifest, and customary law can more readily be integrated in apparent conformity with a theory of the divine origin of law. Similarly, where sacred law prescribes detailed rules, rather than general principles of conduct, it may more easily incorporate specific customs. There may thus be considerable flexibility in the relations between divine ordinance and secular practice.

Two apparently contradictory interpretations of the nature of sacred or revealed law are given by d'Arboussier and Anderson. D'Arboussier criticizes the belief that written law is more rigid and unwritten customary law is more supple and responsive to social change, on the ground that custom (in African societies) is rendered immutable by its sacred character, which links it to the religious beliefs sanctioned by gods or the ancestors. Anderson's discussion of Islamic law shows that the immutability of divinely revealed law is no barrier to change, and that there may be contrary secular developments which are, however, not perceived as affecting the divine law.

Indeed, the very nature of divine revelation, with its otherworldly logic but its this-worldly social context of ancient Judaic or Arabic or African ancestral society, may facilitate the process of legal change by reason of the irrelevance, or inappropriateness, or silence, or lack of precise reference, or mystical or tanscendental quality of the divine law. Similarly, a highly rational and codified system of law, by its very inappropriateness and rigidity when applied to societies of a sharply contrasted character, may impose the necessity for an extensive, flexible, *de facto* adaptation outside the institutional framework of the law.

The adaptation of African systems of law will be affected not only by the theories of law of the colonial powers or of Islam, but also by African theories of law, whether explicitly formulated or implicit in legal institutions.[21] Probably there are many different theories of law in African societies, varying perhaps in their relative emphasis on imperium, tradition, and divine revelation. They have not been much studied in the past. Now emancipation from colonial rule is stimulating this study. Denigration of African society and law naturally provokes the demonstration that traditional African societies were regulated by just and efficient systems of law. This demonstration may take the form of drawing close parallels between African and European systems of law, or of seeking out qualities of law, uniquely African and superior to European. Racial counterassertion may emphasize a more democratic participation in the work of the courts, or deeper concern in African law for the human quality of a person, or stronger group consciousness and a more sensitive awareness of the social context, encouraging the reconciliation of persons rather than the apportionment of blame, regardless of disruptive social consequences.

Many pressures, political, economic, and social, impel the quest for appropriate theories of African law. There is the need for stability in newly independent states, and for unity, transcending the plural divisions within the nation-state. There is the internal struggle for power, in which theories of law may be forged as political weapons. There are economic pressures, and the search for formulas of efficient modernization, socialism finding a charter in the communal organization of African society, and capitalism, perhaps a little more doubtfully, in the scope for African initiative within traditional society. There is the appeal of the political philosophy of Pan-Africanism, which encourages the search for a specifically African theory and system of law on the assumption that the unity of African law will promote the unity of African societies.

It is in such milieus of thought and action that theories of African law may emerge as by-products of political and economic processes. The changed situation from colonial subjugation to national independence, with the realization of sovereignty and the compulsions to modernize, seems likely to encourage an emphasis on imperium as the source of law. The influence of purely legal considerations, such as a tradition of civil or common or sacred law, may not be decisive. In many respects, it may convey more understanding to analyze the new theories of law in the period of their emergence as ideologies. Once established, they no doubt exert an independent influence on other aspects of the society.

Law and Society in Homogeneous and Plural Colonial Societies

The relationship of law to society may be expected to vary in different types of society. Smith suggests (pp. 26-27) differences in the role of law in homogeneous and plural societies:

> Whereas in homogeneous societies it is society that constitutes law, in plural societies, such as those of Africa, there is evidence that law may serve to constitute society. Thus law both derives from and may establish society.
>
> In the first instance the social milieu is typically homogeneous, ethnically and culturally, and the basis of society is primarily consensual; in this situation law may express organic institutional relations. In plural societies, on the other hand, the social milieu is heterogeneous in cultural and ethnic constitution and coercive in base, and the law that seeks to constitute it and serves to regulate it is essentially sectional. In the culturally homogeneous society, the state—that is, the central political institutions—is, like law, a derivative, expressive, and secondary structure. In the evolution of plural units the state preexists society, and provides the legal framework within which the new society may or may not emerge. . . .
>
> While law is a social fact in homogeneous units, as Durkheim holds, in colonial pluralism it is clearly in some sense presocietal. . . .

The distinction in the nature of law in the two types of society is analogous to the one that sociologists have sometimes drawn between folkways, arising out of the "natural," spontaneous, and nonreflective life of groups, and stateways, representing the "artificial," relatively external regulation of groups by deliberate enactment. It is also reminiscent of the contrast between the political theories of Hobbes and Locke, the plural society corresponding in some ways to the Leviathan of Hobbes's theory, and homogeneous society to Locke's concept of civil society.

There are many implications of this thesis, relating to the legitimation of law, the role of repressive law, and the use of law as an index of social relationships. The homogeneous community is autonomous in the sense that its normative order is established by its own members and not imposed by outsiders, whereas in a plural society obedience to the norms of an external power is enforced. Legitimacy in the homogeneous society, where both law and the state derive from society, rests on the traditional acceptance of established patterns of social relationship. In the plural society of the colonial type, law is legitimated, if at all, by the sovereign command of the colonial power. For the subject peoples, law may remain or may become identified with conquest and alien rule, leading to the rejection, not only of specific laws, but of law and order itself—a trend to be observed in the Republic of South Africa. Law and morality may become increasingly detached, as the formal justice of the rulers impinges upon substantive justice, imposing order without morality.

The role of repressive law should be smaller in homogeneous than in plural societies, if the basis of homogeneous society is primarily consensual and that of plural society primarily coercive. Durkheim sought in the very element of consensus in homogeneous society the motive force for repressive law, and in the division of labor and organic solidarity the stimulus for the growth of restitutive law. Plural societies, however, cannot be equated with societies based on organic solidarity. They are *sui generis*. Characterized by a considerable division of labor, they combine in their legal systems an extensive development of both repressive and restitutive law.

The use of law as an index of social life is affected by the difference in the relationship between law and society in homogeneous and plural societies. If the basis of homogeneous society is primarily consensual, and law is a derivative expression of institutional relations, then law may be used as a direct measure of social relationships. But it is difficult to know what law measures in plural societies because of the diversity of legal traditions or systems. There is the "received law" of the colonial powers, related to the social context of British or French society. There is Muslim law, with its varied social contexts: the ideal society of the Koran and the Sunna, or the actual society of the bearers of Islam, whether traders carrying their personal religion and religious law into the interior, or warriors establishing dominion and spreading many of their institutions by conquest. Then there are the laws of different African ethnic units, with their varied social structure and culture, somewhat arbitrarily drawn together into new political societies. And, finally, there is the law arising from the interaction of the different groups in societies dominated by white settlers, or in colonial societies, with their policies of assimilation or differentiation, or in independent African states, formulating political philosophies which express varied conceptions of African freedom, significance, and identity.

Because law tends to be sectional, with dual or parallel systems, it must first be related as a measure of social life to the particular group whose activities it governs. But the relationship is not direct precisely because of the presence of other groups. Where African customary law is retained in the context of colonial or white-settler domination (as is generally true of personal and family law), it reflects aspects of the traditional life of the African society, but as regulated by administrators of the dominant group, and as harmonized with the structure of alien domination. The interests, ideologies, and perspectives of the rulers intervene between African custom and its legal expression. The sectional law both expresses and modifies customary relationships.

The use of the general law to measure the common area of living is even more complex than the use of sectional law to measure relations internal to each of the groups that compose the plural society. Laws linked with industrial society, and regulating behavior in fields new to Africans, become part of the general law of the total society. Some of these laws act fairly uniformly throughout the society, but many, both in industry and in other spheres, have different meanings and functions for the varied groups, again imposing the need for sectional interpretation. Bohannan[22] discusses the different interpretations of the same legal institution in terms of what he describes as the "folk systems" of Africans and of Europeans, and Forde in the present volume shows differences in the concept of "warrant chiefs" among the southern Ibo. While much of criminal law tends to become generally applicable, different meanings may attach to both crime and punishment. Forde points out that among the southern Ibo prison sentences[23] for assaults "deprived the injured of the compensation they traditionally expected, and often came to be seen as a means of escape and even of reward through good food for the violent. Punishment for accusation, as opposed to the practice of sorcery, reversed the order of traditional legal values whereby sickness and misfortune afforded occasions for exposing and punishing those who had long been suspected of malevolence. . . . In sorcery cases . . . the initial assumptions and criteria of the hearing and the judgment appeared to turn indigenous judicial logic upside down."

Our discussion of the relations between law and society in homogeneous and plural societies has been in terms of hypothetical extreme contrasts. These are to be interpreted as referring to dominant tendencies in the two types of society, and not as precise descriptions of actual societies, in which law and society continuously interact. Thus, when a homogeneous society of a segmentary type becomes centralized under the domination of one of its segments, law may be used not only to legitimate the domination, that is to say, a process of law following society, but also to restructure the society in the interests of that domination, a process of society following law. In other words, homogeneity does not exclude such dynamic elements of change as a struggle for power, and the instrumental use of law in that struggle.

The Mayers, in their paper "Land Law in the Making," illustrate this process, though in a situation where the presence of whites is a significant factor. They discuss how, among the Kikuyu, competing interests in land were expressed in the ideological form of conflicting interpretations of customary law, whereas among the Gusii these competing interests led to an extension of an accepted precedent of traditional law relating to bridewealth. Changes in the customary organization of the Gusii became the basis for land law, but these changes, and the legal innovations (by which law followed society), were assisted by the use of traditional machinery for adjudication and traditional legal precedents (society following law). Both examples illustrate the complex interplay of law and society under the dynamic of interest.

Although it is more difficult to think of law in plural societies as derivative from social relationships, there is nevertheless a continuous interaction between law and society. In the early stages of the establishment of the plural society, the socially constitutive force of law is most marked, but even then there is the reciprocal influence of society on law, which may be observed in the frustration of legislative intention, or in the modification of laws under the pressure or resistance of ongoing social processes. Later, law increasingly charts the process of interaction, as social relationships precede and influence law. There is always an interplay between the derivative and constitutive aspects of law. On independence, the constitutive aspects of law gain new significance.

D'Arboussier refers, in the introduction to his paper, to the "faim de législation" which followed independence. The phrase expresses the enthusiasm and the impatience of leaders in the independent African states to shape a new society, freed from the old colonial domination, united, modern, and responsive to African aspirations. It expresses confidence in the role of law as providing the effective means for creating the new society, and the inescapable need for legislation to lay the foundations.

One of the main legislative tasks in the independent states is to use law to resolve the pluralism of their societies. Under the colonial system pluralism did not threaten the colonial power; on the contrary, it facilitated continued rule. Hence the multiple systems of law, expressive of the pluralism of colonial societies, served to support colonial rule by maintaining in some measure the divisions among the plural segments of the society. Colonial power was challenged by the unification of the plural segments, and not by the threatened secession of one of the plural units. By contrast, pluralism threatens the independent states with conflict, or dissolution. A measure of social unity can be maintained by force, and dictatorial trends are no doubt one response to the threat of pluralism. Alternatively, law may be used to create a more homogeneous society, or to contain the plural diversities. The papers by Elias and Allott deal specifically with these issues.

The hypothetical extremes in the legal response to pluralism are acceptance of diversity at the local level with some loose form of association at the national level, and an attempted unification of substantive and procedural law at all levels. Between these extremes lie the actual solutions which attempt a balancing of plural and unitary forces. This balancing may rest on locality; or it may rest on role, the plural principle being recognized in respect to certain roles and the unitary principle in respect to others; or it may rest on a combination of locality and role. For example, while general policy may be directed toward unification of the law, the plural structure of the society may be recognized in an advisory or legislative role for the traditional chiefs. Or, the plural principle may be expressed in the provision that customary law or religious law should govern roles in the family, while the unitary principle is expressed in the definition of political and economic roles, such as the rights and duties of citizenship, wage regulation, industrial conciliation, trade-union organization, and so on.

Far from achieving a balance, the unitary and plural principles are likely to be in continuous tension. These tensions are dramatic and disruptive when they directly affect relations between local and national units. Tensions are also present in the relations between plural and unitary roles. For example, the recognition of religious differences, as in the concessions to Islamic principles in the new Northern Nigerian Penal Code, mentioned by Anderson, may have the effect of imposing more onerous obligations, or different obligations, on citizens of a particular faith, in tension with the unifying principle of equality before the law. These tensions between roles may activate conflict among the plural units themselves.

Where some measure of recognition is accorded traditional law, it generally includes the family. But the preservation of pluralism in family structure may have consequences that conflict with national unification. Influenced by the image of the family in industrial societies as relatively detached, there is a tendency to underestimate the significance of family structure for the general structure of the society. In fact, different family institutions often sustain plural division. They may be associated with differences in education, and in economic and political participation; and they provide a basis for exclusive perspectives and the conservation of divisive custom. In resolving pluralism, the family may be a fundamental area for change. Allott expresses the significance of family law for the maintenance of custom when he observes that if the succession law goes, then the whole fabric of customary laws will go with it.

Other approaches to unification may be distinguished in terms of an emphasis on law shaping society, or society shaping law. Programs for the unification of different customary laws, and of law received from the colonial power, give primacy to law. There may be an element of false deduction in this approach. Since the unity of a society is often expressed in a unified system of law, the unity of law becomes associated with the unity of society, and from being an index or consequence of that unity is transposed into a cause. One of the results of a hasty unification of law may be to stimulate the growth of a diversity of deviating customs.

The movement from society to law is encouraged by mechanisms through which unifying currents in the society find expression in law, as, for example, a measure of unification of the courts, as distinct from unification of the law, or provision for appeal from customary to general courts. Similarly the legal guarantee of fundamental human rights in the constitution may initiate social processes that encourage members of the different plural units to leave the tenuous security of their groups for the more varied and extended relationships of the wider society, and in this way ultimately promote unification of the law.

This volume deals with the development and the adaptation of law in Africa, but has a wider than regional relevance. The societies of Africa are themselves highly diversified in structure and history, and the essays analyze problems pertinent to the broad field of the sociology of law, in both theory and application. They indicate complexities in interpreting legal systems and in relating them to the process of change, and they reveal some of the difficulties confronting governments in their efforts to shape social relations by deliberate legislation. The new national governments of Africa are not alone in the enormous task of relating law to the requirements of economic growth, political independence, and national unity in a divided world.

2.

THE SOCIOLOGICAL FRAMEWORK OF LAW*

by M. G. Smith

My main objective in this paper is to show the relevance of a comparative history of the growth of legal systems and theory to the sociological analysis of jural institutions and legal development, with special reference to Africa.

Law in Africa is only in part African law. It includes also certain elements of European law—Roman-Dutch, Portuguese, Belgian, French, or British—together with their local development in the African context. Further, there is a substantial body of Muslim law, often claiming greater local antiquity than European codes.

Under various accepted definitions of law, indigenous African societies may be said to have lacked law, or at best to have had an exiguous and erratic public law. On such views, before the Muslims or the Europeans overran tribal Africa, its peoples knew only custom instead of law. Sociologists and anthropologists have debated these notions at length, as features of a general difference between "primitive" and "modern" law, but as yet have reached no significant conclusions. As a rule, all parties to this debate have assumed that European legal theory and framework provide the appropriate standard, and arguments have accordingly centered on the presence of comparable or substitute patterns or their functional equivalents among primitive peoples. It seems possible, however, that the differences between European and Muslim law in sources, content, procedure, development, and political framework are quite enough to suggest the inadequacy, in a cross-cultural framework, of those European axioms that identify law with centralized administration and its apparatus of tribunals, registries, legislatures, or police.

An independent African state has to select the legal framework it

*I am grateful to Professors J. N. D. Anderson and G. E. von Grunebaum for their comments on an earlier version of this paper.

will use. To date, the evidence suggests that Europeanized Africans, the political elite in most new African states, may prefer to retain the basic framework of European law inherited from the previous regime, with such modifications, especially in constitutional spheres, as seem immediately appropriate. Likewise, African Muslims prefer to retain traditional Islamic law, with modifications in the penal code and in personal and commercial law appropriate to modern circumstances. Tribesmen, lacking alternatives, continue to observe or modify their tribal laws as the political superstructure permits. One issue that no new African government can indefinitely avoid is the integration of these tribal traditions in the law of the state. Before independence, this problem preoccupied the colonial regimes; and before the establishment of European rule the problem of tribal jurisdiction confronted all Muslim and non-Muslim conquerors who subjugated culturally alien groups. Today, when new elites proclaim the African personality and the African heritage, it is well to recall that African tribal tradition, law, and custom are clearly among the most authentic and fundamental expressions of this heritage. It would be ironic if these new ideologies functioned to legitimate further displacement of tribal law and custom by state rules based on alien models.

There are many sociological frameworks of law. The sociologist examines law in the broad context of social relationships. Thus, for Durkheim, law is the prototype of social fact: the sociological framework in which law arises, develops, and operates is society itself. But law is also a rather special type of social fact because it is regulatory in distinctive ways and spheres. In this sense the sociological framework of law consists in the institutional machinery through which its regulation is manifest. In another sense, we may identify the sociological framework with the milieus of thought in which systems and theories of law develop. As these systems of thought directly influence the operation of law in societies, this framework may be the most fundamental of all.

Until recently, the African continent was almost entirely partitioned into colonies. Thus the most important general experience shared by Africans was the colonial situation. Adriano Moreira has defined this situation rather neatly: "There is a colonial situation whenever one and the same territory is inhabited by ethnical groups of different civilization, the political power being usually exercised entirely by one group under the sign of superiority, and of the restraining influence of its own particular civilization."[1] After 1945, and mainly in Africa, there was a "sudden awakening of racial groups which had no political power, the emergence of an elite struggling for political supremacy, and, in consequence,

[1] For notes to chapter 2, see page 245.

all problems of citizenship, of representation, of the communities on an equitable basis, of the right of the people to self-determination."[2]

Moreira identifies this situation as one of social and cultural pluralism. The basic character of colonial pluralities is worth attention:

> By virtue of their cultural and social constitutions, plural societies are only units in a political sense. Each is a political unit simply because it has a single government. . . . Democratic governmental forms appropriate to plural societies are usually federal. Autocratic governmental forms reserve the ultimate political functions for one or other of the constituent cultural sections, even where other sections are separated territorially, for instance on reservations, and are allowed some internal autonomy. But some uniformity of laws and government is essential, if the society is to remain a political unit at all. Excluding government and law, the institutional differences which indicate plurality relate to marriage, family, education, property, religion, economic institutions, language and folklore.[3]

In this sense these Africans states, colonies, and protectorates were all plural societies, and their colonial character directly confronts us with the basic significance of the sociological framework of law.

Such pluralisms generally arise through the domination of one culturally distinctive collectivity by another, and, as Moreira says, in this condition the dominant group is subject only "to the restraining influence of its own particular civilization," especially its own laws, customs, and morals. The effective limits of political power may determine the boundaries of dominance thus established; they cannot directly account for the form, administrative or legal, which this dominance takes. Whereas in homogeneous societies it is society that constitutes law, in plural societies, such as those of Africa, there is evidence that law may serve to constitute society. Thus law both derives from and may establish society.

In the first instance the social milieu is typically homogeneous, ethnically and culturally, and the basis of society is primarily consensual; in this situation law may express organic institutional relations. In plural societies, on the other hand, the social milieu is heterogeneous in cultural and ethnic constitution and coercive in base, and the law that seeks to constitute it and serves to regulate it is essentially sectional. In the culturally homogeneous society, the state—that is, the central political institutions—is, like law, a derivative, expressive, and secondary structure. In the evolution of plural units the state preexists society, and provides the legal framework within which the new society may or may not emerge. This distinction between society and polity, or, as it is often phrased, between society and the state, combined with the basic differences in structure and function of governmental institutions in these two differing types of society, indicates yet another range of problems that lurk in the general concept of law.

While law is a social fact in homogeneous units, as Durkheim holds, in colonial pluralism it is clearly in some sense presocietal. In the homogeneous society the state claims legitimacy as the derivative authorized regulatory institution. In the plural society, whether protectorate, colony, or racially exclusive union, the state seeks to constitute a new society within a legal framework which it legitimates independently. Given the profound differences in legal, political, and communal structure between these two social contexts, it would be surprising if they did not also exhibit comparable differences in legal form, substance, and mode of operation, even where the rulers hold to a doctrine of the state which Dicey and others have summarized as the rule of law. For an example, Sir Ernest Barker's statement of this widely accepted doctrine serves well:

> The purpose of the state is . . . a specific purpose of law. Other purposes, so far as they concern or affect this purpose, must necessarily be squared with it . . . but the adjustment is not a matter of discretion, and it is not absolute: it is controlled by the purpose of the state. . . . In a word, we see and accept the Sovereignty of Law—both the Law of the Constitution which expresses the fundamental purpose on which the State is based, and the ordinary law of the courts, duly made in accordance with the Constitution which expresses that purpose in detail.[4]

These are the final self-restraining influences to which Moreira refers.

The significance of the doctrine of the rule of law is no more deniable than its ethnocentrism, which imposes on sociologists the important task of formulating culture-free definitions of law and government which may have comparable significance. But we shall advance nowhere if we adopt the current formulas of European political and legal philosophy without a careful comparative study of their histories. Manifestly, also, the culturally neutral analyses of developments in African law and politics may contribute much to such understanding.

The history of law and government in Islam presents a vivid contrast to European developments, and may accordingly show how inadequate for comparative study are conceptions of law and the state drawn solely from Europe. Attention to Islamic law is also relevant here, for Islam has been one of the major sources of external influence on Africa. Formally and otherwise, European colonial powers in Africa have made various special provisions to accommodate their Muslim populations.

Islamic law developed by paths and mechanisms almost exactly the reverse of those by which European law developed. Until Muhammad's time, the Arabs had lived in tribal communities with temporary confederations, following an unwritten, variable body of custom in which agnation, the jural autonomy of lineages, *lex talionis*, and jural subordination of women were the principal elements.[5] As Allah's Prophet and

Messenger, Muhammad simultaneously proselytized, organized the Muslim community, and delivered Allah's pronouncements in the Holy Koran. On his death, this book became the unquestioned basis of Islam, regarded both as a faith and as a system of law, divinely ordained to regulate and protect the faithful. The serious incompleteness in koranic rules, however, soon became evident through the rapid expansion of Islamic territory by conquest in obedience to the Prophet's command of jihad (holy war). Muhammad's death also raised certain central problems of succession, of continuity and coordination in Islam, which had important legal and political as well as religious implications.

To rationalize their procedures of adaptation in accordance with the requirements of the Faith, Muslim doctors compiled the Sunna, or traditions of the Prophet and his Companions, and used these as a source of guidance to supplement and interpret the Koran. A number of other principles were also employed to amplify and develop a substantial code of laws from the slim body of given rules. These include exegesis, opinion (*ra'y*), analogy (*qiyās*), and consensus (*ijmā'*) as elements of *fiqh*, or the finding of judgment. Of these, *ra'y* was the first to develop; a tradition of the Caliph Omar II (717-720) authorized its use by a *qāḍī* where the texts gave no guidance.[6] Analogy, which rests on the interpretation of Sunna or koranic rules to identify the reason or purpose (*illa*) of particular passages so that it may then be validly extended to other circumstances, sought to limit the scope for independent opinions, to exclude arbitrary judgments. *Fiqh* originally meant finding (the basis) of judgment by knowledge of the Koran and the Sunna, or by analogy. Later, in consequence of the development of formal law, it came to mean knowledge of the practical rules of religion.

Ijmā' was a further important source of law legitimated by the Sunna. "The Prophet said, 'My community will never agree in an error.' " By inference this saying came to mean that the agreement of the community could supplement revealed law by further rules. Opinions would inevitably differ, as the Prophet, according to tradition, had anticipated: "The Prophet said: 'Difference of opinion is a gift of Allah.' " These two sayings of the Prophet "were destined to explain the variety of legal schools and also the origin of *ijmā'*." [7]

Opinions initially varied about the membership and the location of the community whose consensus was relevant as a further source of law, and also about the legal status of minority views. Eventually the *'ulamā'*, or body of devout and learned Muslims, was identified as the relevant group. On this basis jurists and doctors sought to develop a law consistent with koranic directions and adequate for daily use.

General agreement obtained about the need to restrict the scope for arbitrary opinions (*ra'y*) by means of precise legal rules. As each successive school of law emerged, the scope for *ra'y* decreased. Opinions differed among the founders of these schools about the admissibility of analogy as a source of law, and about other details of substance. The founders of the four orthodox rites or legal schools—Abū Ḥanifa, Mālik b. Anas, Ash-Shāfi'i, and Aḥmad b. Ḥanbal—all owed their authority and legitimacy to the doctrine of *ijtihad,* by which the right of the most learned to initiate new interpretations of Sunna or koranic texts, independent of previous exegesis or traditional glosses, was admitted. The doctrine of *ihtilaf,* or divergence of opinion, itself served to legitimate the division of Islam among the followers of these four jurists.

This sketch of early Islamic legal development focuses on sources of law internal to the law itself. Along with the Sunna and the Koran, from which their legitimacy derives, opinion, analogy, interpretation, *ihtilaf*, and *ijmā'* are the principles that constitute the law (*shar'*, *sharī'a*). Two other sources of law, political and customary practice, remained outside this logical framework. Islamic expansion did not await the development of legal codes; neither were the political problems of succession and administrative continuity which followed Muhammad's death resolved by earlier directives from Allah. *Ad hoc* adaptations to these new situations which were simultaneously consistent with Islam and appropriate to the circumstances were the best the faithful could do. Later generations in unforeseen circumstances likewise sought the most advantageous accommodations consistent with their Faith and its obligations. The alternatives open to believers in these conditions were strictly limited. If Islam was to prevail politically and socially, as the Prophet had enjoined, it was necessary for Muslims to allocate substantial discretionary powers to their ruler the caliph, his official, or the local chief in his capacity as *imām* or head of their community. From this developed the doctrine of *siyāsa,* which empowered rulers to exercise discretion corresponding to their responsibilities for the maintenance and spread of Islam. In theory, the ruler should be a *mujtahid,* which means that in the absence of qualified legal advice he must be capable of finding the appropriate solution in keeping with accepted principles and precedents. In effect, the *siyāsa,* or political jurisdiction, guided by reasons of state, could supersede, supplement, or, on occasion, abrogate the *sharī'a* with a legitimacy that varied with the *'ulamā'* 's consensus or the force of circumstances.[8] As the Koran enjoins obedience to the ruler,[9] however, this discretionary power could also claim the ultimate legitimacy of koranic sanction, even when it directly contradicted the *sharī'a.*

This basic ambiguity in the relation of *sharī'a* and *siyāsa,* code and discretion, has always exercised a profound influence on legal administration in Islam. Even under the early caliphates, "the *qāḍī*'s jurisdiction was handed over to the executive arm of the government to be decided by the vizier, or the governor, who presided over the so-called *maẓālim* [lit., wrongs] court" [10] which exercised a jurisdiction in some ways similar to the French *droit administratif*. Gustave von Grunebaum holds that "this innovation . . . fatally wounds the idea of uniform administration of divinely ordained justice among the Muslims." [11]

A religious obligation which no Muslim ruler should disregard requires that he establish or maintain a *qāḍī* court to administer the *shar'*. In the western Sudan, one of the grounds by which Fulani Muslims justified their jihad of 1804-1810 was the absence of such courts in the Muslim Habe states they overran.[12] But the functional significance of these *qāḍī* courts varies with their number, distribution, and independence of the executive *siyāsa*. No rule of religion clearly regulates the distribution of such courts in terms of area or population. One *qāḍī* court seems both essential and formally sufficient for qualification as a Muslim state, but it may have little work if the court of the *naẓr al-maẓālim* is very active.

One implication of this situation is the recognition of non-Muslim practice or custom (*'urf, 'ada*) as valid in regulating social relations. Another implication is that deviant practices which arise may also be recognized among Muslims as valid tradition (*'urf*). For example, in northern Nigeria it is now accepted as local custom that issues involving claims in land should be reserved for the ruler's courts or handled by executive officials.[13] This executive jurisdiction over suits involving land persisted after the Fulani jihad which expressly sought to enforce Islamic observance.

The simple absence of an effective administration of the *sharī'a* through *qāḍī* courts, itself in part a correlate of the *siyāsa* power to create and maintain or quietly to ignore such courts, suffices to perpetuate adherence to old customs and to promote the recognition of new ones as further indirect sources of law. Levy points out that this position was held even during the Prophet's lifetime: "The Koran declares that no Muslim under penalty of everlasting torment in Hell may slay another who is innocent of offense. Yet to this day the exaction of blood-revenge remains an important part of tribal life." Further, "Where family life is concerned, in marriage, divorce and the distribution of inheritance, the provisions of the *shar'* would appear to be very widely neglected." "There have not been lacking attempts to regard *'urf* as one of the roots of the *fiqh*, but excepting the works of the early Sunni *mujtahids*, the customary laws have generally gone unrecorded by the legists. Yet they have not gone unrecognized, for by some *faqihs* they were preferred to laws derived by means of *qiyās*, and where local influences have been strong, custom has frequently been held to be decisive." [14] Thus, although various customs have been integrated in the law by special devices, the total body of custom as such has not been integrated, perhaps because such integration would formally abrogate the *sharī'a* in many areas. The integration of specific customs is more readily achieved because Muslim law is a deontology, a series of moral injunctions, rather than a logically systematized body of law, although the Mālikite elaboration of the sacred law comes perhaps closest to a system owing to its concentration on the *furu*, that is, the substantive regulation of detail. From the earliest times, elements from *'urf* entered the *sharī'a* through *ijmā'* and judicial decision.

In its own theory, then, Islam is a theocracy, based on and regulated by a divinely revealed law, the *sharī'a*, which is developed by *fiqh* on the foundations of the Sunna and the Koran. In practice, the *sharī'a* has various sources and an application that varies inversely with the range of *siyāsa* and *'urf*. Under these conditions Muslims stress the diacritical significance of certain symbolic, formal acts, such as Ramadan, pilgrimage, or the daily prayers, by which adherence to Islam is expressed. The *sharī'a* as an ideal system of law is dependent for its realization on secular pragmatic considerations, as well as on historic political precedents. Thus Muslim law as applied represents a system based on revelation, rules of interpretation, precedent, and consensus, as well as on custom and reasons of state expediency. The basic religious premise and goal set certain limits to the variability this mixture of elements might otherwise exhibit. The Sunnite world formally subdivides among the followers of the four orthodox legal schools, West Africa being mainly of Mālikite persuasion. In practice, legal recognition of *'urf* considerably increases the variety of substantive laws, whereas *siyāsa* introduces comparable variations in procedure. Political fragmentation of the Muslims further enhances this diversity. The overriding religious obligation of rulers to maintain and expand Islam serves to legitimate expedient deviations. In consequence, local differences in political and legal administration are quite as impressive as Muslim continuities. Moreover, much of the operative law, both *'urf* and *siyāsa*, remains unwritten, applied by Muslim courts but forming no part of *sharī'a*. The theory of Islam as a theocratic civilization, regulated by God's revealed law, accordingly remains unaffected by these contrary, secular developments.

Legal theory and institutions in Europe developed on lines sharply different from those in Islam. From Rome to the present, European law has had a secular base and orientation even where formal structure or theory was absent. As we shall see, such qualities are not easily integrated with the requirements of theocracy.

Greece did not produce a theory of law before Zeno, mainly, it seems, because of the character of the polis. Cities varied widely in their political constitutions, but in the typical city the assembly of notables which decided policy also decided important legal issues, and no clear distinction between the two was consistently maintained. In effect, Greek thinkers directed their attention to the requisites of the desirable polis, that is, to social and political philosophy, rather than to the theory or analysis of law. In such conditions, legislation and jurisprudence are equally inhibited. Moral, political, and religious issues tend to invest the judgment of critical cases of law.[15] Nonetheless, the seeds of a future theory of law are to be found in Aristotle's casual references to natural law as both general and inherent in human nature, in contrast with particular positive rules.[16] With the decline of Hellas, Stoics developed the notion of natural law both as empirical truth and as normative ideal.

Rome lacked speculative philosophers, and produced little literature of a theoretical sort. Instead, from an early separation of judicial and political functions, the Romans gradually developed a refined and inclusive system of secular law, backed by a technical jurisprudence directed toward the clarification of precedents, legal conceptions, and the like. The nearest approaches to a formal theory of law in these Roman writings center on discussions of natural law and of the imperium or sovereign power. As Roman jurists and praetors developed the *jus gentium* to supplement the ancient civil law, they identified the idea of natural law with this emerging law of nations and used it to rationalize innovations of procedure and substantive law. Such jurisconsults as Gaius, however, undertook no formal discussion of the notion of natural law. In their responsa (as in the responsa of the rabbis and the *fatāwī* of the Muslim legists) they simply gave their opinions on specific issues of law put to them, initially by praetors, and later by the emperors, citing appropriate precedents, distinctions, rules, and reasons for their conclusions. The results were valuable manuals of a rational, technical kind suitable for practicing lawyers, but devoid of general theoretical content. In due course codification followed, to eliminate conflicting responsa and reduce the corpus to an authoritative order. It was at this point that the nature of imperium, the source of authority for this finished code, emerged as a theoretical problem. Under the republic, the nature and the locus of imperium had, perhaps deliberately, remained obscure, the relative powers of senate, *populus*, and tribunes varying within certain ill-defined limits which constitutional history, unwritten traditions, and the political situation sanctioned. Under the principate and the early emperors these ambiguities persisted, though in a differing form. Justinian, in the preface to his *Institutes*, first sought to define and rationalize the imperium, and did so on logically inconsistent grounds, claiming the sovereign power simultaneously as the ruler appointed by God, and also in accordance with secular constitutional practice. In his code, then, the source of law is imperium or sovereignty, but the source and the legitimacy of this sovereign power remain obscure.

A formal theory of law in Europe derives from the competitions of Church and state during and after the twelfth century. In outline this struggle had long been foreshadowed. Even before Justinian based his claims to imperium on divine appointment as well as on secular practice, in the politically insecure West, Augustine had stated the superior claims of Church to state and the incompatibility between the laws of human society and those of the City of God. With the rise of the Holy Roman Empire and the political dominance of the Western Church under and after Gregory VII, relations between Church and state, and between divine and secular law, became problematic. Implementation of Augustine's ideals seemed quite possible for the popes. Feudal Europe was at this time a patchwork of loosely connected jurisdictions. The Holy Roman Empire itself was an *ad hoc* assemblage of scattered principalities, often held by the same individual under quite different titles, and typically distinguished by differences of law and jurisdiction. Of contemporary systems, canon law was superior in its rational structure, and appeared likely to develop the only universally applicable law. In between estate-stratified feudal jurisdictions, during these centuries, the law merchant gradually emerged as an applicable autonomous code based on elements of old Roman law, supplemented or modified as conditions required. In Britain there was the further peculiarity of an evolving royal law, relatively centralized, and superior to that of the courts baron and leet in range and scope as well as in structure.[17]

Papal dominance produced its own crop of problems, initially in papal control of political appointments, but also in the relations between canon and secular law. Aquinas, for instance, sought to harmonize the notions of Aristotle and Augustine with the realities of the early thirteenth century. He proposed a classification of law into four species: divine law, most nearly represented by ecclesiastical law; positive law, enforced in the courts of princes whose authority derived principally from God; the *lex aeterna*, or divine purpose immanent in all creatures; and natural law, identified with man's rational faculty as applied to the understanding of divine rules and purposes. St. Thomas supplemented this hierarchy of law with injunctions requiring Christians to fulfill the obligations of their social status, and appealed to the feudal nobility to practice *noblesse oblige*.[18] Thus Aquinas ultimately sanctioned the heterogeneity of feudal jurisdictions while seeking to subordinate them to the higher, divinely sanctioned jurisdiction of the Church.

This papal theory of law was challenged sharply by Marsilius and Dante, who drew on the studies of Roman law carried out at Bologna.

Marsilius bluntly denied the legitimacy of papal claims to the religious leadership of Christendom, recommended a democratic collegial system of government for both Church and state, and advanced a utilitarian theory of reason and natural law. Dante preferred a secular autocracy to that of the Church, and harked back to Byzantium and the Antonines.[19] This competition between secular and theocratic ideologies and interests accordingly focused attention on the problem of the nature and functions of law, especially since both theses drew their inspiration from common sources, the Roman codices and late classical doctrine of natural law. Both these schools of opinion were also disturbed at the legal chaos of late feudalism, and sought to replace it by a uniform and universally applicable system, in one instance with secular base and rational orientation, in the other with a theocratic order. In this period the Holy Roman emperors began to refer legal cases to jurists trained in civilian (Roman) law in order to promote some uniformity of legal administration within their diverse territories.[20] Other monarchs followed suit. In consequence, the Roman civil code came to serve both as a reservoir from which positive law could be borrowed and adapted for current application, and as the model from which systems of natural law could be developed. The civilians whose technical knowledge facilitated this process rationalized their activities by doctrines of natural law which inevitably drew their attention to problems of jurisdiction and its sources, and thus to the theory of society, government, and law. Their position as jurisconsults of the monarch further encouraged these thinkers to formulate their problems on secular lines, favorable to the rulers' claims.

It was in this context that the theories of social contract were developed to provide a logical basis for the secular theories of state and law necessary to legitimate a structure of centralized administration.[21] Grotius and Hobbes are admirable examples of these dual concerns, the development of a social philosophy appropriate to centralized administration and of a rational universally applicable code. To institute this rational legal structure, political centralization and the elimination of feudal jurisdictions were both prerequisite. The competing theories of natural law and social contract which advanced solutions to these questions were thus no less significant for men of the sixteenth to the eighteenth centuries than theories of democracy or communism may be for us today. The first direct political expressions of this movement took place during the Thirty Years' War, after which secularization and centralization proceeded apace, and absolute monarchies replaced feudalism in most of Europe, their ideologies and legal systems alike being shaped by doctrines of natural law and social contract. As Weber has shown, Britain escaped the legal reforms linked with this development, owing partly to an earlier centralization and partly to the presence of a well-entrenched professional group with vested interests in the maintenance of common law.[22]

A pivotal element in these theories of natural law and social contract is imperium or sovereignty. As legal unity and uniform administration presume an imperium, these two doctrines reinforced each other and also supported centralization. In Rome, legal unity and centralization had obtained without any formal theory of imperium. In the modern Europe emerging from theocracy and feudalism, an explicit theory was indispensable, as well to legitimate absolutism as to determine the most suitable form of political reorganization. Theorists differed. Grotius, though advocating the sovereign power of the monarch, derived such power from the people, with consequent ambiguities about the final locus of imperium.[23] Althusius advocated a federal type of structure based on the historical priority of lesser corporations to the state they composed. This federalist view denied an unrestricted absolute sovereignty to the ruler, whose role and powers were thus defined as in essence representative.[24] The practical difficulty with this thesis is that it implied the preservation of the historical feudatories as modal units of political and legal administration, thereby obstructing the desired growth of central power. Hobbes, seeking to cut this Gordian knot, in his theory derived social unity entirely from the prior overriding power of a central absolute ruler. In this view the imperium and the system of law were virtually identified, and the legal validity of any corporations not explicitly created by or based upon concessions by the state was denied.[25] With the triumph of these ideas, the essentials of the modern theory of the law and the state were complete.

Later reactions against monocratic centralization took the form of a doctrine of natural rights, itself clearly derivative from earlier natural law. In Britain, Locke employed this notion to advocate the sovereignty of Parliament. In America these "inalienable rights of man" helped to dissolve the British connection; in France they helped to overthrow the monarchy. In neither revolution do we find successful movements toward decentralization. In both instances arguments center upon the locus and the exercise of imperium, but its indispensability for law and the state remains unquestioned. These three notions—sovereignty, law, and the state—once related in this way, may thereafter have seemed to lawyers and political philosophers alike almost inseparable. Each presumes and expresses the others.

These historical developments furnish the essential background for evaluating the modern European theory of law. After movements for the introduction of civil law in Britain and Blackstone's defense of custom and common law, British legal reformers such as Bentham and Austin were driven to examine the relations of custom and law, questions of significance to continental jurists only where custom competed with civil law. Thus the search for a general theory of law developed in Britain and America, in countries committed to common law as well as to a central imperium. The apparent logical indispensability of the central imperium for the existence of law to these theorists is striking, given the history and composition of Anglo-Saxon common law.

Thus Austin defined law in clearly Hobbesian terms as the commands of a sovereign which his subjects must obey. This Austinian emphasis on sovereignty and centralization persists despite other modifications in the writings of Salmond, Holmes, Pound, and Cardozo. It represents the received tradition and theory of law in Europe and the Anglo-Saxon world, one that sociologists and anthropologists have borrowed and applied or debated without adequate scrutiny of its historical basis.

For Salmond, "all law, however made, is recognized by the Courts, and no rules are recognized by the Courts which are not rules of law." [26] For Holmes, law is simply "the prophecies of what the Courts will do in fact." [27] For Cardozo, law is "a principle or rule of conduct so established as to justify a prediction with reasonable certainty that it will be enforced by the Courts if its authority is challenged." [28] In place of Austin's sovereign, these views identify law solely by reference to courts, without considering legislation or other processes by which courts are constituted and maintained, but denying the possibility of law where courts are absent. Notably all these definitions share Austin's preoccupation with a centralized imperium, although, unlike Austin, later writers presume the imperium without direct mention. Like Austin also, these later definitions focus on substantive rules, the form of legal procedure and machinery of administration being assumed as essential for the existence of law.

Long ago, Sir Henry Maine, defending common law against advocates of codification, the derivative of natural-law theory, questioned the relevance of imperium for the existence and recognition of law: "It is certain that in the infancy of mankind, no sort of legislature, nor even a distinct author of law, was contemplated or conceived of." In such states of social development, says Maine, "law has scarcely reached the footing of custom: it is rather a habit." [29] In Allen's words, however,

> To call these legal rules is something of an anachronism, for in many cases they are equally rules of religion and morality, which, at this early stage, have not become distinguished from law; but they are "legal" in the sense which is nowadays attached to that term, inasmuch as they are binding and obligatory rules of conduct (not merely of faith and conviction), and that the breach of them is a breach of positive duty. Austin denies them the force of law until they have been expressly recognized by the sovereign.[30]

Holmes, Cardozo, and Salmond agree that these rules are legal only when courts exist to enforce them.

Anthropologists and sociologists have tended to adopt one or another of these two opposing views, without adequate attention to their place in the historical development of European legal and political theory. Malinowski aligned himself on the side of Maine, while Radcliffe-Brown adopted Roscoe Pound's definition of law as "social control through the systematic application of the force of politically organized society," [31] and on this basis concluded that many primitive societies lacked law because they lacked "political organization." In his classification of sanctions, only those "imposed by a constituted authority, military, political, or ecclesiastical," rank as legal.[32] Here, also following Pound, Radcliffe-Brown assumes a particular type of machinery and procedure as a precondition of law. In both writers the underlying assumption is that of the modern state, defined by MacIver, for instance, as "an association which, acting through law as promulgated by a government endowed to this end with coercive power, maintains within a territorially demarcated community the universal external conditions of social order." [33]

The retreat from Austin's position we have observed in the views of Cardozo and Holmes is continued by Pound. Whereas Cardozo, Holmes, and Salmond replace Austin's ruler by the courts, Pound replaces the courts by the "systematic application of force," a criterion that led Radcliffe-Brown to wonder whether feud is law or war, while denying that obligatory compensation or indemnification was legal.

The opposed view is presented in its most extreme form by Sidney Hartland, who asserts that the law of savage societies consists in the totality of tribal custom.[34] "The core of legislation is a series of taboos; . . . an atmosphere of terror is sufficient to prevent a breach of custom; . . . the savage is . . . bound in the chains of an immemorial tradition. . . . These fetters are accepted by him as a matter of course; he never seeks to break forth." [35] In this way, Maine's "legal habits" are made to include all tribal culture, but since in this view primitive man is the willing automatic slave of tradition, there can be neither lawlessness nor law.

It is clear that the problem that confronts these writers with both these differing views is in essence the problem that social-contract theorists sought to resolve: What is the logical relation of the state, society, and their components to one another? And what are the minimum reciprocal relations of law and polity? I have already suggested how the doctrine of the necessary priority of sovereignty came to seem historically indispensable in modern Europe for the movement from theocracy and feudalism toward a secular centralized state. If my interpretation is correct, then we should expect that these rather special historical circumstances and interests would produce equally special theories of law, society, and the state. Insofar as sociologists and anthropologists have adopted this special frame of theory, it furnishes the decisive element in the sociological framework of law, for it guides their hypotheses, research, and analysis on lines consistent with its own axioms and equations.

For a neutral comparative sociology, these European developments and definitions have no superior claim to furnish general categories or guidance over comparable developments in other cultures, such as Islam. In fact, the inadequacy of a framework preoccupied with the problem of political centralization and indivisible sovereignty or its opposite is readily apparent from the history of Islam. This civilization owed its religious and political impetus and the territorial basis of its establishment to central sovereign direction. It persisted despite dispersal of sovereignty as a unit with a common basic law. This law itself has positive validity, even though it incorporates unwritten customs, both ancient and modern, and applies in courts authorized by religion, in strictly executive courts, or informally and by various means. I am therefore suggesting, first, that the traditional preoccupation of Western sociologists with legal uniformity and centralized administration—"the systematic application of the force of politically organized society" —is intelligible only in terms of criteria drawn from Western political and legal development; and, second, that these criteria are inadequate as a basis or sociological framework for the comparative study of law. Indeed, some inadequacies of this special viewpoint are well known. International law obtains even without "machinery for enforcement," and perhaps precisely because societies are politically organized. In Celtic Ireland, Brehon Law flourished without courts, without central authority, and without any enforcement machinery, even after conversion of the Irish to Christianity had removed its original ritual sanctions.[36] In Sweden, the law delivered by *lagmen* likewise took effect without direct sanctions.[37] In Anglo-Saxon law as well as in Islamic law, where custom enjoys legal status with judicial precedent and legislation, further difficulties arise.[38]

The adherence of many British sociologists to a theory of law which is essentially derived from Hobbes and Grotius presents a problem of some interest, especially because it seems that preoccupation with the problems of law, its nature and place in society, has been confined mainly to scholars who live under common-law systems rather than codes, and also because in essence the theory they espouse is at odds with common law. Durkheim's role in promoting this viewpoint may be decisive. He restated Maine's evolutionary movement from societies based on kinship and regulated by customary status to those based on territory and regulated by legal contract in terms of a movement from extreme decentralization and mechanical solidarity toward centralization and organic solidarity. According to Durkheim, only a repressive public law, such as Radcliffe-Brown claimed among Kikuyu and Akamba, obtains in the earlier phase, whereas the latter exhibits restitutive private law administered by tribunals.[39] The crucial criterion of law advanced by Durkheim and Radcliffe-Brown is thus the repressive sanction backed by collective force. A moment's thought will show that this sanction might as easily characterize lawlessness.

Durkheim's difficulty may have been cultural. As a Frenchman, he lived in a climate of thought structured by doctrines of natural rights and natural law and by the Code Napoléon, the crowning triumph of the movement for legal rationalism, and the prototype of other modern codes. He could not therefore recognize the independent jural significance of corporations, other than those created or formally acknowledged by an evident state; in consequence, he could not initially discern their evolutionary and structural significance as units of jural regulation. Later Durkheim was to change his view, and to advocate the establishment of occupational corporations, intermediary between individual and state, on historical and functional grounds.[40] But the difficulties that invest his earlier treatment of law persist in Radcliffe-Brown's emphasis on "constituted authority, political, military, or ecclesiastical," as the agent disposing of legal sanctions. Radcliffe-Brown makes no attempt to elucidate the constitution of authority. The attempt might have led directly to a formal theory of corporations.

In developing the ideology appropriate to institute and guide and legitimate the modern bureaucratically centralized state, with its unified form of legal administration, political philosophers and lawyers alike had logically to exclude recognition of independent or antecedent corporations; hence arose certain peculiarities of social-contract theory. By these means they denied the legal existence of corporations, save those derived from the imperium. Any other course might simply have permitted the perpetuation of feudal elements such as fiefs or guilds, which it was necessary to eliminate in law and state if the requisite centralization and uniformity were to obtain. In Britain, Maine reopened this subject by directing attention to the historical priority of corporations aggregate over corporations sole. In Germany, the status of precivilian Teutonic corporations was keenly contested during the process of drafting the Civil Code of 1898, following the work of Savigny and Jhering. It was in this context significantly that Tönnies contraposed gemeinschaft and gesellschaft, and Gierke undertook the historical analysis of natural law in Europe, seeking thereby to reinstate as legal units the ancient Germanic corporations, fraternities, local communities, and the like. The curious convergences on the subject shown by syndicalism, by the Fascist theory of the corporative state, and by advocacy of intermediary corporations, are also significant. In different ways and for different ends, these were all attempts to reintroduce corporations as units of legal jurisdiction, after their virtual elimination as autonomous units from the legal systems of modern states.

Malinowski, in his attempts to redefine and analyze primitive law, reacting against the presumption of central power, began by looking for "rules regarded as compulsory obligations of one individual or group towards another."[41] He found that "the whole structure of Trobriand society is founded on the principle of legal status. By this I mean that the claims of chief over commoner, husband over wife, parent over child and vice versa, are not exercised arbitrarily or one-sidedly, but according to definite rules, and are arranged into well-balanced chains of reciprocal services. . . . Social relations are governed by a number of legal principles . . . mother-right, . . . succession to rank, power and dignities, economic inheritance, rights to soil and local citizenship, and membership in the totemic clan."[42] In short, legal relations are embodied in and expressed by social structure which analytically reduces to a distributional network of reciprocal jural rights, privileges, and obligations. The primacy of corporations as units of this social structure is owing partly to their qualities of persistence, to their estates which include rights in the persons of their members, to their external unity and identity, to their internal jural autonomy, which defines the essential conditions of membership, and above all to the fact that together, and in their interrelations, they constitute the society and the polity. Given these characteristics, the procedural features which writers like Roscoe Pound or Radcliffe-Brown have stressed as essential prerequisites of law cease to be meaningful. The primitive corporation is simultaneously a unit of social structure and of social procedure; these two aspects cannot be separated.

Thus, when Hoebel defines law as a social norm, the neglect or infraction of which "is regularly met, in threat or in fact, by the application of physical force by an individual or group possessing the socially recognized privilege of so acting,"[43] two comments are in order. First, the unit of reference and authorization is a corporate group of some kind, and the authority varies with regard to issue and as the corporation is autocephalous or heterocephalous. Second, binding obligations are law, even where physical force is rarely or never applied, provided that their breach effects some alteration in the jural status of the corporation or any of its members.

The appeals of legal uniformity, coherence, and efficiency for lawyers and theorists are quite understandable. We should not, however, allow these normative qualities to lead us astray. Regularity and effectiveness in legal operations have directed attention to the efficiency of sanctions in the process of law; hence there is stress on centrally administered coercive sanctions to enforce decisions made by authorized tribunals. Certainty in the application of sanctions is one but not the only characteristic of "perfect"—that is, predictable—legal process. Such certainty may be irrelevant when law consists in skillful guesswork, or in the words of Judge Holmes, "prophecies of what the courts will do." Here, near perfection or predictable regularity in the application of sanctions fails to compensate for irrationalities in legal decision making. In this situation, the routine, predictable administration of sanctions is clearly no adequate basis for identification of law.

In societies that are imperfectly centralized, we may expect an imperfect or irregular application of sanctions, and perhaps even of judgment also. These are both quite consistent with the presence of law. Difficulties arise only when we accept the ambiguous ideals of perfect law, that is, of routinely enforced judicial decision, which is clearly a lawyer's desideratum, as the basis for a minimum general definition of law. It is clear that this ideally perfect law, the derivative of natural-law theory, represents an extreme of legal development in which many differing levels and types of imperfect law are also important. In simple societies, legal imperfection obtains, both as to recourse to law and in regard to the enforcement of decisions. Typically, the tribal law is unwritten, and judgment considers many particulars which Western rules of evidence would exclude. Such systems of law have predominant commitments toward rationality of substance rather than form, using these terms in Max Weber's sense. One basic reason for this difference is that the primitive law normally operates without the overriding sanction of central political institutions, and accordingly requires consensus and support among members of the corporate groups it affects. Where overriding repressive sanctions are available to enforce judicial decisions, lawyers and judges are free to pursue formal rationality and coherence at the public expense.

Undue attention to substantive rules and their codification, coupled with the assumption that only perfect law is law, has diverted the attention of sociologists from the significance of procedure in defining legal events. Even the catalog of Radcliffe-Brown, despite his procedural concept of law, does not include the sanction of nullity, which is essential for valid legal form. Sir Paul Vinogradoff identifies this sanction when he says that "unless certain rules are observed, an intended result cannot be achieved."[44] The effect of this sanction is to distinguish jural from other types of social procedures and rules, whether recorded or not. Feud, compensation, arbitration, appeals to divination, ordeals, oaths, councils, and the like are all procedures institutionalized within social units to publicize, regulate, and resolve intercorporate disputes.

Only when writers, having assumed a very specific procedural basis, define law substantively and as a perfectly effective system, are these imperfect modes of procedure theoretically problematic. Thus Weber, having initially identified law as an order "externally guaranteed by the probability that coercion (physical or psychological), to bring about conformity or avenge violation, will be applied by a staff of people holding themselves specially ready for that purpose,"[45] soon has to admit that "not all law is guaranteed law," and thus to recognize "indirectly guaranteed" and "unguaranteed" law, where enforcement staffs are absent.[46] The distinction Weber makes here corresponds closely to the differences between perfect and imperfect law mentioned above. But there is also a special normative quality of perfect law which derives from its basis in the programmatic theory of natural law, and which, aiming at a perfectly coherent, formally closed, and independent system of law, directly excludes all that might obstruct its objective, and rejects the incorporation of all elements extraneous to the imperium with which it identifies itself.

We can provisionally test and refine this analysis by a brief review of the framework of legal development in certain African colonial societies. For this purpose, I shall consider only three bodies of legal tradition—French, Muslim, and British—which interacted with native African society and law. In various parts of Africa these foreign systems were established by treaty, force, or other means as the law of the dominant group, in "territories which never showed signs of national life . . . and where the principle of unity is fundamentally due to the action of the dominant group."[47] In all such situations the native society and legal tradition were officially subordinate to the foreign law. The new state was constituted by its rulers in the context of their own legal tradition, and the forms of law familiar to them served to limit or regulate their relations with native institutions. We have seen that these three dominant traditions differed significantly in their development and constitution. They differed also in their accommodations to the common situation of African overrule. It is therefore worth asking to what degree their differing theories of law and government may have guided or limited the adaptive capacities of these ruling groups to the colonial condition.

We may regard French law after the Code Napoléon as a fine expression of systematic legal rationalism developed and advocated by theorists of natural law. The sole and ultimate source of this law is the imperium of the French state. It is not directly crucial for this theory of law how the imperium is distributed among the central corporations that constitute the state, providing only that there is a definite, recognized procedure by which all laws are instituted and applied. In theory and fact alike, this body of law begins with a systematic coherent code, which is subsequently modified and supplemented by statute, including rules made by particular organs of state in the exercise of powers delegated by statute. The result is a formally perfect legal tradition which excludes all units, relations, and processes not directly or indirectly represented in the statutory law. In this system procedure and substantive law are both well defined, the distinction between public and private law is central, and there is great refinement of form. High levels of certainty obtain in regard to both adjudication and the application of sanctions. The code expresses a classical tradition aimed at perfection in law. The state itself has as legal basis a written constitution, and all the organs of government are defined and identified by law.

Muslim law, like Islam, derives from Muhammad's mission. Its base is the Koran and the Sunna. Its object and limits are Islam, as both the Faith and the community of the faithful. In theory, this law expresses God's *religio* (or binding ordinance). In practice the sources of law are heterogeneous, and the *sharī'a* is furthermore mixed with or supplemented by regulations derived from *'urf* or *siyāsa*. In theory, then, legal procedure and substance are well defined. In practice both are somewhat ambiguous in various spheres. Muslim law as we actually encounter it in Africa embodies all these elements, some directly at odds with the Koran and the *sharī'a*, others supplementing their prescribed procedures or substantive rules. In this legal tradition there was initially no legitimate place for statutes, other than those contained in the Sunna or the Koran, although they may derive legality from the ruler's authority as sanctioned by the Koran. In a word, the tradition is one of theocratic pragmatism with a predominant focus on substance or content.[48] In this system uncertainty attaches, *ceteris paribus*, both to judicial decisions and to the application of sanctions.

British common law is almost equally complex. Besides custom, its sources include precedent, judicial decisions, legislation, equity, and various rules made by subordinate units with autonomous powers.[49] It is equally consistent with an imperium based on organic historical growth and expressed in an unwritten constitution, or with one defined by a formal document, such as the American and Australian constitutions. Where, as in Britain, there is an unwritten constitution, the legality of law ultimately reduces to the observance of certain accepted procedures by legislature and courts alike. In such a system, if it merits that term, the traditional diversity of sources of law is linked with and maintained by rejection of systematic codes. In consequence, conditions conducive to conflict of laws arise, and uncertainty attaches to legal decisions on both formal and procedural grounds, though the application of sanctions is sure. In keeping with this secular empiricist tradition, periodic compilations of the current law are undertaken as part of a more or less continuous process of adjustive activity in which legislature, courts, jurists, and others are involved. In general, the law of procedure exceeds substantive law in clarity and certainty.

Indigenous African law varied widely in procedure and substance, in sources, theory, and scope, perhaps as an expression of differences in social organization too numerous to catalog. The extremes of this variation may be illustrated by the Bushmen and the Baganda. In Buganda, Muteesa I (1856?-1884), following Kabaka Mutebi, exercised an absolute and despotic power, the autonomous jurisdictions of clans having been circumscribed, hereditary chiefs and officials eliminated, and the ruler's orders enforced as supreme law. During these developments, the political constitution and legal procedures and content underwent simultaneous complex changes which we may summarize as the modification and replacement of an old corporate structure by a newer highly centralized despotism. These changes were partly legitimated by the Ganda theory of the Kabaka as the sacred personification of their unity as a nation.[50]

Within a Bushman tribe, bands are the only corporate groups, and band headmanship, which is often held by infants and occasionally by women, is the only corporation sole. Band and headmanship are identified with each other and with certain properties, such as water holes, veldkos areas, and the like. Both persist, with their estates, even when the band has ceased to exist. Jural rights over property—that is, over Bushmen resources—vest entirely in bands, and the Bushman's habitat is divided accordingly. There are no legal tribunals, unless the flurries of excited collective jabber in which members of a band engage to "talk" some offender into retribution are so regarded. But crimes such as theft, though rare, are recognized, and violent punishment by the injured person is sanctioned, no protest arising even though the thief is killed.[51]

Between these extremes we find a wide variety in the corporate constitution of African societies: age-sets, age-regiments, age-villages, lineages, clans, local communities, associations, secret societies, castes, offices, and various types of chieftainship. In all instances an individual derives his jural status and rights from membership in some corporate category or group, or from tenure of some corporation sole. Thus the subordinate Hutu in Ruanda, like the slaves in West Africa, shared the jural disabilities attaching to the corporate category to which they belonged. These corporations, in their differing constitutions, bases, ideologies, and interests, provide the sociological framework of indigenous law. As Gurvitch points out, "the real collective units only, e.g., groups, give birth to the frameworks of law," the legal system of a given society "representing already the syntheses and the equilibria among different kinds of law."[52] Moreover, as corporations defined the scope and the source of the law, they embodied its theory and procedural forms and established the frame within and through which legal relations and processes obtained. The nature, form, and content of these jural relations and processes will therefore change with the identity and characteristics of the corporations involved, directly or indirectly, through the parties to the relation in their representative capacities. In this context law provides the medium for expression and adjustment of the corporate relations which constitute the framework of society.

Perhaps the most important structural difference among the French, Muslim, and British legal systems lies in their treatment of corporations. In English law, corporations emerged as independent juridical personalities endowed with continuity and exercising legally valid powers. The law accordingly admitted the existence of a certain type of unit which may or may not have been formally acknowledged by the state. In the developing English law of corporations, the legal capacities of these units were taken to include powers of rule making for their membership, where not inconsistent with the laws of the land. In short, common law, with its feudal basis and heterogeneous sources, accepted corporations constituted on various principles as relatively autonomous legal units.[53] The position in Muslim law seems curiously similar. Muslims were free, through the *siyāsa* and the doctrine of *'urf*, to suspend application of Islamic rules in favor of local practice, and could thus recognize and use the corporate organizations of those they ruled. They could also, with fewer procedural problems than the British, institute new corporations, both group and sole, as social or political conditions seemed to warrant. In the French legal system corporations exist as juridical units only by virtue of specific recognition or acknowledgment by the state. The French legal framework, being logically coherent, complete, and closed, cannot admit the logical or historical existence of native corporations independent of or antecedent to the colonial regime. On this basis the French theory of law denied recognition to African custom and polities.

Inevitably this consequence follows from the French view of law as a statutory code, properly authorized by the French state or by some other state that France recognizes. Only by special legislation could such law admit the existence of other old or new units. Even then it had difficulty in recognizing custom. With these bases the French had little alternative except "to regard their oversea territories as an integral part of the national community."[54]

One case discussed by Delavignette makes the position plain.

> For a long time African customary law was not legally recognized, since the situations to which it applied did not fall within any of the categories provided for by French law. Supposing a Chief tried to establish in the Courts, in accordance with the Code, the traditional rights exercised by a village over its own land. ... The magistrate inquired in what capacity the Chief appeared. As representing the village—true, but what, according to the Code, is the legal status of the group known as a village? Is it a public utility company, a society, an association, a syndicate, a corporate body, an association of owners? The magistrate searched through the Code and found nothing. The African village exists in fact but has no means of proving its existence in law. It exists within the framework of customary law, but has no power to act within the framework of French law. . . . Now on 3 November 1934 the Court of Appeal at Dakar, the supreme court of French West Africa, for the first time took cognizance of the nature of customary law in its own legal practice. . . . The court decided two questions: first—what was the legal basis of the African village? The court's decision was that the French legislature, by proclaiming its recognition of local custom, placed the village on a legal basis entirely distinct from anything provided for in French law. . . . In order to recognize the legal status of the village and of the land rights it asserts, the court must define custom and legislate in accordance with it. The second question was, who is qualified to represent the village in law? . . . The decree of 3 November 1934 [points] . . . the way to a solution of the conflict between Code and Custom by means of a development of French law.[55]

This involved a major modification of French legal theory.

The British, with their inadequate theory of law, and the Muslims, with a religious conception liberally modified by and adapted to circumstance, escaped the difficulties that faced the French because of the logical closure of their system and the extreme integration of legal theory with the theory of the state. Common-law willingness to accommodate corporations allowed the British to deal freely with tribal units whose forms and boundaries they could identify. Given prior experience with custom in common law, in Africa the British were well equipped to incorporate traditional social units and custom within the framework of their colonial administration, both legal and political, under the general rubrics of native authorities or native law and custom. Moreover, again on the basis of common-law experience, the British were well placed conceptually to admit that customs have a capacity for change, and thus tapped an essential source of adjustive development. As native law and custom changed, the British were therefore free to admit changes in the boundaries, character, and identity of the representative native corporations.

For Muslims, Islam imposed the obligation of jihad and thus legitimated their conquests. Under the Koran, the Muslim ruler also enjoyed a discretionary power of pragmatic accommodation to secular conditions. The adaptive capacity of *siyāsa* has enabled Muslim law to harness the regulatory powers of custom and local corporations to the service of Muslim rulers. In practice, only those who identified themselves by the essential religious observances as Muslims had access to the *sharī'a*, all others being subject to the poll tax (*jizya*) and irregular levies or demands, as well as to effective official disenfranchisement, although under *siyāsa* and the doctrine of *'urf* they were free to maintain their traditional custom and social groupings.

I draw two conclusions from this review. First, as a rule of method, in the comparative sociology of law, it seems as essential to examine the history of legal theories as to observe the operation of legal systems themselves. In a very special sense, these theories and ideologies, however imperfect they may be, as in modern Britain or ancient Rome, serve to define the framework within which law proceeds. It is furthermore possible, given suitable data, to refine an initial analysis of the special properties and assumptions of differing systems of law by comparing their adaptation to a common situation such as African pluralism provides. Perhaps only by some such procedure are we likely to develop a culture-free notion of legal facts significant for theory and practical affairs alike.

My second conclusion relates to the theory of law itself. We have found that the critical element in three traditions—Muslim, British, and French—is their treatment of corporate bodies other than the state. Muslim law apparently ignores the question, but thereby permits great adaptive freedom; British law explicitly provides legal recognition for autonomous corporations; French law as explicitly excludes them. It seems possible that law is both the process and the product of processes by which corporations emerge, acquire definition, and articulate with one another within a wider unit. In Muslim theory, the most inclusive corporation is the House of Islam; but when dominant, Muslims are legally free to acknowledge the corporate organization of their pagan or *dhimmī* subjects, whose traditional customs are accordingly recognized as valid in regulating their internal affairs. Without any overriding religious commitment or classification, British law permits equally flexible accommodation. Per contra, French law, which most perfectly expresses the dominant rational Western theory of law, assumes a primary sovereign corporation, the state, and accordingly denies the legality of prior or independent units unless the latter are expressly recognized by the state. In their common African situation, the responses of these dominant legal traditions inevitably differed; and their relative capacities to absorb native legal and political institutions into their framework varied inversely with their logical closure and formal completeness, that is, with the specificity of their political presuppositions. If this conclusion holds, its pertinence for sociologists concerned with the general problem of law and social control may lie in its stress on corporations as modal units of social and legal structure.

PART II.

TRADITIONAL LEGAL SYSTEMS

3.

LAND LAW IN THE MAKING

by Philip Mayer and Iona Mayer

Introduction

In this paper we apply the anthropological microscope to a specific case of law in the making: the genesis and the development of one branch of law—land law—among a given people at a given time. The people are the Gusii of western Kenya; the time is 1925-1950.

The kind of study undertaken here is theoretically relevant because it can help us to test, by reference to concrete material, the soundness of ideas that have been worked out in the field of theoretical jurisprudence, that is, historically and sociologically oriented theories about the origins and the development of law. It is, however, beyond the scope of the paper to analyze in detail how the material bears on specific hypotheses.

The material shows a new body of law developing, at a time that is still recent and for which official written records exist, without deliberate guidance from either legislators or authorities, colonial or indigenous. It was an apparently spontaneous emergence of a new branch of common law. In other parts of the world it may still be possible to watch and record such a process among a tribal people. British East Africa, to which Gusii country belonged at the time under review, would doubtless have afforded many good examples; East African official files and court records of the colonial period must be rich in similar material, which seems not to have been sufficiently exploited by anthropologists or by lawyers.

The declared policy of noninterference with native laws and customs except on grounds of repugnancy, in Kenya, was not always practicable in regard to land law and custom, especially in the face of the serious land problems and conflicts that developed in some areas. Even before World War II, royal commissioners and others from time to time recommended the use of legislative power to guide the development of land systems.[1] Nevertheless, so long as things went on reasonably smoothly,

[1] For notes to chapter 3, see page 247.

the most common policy was to "find" rather than to "make" civil law for the tribal peoples, in this field as in others, and to let development proceed along its own lines. It was under this policy of laissez-faire that a new land law emerged among the Gusii within a generation.

Like many East African peoples, the Gusii traditionally had only a rudimentary land law, though some other branches of substantive law were highly developed. The simple reason was that land had always seemed abundant in relation to demand. The Pax Britannica brought in its wake three events that together made for land shortage: freezing of boundaries; population explosion; and, eventually, the introduction of cash crops in a market economy. As was to be expected, Gusii land law first developed during the colonial period,[2] when a new form of competition arose, necessitating social control. We are mainly concerned with the further question as to why it developed along the particular lines it did.

Authority, Competition, and the Rule of Law

In leaving the Gusii to develop land law along their own lines, British administrators were not leaving it to traditional authorities—chiefs, priests, councils of elders—for there were no constituted authorities in the indigenous society. The Gusii were an extreme example of the acephalous pattern, which was not uncommon in East Africa. The only controllers of or spokesmen for groups of persons had been fathers/grandfathers, each of whom, as head of a family, represented authority to his own wife, children, and grandchildren. Outside these narrow limits the cohesive principle was not common authority or leadership, but mutual loyalty or solidarity conceptualized as common descent (of lineages, clans, tribes, and the nation as a whole). Not even minor lineages vested authority in recognized elders, as was true of some neighboring chiefless peoples.[3]

In some parts of Africa the segmentary descent system is associated with a more or less centralizing ancestor cult, with recognized priestly authorities. Although the dominant religious system of the Gusii was indeed an ancestor cult, it required no large cooperating unit and no priest other than the father/grandfather officiating for his own family.

Shortly before World War I, native authorities had been created by the British administrators, who had divided Gusii country into seven chieftainships. Each chieftainship was further divided into a number of headmanships, corresponding on the whole to traditional areas of solidarity, tribal and clan areas defined by the inhabitants' claim to common descent. The chiefs and headmen were not legitimated in any traditional way, and remained in principle simply agents of the new administration.[4] The powers and the tasks entrusted to them did not include legislation or anything else that would affect the development of land law. Thus, as noted above, the Gusii had no indigenous authorities or elders, secular or sacred, traditional or modern, to whom the allotment of land or the enunciation of land law would naturally fall when land shortage became a problem. Their land law developed as an apparently spontaneous movement by the people themselves, driven into competing for land and eventually into seeking ways whereby the competition could be regulated.

Traditionally, Gusii society had been organized for overt competition, to which the new land shortage merely added a new dimension. All the lines of social cleavage had been vertical, not horizontal; rank, caste, and class, strictly speaking, had not figured at all, any more than constituted authorities[5] and these lines of segmentation had been associated with the acknowledged rivalry at every point—between tribe and tribe, clan and clan, lineage and lineage, family and family, and even between brother and brother. These oppositions and rivalries had expressed themselves principally in competition for certain desiderata. Between large political corporations competition had been mainly for territory and power; between families and individuals, mainly for cattle, women, children, and personal influence. (These were intimately associated, because cattle, as bridewealth, were needed to obtain women and children, and men acquired influence through having plenty of all three.) To the Gusii all such competition seemed natural and not reprehensible; that "brothers fight for the mother's breast" was a favorite axiom. But precisely because it was natural, or inevitable, it had to be disciplined by certain regulating codes of law and convention, which everybody included within Gusii society must accept in principle. Indeed, in the absence of institutions of centralized authority, a national cult, and so forth, the acceptance of these codes could be called the principal defining factor of Gusii society. The nation was defined by descent from Mogusii; the society, by the rule of law.

Before the British occupation, Gusii clans, each being sovereign in both a political and a military sense, fought one another for territory and cattle much as they fought Kipsigis and Masai. The Gusii codes, however, prohibited the killing of women and children and the burning of houses (which were in order when fighting non-Gusii enemies), and required that compensation eventually be offered for men killed. This regulation governing the relationships of sovereign clans was a rule of law in only a loose sense; it might be called customary or conventional, rather than strictly legal, especially as the sanctions were simply reciprocal (fear of retaliation) and there were no agents of reconciliation who were not internal to one side or the other. But when competition was between families or individuals—whether of the same or different clans—there were mechanisms that deserved to be called "legal." Competing claims to women, cattle, or children could be brought before supposedly disinterested third parties, the *etureti* elders, who were required to apply a code of specific legal rules, the Gusii law of bridewealth.[6] The bridewealth code, the main corpus of traditional Gusii law, had special significance for the emergence of land law, which derived mainly from the application of bridewealth-law procedures and principles to the settlement of land disputes.

Land law developed after shortage had motivated Gusii families to give up their old rights to scattered arable plots in exchange for compact farms which were easier to defend against competitors. Subsequently, judicial elders were called upon to define the boundaries of such farms more exactly. Lacking substantive law to guide their boundary definition, they had to reconcile competing neighbors as best they could. Once drawn, however, the boundaries made it possible for ownership to emerge out of possession. Gusii themselves say of this process that "land was becoming *etugo*" (i.e., patrimony or heritable family property). Since the word "etugo" had normally applied only to livestock, the saying indicates the Gusii's awareness that the developing land law was closely modeled on the older bridewealth law. Gusii apply the statement especially to the parceling out of land among members of a family, which came to follow much the same lines as the distribution of patrimonial cattle. But the negotiation of boundaries between neighbor families, as a process, owed much to the concept of contract obligation existing in the law of bridewealth exchange.

Judicial Process and the Development of Land Law

Traditionally, Gusii law (bridewealth or other) was expounded and applied by the etureti elders. In terms of rank they were ordinary men who had no ascribed authority or status; their position depended on skill in reconciling disputes and on "knowing the law well." People would patronize them for these special abilities in much the same way as a skilled herbalist or a harp player might be patronized. The word "etureti" means the extra hut in which a Gusii husband may receive other men, away from women and children. Any married man may have an etureti hut, but "etureti elder" signifies the man to whose etureti hut people of the locality most often turned when they wanted legal advice or arbitration. The renown of an etureti elder was gauged by the distances that people came in order to consult him.

In this traditional system, the decisions of etureti elders were not backed by force, but by the moral consensus of the community. The promulgation of a decision gave the successful disputant an assurance of his legal and moral right, and, if satisfaction was not then made, he might forcibly seize his due—cattle, child, wife, and so on—with the community's approval. In cases involving people of different clans, both sides might bring in etureti elders, but, in theory at least, their status was still that of third parties or disinterested technical experts.

It was largely at the etureti level that the Gusii began to evolve a new code of rules about land in the period under consideration. The colonial administration, however, had also introduced new judicial authorities. At first the government-created chiefs and headmen were empowered to try cases, but these powers were removed *de lege,* if not entirely *de facto,* before the period we are concerned with. Considerable judicial power was vested in the British district commissioner and district officers, who were magistrates ex officio and could hear cases either at the administrative headquarters (Kisii Boma) or on their periodical tours of the country. Even more significant for ordinary people was the introduction of native tribunals, one for each half of Gusii country as well as one district appeal tribunal which the Gusii shared with the Luo peoples of the district. These tribunals consisted of panels of native elders appointed by the government specifically to hear and judge cases "according to native law and custom" (Gusii elders for Gusii litigants and Luo elders for Luo litigants).

The administration gave formal recognition and blessing to the etureti system by maintaining an official list of all etureti elders in each clan area. It thus in fact introduced a new element of rigidity and permanence. It did not, however, attach *askari's* (constables) to the etureti elders, as it did to the native tribunals and the district officials and chiefs. Nor did the etureti keep case records, as did, in some periods at least, both the magistrates' courts and the native tribunals. Some kinds of cases could, if desired, be taken directly to the British magistrates or the native tribunals, but not always land cases. Magistrates and tribunals preferred these cases to be considered first by the local etureti elders, who could more conveniently make an on-the-spot inspection. At the time of our fieldwork (1946-1949), a Gusii who brought a land complaint to a tribunal or a magistrate had to be able to report "what the local elders had said."

The judicial innovations of the colonial period, then, meant that any contestant who felt dissatisfied with an etureti verdict could take his case up to a new kind of constituted judicial authority, which kept records and dispensed justice. As competition for land was becoming keen, and as etureti elders had no halo of ascribed authority and no means of enforcing their verdicts, many contestants gladly turned to the new fountains of justice. They did so with such alacrity that the Gusii became officially known as the most litigious people in Kenya. Arthur Phillips, in his *Report on Native Tribunals* (1945), made reference to the "comments on the intensely litigious disposition of the Kisii" (i.e., Gusii) which "are to be found in official reports for at least thirty years past." Figures are given which show that the Gusii, with only two-thirds the population of the neighboring Luo, brought to the tribunals three or four times as many civil cases, and four or five times as many appeals, in a given year.[7]

It was within this framework that the new land law emerged. As the old communal agrarian system was in process of disruption, families and individuals quarreled over land more and more frequently. At times local etureti elders tried to reconcile the disputes without the guidance of legal rules; at other times they applied rules proper to a more familiar type of quarrel, that is, over bridewealth rights. Cases already digested by etureti elders on these lines proceeded to the two native tribunals, where again they were heard by Gusii elders pledged to apply native law and custom. Here they were given further consistency, and the common law began to crystallize, with bridewealth-law features more or less firmly embedded in it. Some cases went on further appeal and reached British magistrates who, reluctant to interfere with native law and custom, made no deliberate alterations of principle.

In the course of our fieldwork we scrutinized and analyzed some hundreds of tribunal and appeal tribunal land case records. We attended scores of etureti hearings and took notes of the proceedings, as there were no official records at this level. In addition, we interviewed many tribunal and etureti elders, as well as ordinary people.

The need for land law arose from the the factor of land shortage, which made every Gusii family anxious to secure sufficient land for itself in the face of increasing competition from others. There would have been various ways, in theory, to apportion the limited cake among the growing numbers of the hungry. For example, full landrights might have been reserved to eldest sons or senior houses, leaving the rest to become their dependents or tenants or to be forced off the land altogether. Or, as many Gusii had taken to labor migration (spending periods at work on white-owned farms, in towns, or in the army), full landrights might have been reserved to the stationary subsistence cultivators, and the migrants forced to give up their land claims. But no such solution, involving a division into haves and have-nots, would have been likely to suggest itself to the Gusii at the grass-roots level where the new law was being evolved. To them, just as every mature man must have cattle and a family of his own, so every mature man must have land of his own for his family. The evolving legal system may be read as a commentary on the tendency of the Gusii social structure to insist on fair shares for all.

Law, Dominion, and Communal Landright

Landright in the old Gusii system (up to about 1925) was largely communal, with active competition for land occurring mainly between communities or large corporations—clans or neighborhoods—which were confronting each other on a political level. Such competing territorial claims were settled through a trial of strength, by fighting or negotiation. To some extent even the land claims of families and individuals within the group were settled in a similar manner. In this sense little actual land law prevailed. We shall see how, at first, legal process was invoked in land disputes as another form of the trial of strength, with no significant legal principles at stake.

A distinct area (clan land), traditionally occupied by each clan community, was isolated from its neighbors by buffer zones of unclaimed land. The clan land typically took the form of a long strip, which fell into two parts, the settlements (*amatongo*) area at one end and the bush (*oborabu*) area at the other. At the settlements end were the scattered homesteads in which the families of the clan community lived, and the arable fields where they grew their staple crops. The bush end (clan bush) was their common pasture; young men and boys camped out there in specially built cattle posts (*ebisarate*), with their parents' cattle under their care.

Besides enabling cattle to be pastured at a suitable distance from crops and concentrated for defense purposes, this division of the clan land was directly relevant to the mode of territorial expansion. If land grew scarce in the settlements area, the community could expand onto the clan bush area, and warriors and cattle would then move on ahead, staking out a claim to new clan bush. As they felt their way ahead, the clan community next door might counterclaim, sending its own warriors with their cattle to drive off the first comers. (To drive one's cattle toward an enemy was a common challenge or symbolic aggression.) We believe that the characteristic shape of Gusii clan lands, the elongated strip, resulted from the successive staking of land claims by groups advancing side by side toward enemy borders (Masai, Kipsigis, Luo, or hostile

Gusii tribes), each determined not to let its line of future expansion be cut off. The danger that the neighboring clan community might get ahead and spread out in front would be an incentive to keep abreast, even without an immediate need for more land.

The settlements area of a clan strip comprised a series of subcommunities, the neighborhoods (*amasaga*; sing., *risaga*). The people of each neighborhood were internally organized for agricultural cooperation.[8] Normally these people would send their cattle and youths jointly to the same cattle post. At home they would join in reciprocal work parties; but, more significantly for our purposes, they joined to grow their staple crops side by side, forming large common fields (*chindemero*; sing., *endemero*; cognate with *okomera*, to cultivate). Insofar as law applied to land at all, it applied mostly to the plots that made up the common fields.

The common field contained a plot for each active cultivator who belonged to the neighborhood, perhaps ten to fifty or sixty in all. Every married woman had a plot as a matter of course, to feed her own household. Some men chose to cultivate for personal profit, to exchange the grain into livestock. The whole field was under one crop at one time. The staple crops—eleusine, millet, and beans (maize was a later introduction)—were grown in rotation, the cycle requiring about two and a half years; after that the field was allowed to lie fallow for five or six years. As all the staple foods were needed all the time, each neighborhood required a sizable number of different common-field sites at various stages of rotation.

Normally the neighborhood cultivators returned to the same sites after each fallow period. But sometimes a few men would clear new plots for their wives on a new site, and others would follow until a new common field was established. Just as the driving of cattle onto new pastures was a potential challenge to the people of the next clan, so the clearing of new common-field plots was a potential challenge to the people of the next neighborhood. At the first signs of activity men of the other neighborhood might appear and claim the site as theirs, and perhaps actually start rival clearing operations. Again, there was no law to settle the dispute. The neighborhoods faced each other as competitors between whom the only real argument was force, or negotiation. But, whereas rival clans could fight for territory with spears, rival neighborhood communities within the clan could fight only with sticks, or with fists or words. A common-field site, once successfully occupied, became an acknowledged part of the neighborhood territory, and could then be used again and again by the same group.

The general principle may thus be characterized as the staking of claim by taking possession, and the defending of it by force; only then was possession fully acknowledged by the competitors. A similar principle may also be seen in the delimiting of individual plots on a new common-field site. Initially it was left to each cultivator to assert the limits of his own proposed plot. Those who came next would inquire, "Where have you eaten?" (i.e., "How far have you reached?"), and accommodate themselves accordingly. To anyone who complained the retort would be, "Why didn't you get here earlier?" When disputes arose over the best patches (meaning, in Gusii terms, the most easily worked rather than the most fertile), there would be a quarrel or a fight; the stronger party would force the weaker to withdraw. At the stage of first acquisition, then, there was no law to appeal to, even about individual plots. There was no disinterested third party; elders would simply look on, saying, "Let them fight it out," or, "Why quarrel over land when there is plenty more?" But whether delimited first by peaceful cooperation or by open conflict, the individual plot, once established, came to belong to its proprietor by firm legal right. He was explicitly entitled to take up the same plot again whenever the group returned to an already used site for another rotation. Boundary stones were usually left in position through the fallow period. If the "owner" had left the neighborhood, the plot could be taken and divided by those working the plots on either side; but if he returned within a reasonable period, the right would revive. Then it was obligatory only to let the present users harvest their current crop.

Disputes about these established plots, unlike disputes over their first acquisition, were matters for the legal skill of elders and the witness of neighbors. It is fair to say that the right to the plot, plus the right of a temporary user to harvest his current crop, or in some instances to complete a rotation, constituted all there was of Gusii land law, as opposed to political regulation under the dominion principle.

The Principle of Dominion

Under the traditional system, all land either was unclaimed no-man's-land or was under the exclusive dominion of a particular clan; there was no legal basis for saying which land belonged to which clan. Even old settlements (and, a fortiori, newer ones) were not guaranteed to the occupying clan by anything more than the fact of occupation, or dominion, itself; they had never been sacralized by a mystic charter, for example, or by a historic claim to ancient settlements. Clan boundaries were simply political; that is, they were where the neighbors for the time being would concede them. They shifted according to the fortunes of war. Furthermore, whole clans might abandon their territories and migrate to new ones, driven by famine, disease, or military insecurity. Many Gusii clans commemorate such migrations in their oral historical record.

The proper land of a clan was the land on which it had settled and, for the time being, had resisted challenge. The acquisition of new land was the act of obtaining dominion by establishing cattle posts and sending out warriors and cattle, and subsequently by building homesteads and starting cultivation. Use would come first and title afterward. If two clans wanted the same piece of land, both would try to establish a claim by use, and the question of title would be settled by fighting, which ended in one side withdrawing. The position was the same, as we have seen, with competing claims of neighborhoods to common-field sites within the clan area, and again with the definition of individual plots on a new common field. In none of these instances was there any law to which groups or individuals could appeal.

Another common feature, besides the absence of law proper and the dependence of title on actual dominion, was the idea that dominion, and therefore title, could be maintained only over a continuous area. This second point, minor though it may seem, has been of importance in shaping present-day Gusii land tenure. The two together are implied in what we are calling the dominion principle.

That each clan land formed a continuous area needs no special explanation. If some of the clanspeople were cut off from the main body by a neighboring clan driving in a wedge, or if they hived off on their own account to virgin land which was separated by the settlements of other clans, or by large expanses of no-man's-land, they had effectively left the parent community, and formed the nucleus of a new, separate clan community as dwellers on its territory. It is not uncommon to find two not quite neighboring clan communities that say they owe their separation to a history of this kind, and still retain a common exogamic bond to commemorate the fact that "formerly we were one." The point in question here is that their territories are spatially and functionally distinct; there can be no such thing as a clan land in two places.

The same applies to the neighborhood community. Its members were neighbors in the literal sense. Any new cultivation or settlement that they claimed as theirs would have to be a direct extension of their present territory; otherwise it would constitute a new separate neighborhood, or fall within the orbit of another neighborhood.

The clan pastures, too, while theoretically open to the whole clan community, tended to be marked out into separate areas on the dominion principle. We have seen how the cattle camps collectively proclaimed the clan's dominion over the pastures as a whole, but each separate cattle camp also asserted the claim of its own inmates to pasture their beasts in a certain place, or to start cultivating there if they eventually wished, or to have their own neighborhood group start cultivation.

The general picture, then, was one of communal dominion, strong and incontrovertible at the place where the group actually lived, and thinning out from there toward somewhat indeterminate boundaries; the title would be lost if the group moved away, whether voluntarily or dislodged by conquest. In short, as the ultimate arguments were physical presence and the power to defend the area, there was need for concentration of the group and for continuity of its area.

These themes may now be traced in the consolidation process that produced a new type of compact family farm, the kind of farm which almost all Gusii had by about 1940. The driving force was the desire to keep arable land under the family's control, especially during the long fallow periods. In the old system, the legal right to plots scattered on the various common-field sites was sufficiently guaranteed by the witness of neighbors and the moral backing of elders. Under changing conditions this legal protection seemed inadequate, and most cultivators preferred to exchange it for personal dominion, that is, for the effective physical control of one continuous area. The dominion principle came down from community to family level.

Individualization without Law

The communal land system underwent profound changes when population began to expand rapidly, and clan boundaries at the same time became frozen. Interclan fighting was stopped, so that there could be no more spreading forward onto no-man's land. A new land law emerged, but only after an intermediate stage in which possession was the only real argument.

Through all the changes the clan and neighborhood communities continued to be firmly contained within territorial bounds; the neighborhoods continued to be organized for many of the old forms of cooperation; the people still mostly grew the old staple crops in the old rotation; and the large common fields could still be seen, with their individual plots all under one crop at one time. But by about 1940 the bush strips that formerly separated clan lands could no longer be seen; nor could the clan bush areas at the forward end of each clan land. There were homesteads and cultivation wherever physically possible. People would still point to what they called the settlements and the bush of their clan land, but the division was only the invisible one between settlements of earlier and later date. The cattle posts had disappeared, along with the old common pastures; cattle were all kept in the homestead and pastured as near there as possible.

These physically visible changes had been accompanied by other changes, amounting to the start of a revolution in land tenure. By the time all bush land had been taken up for settlement and cultivation, the replacement of scattered plots by compact family farms was also more or less complete. The common fields, where they existed, were only outwardly the same. The fact was that the old legal right of each neighborhood cultivator to his own plots had lapsed, and plots could only be borrowed, subject to the overriding right of the nearest homestead farmer. This type of consolidated homestead farm is called by the Gusii the "in-front land" (*egeita*) of so-and-so's homestead. The substance of the revolution in land tenure is that "in front" today is not only meant literally, but implies legally protected possession and even ownership.

The consolidation came about initially, without legal regulation, as a direct expression of the desire to exercise physical control, to secure actual possession of arable land which was becoming scarce and coveted, and literally to seize enough land for one's own family before anyone else could get it. The old legal right to return to an established common-field plot would be tacitly or explicitly surrendered in return for the advantage of having more cultivation space here and now, next to one's own homestead, and being able to control it accordingly. According to eyewitnesses, "When the people of a neighborhood came to an old common-field site at the beginning of the new season, expecting to cultivate there as before, somebody whose homestead was nearby would refuse to let them. He would say, 'I am going to cultivate all this land myself. But if you keep away from this place, then I also will keep away from your places. I don't want to cultivate near your homestead any more and I don't want you to cultivate near mine.' "

The land directly in front of a homestead was the easiest to oversee and control, particularly as it was always below the homestead. (Gusii country is hilly, and the people always build facing downhill.) From the homestead the claim would thin out by degrees that were as yet undefined; during this consolidation stage there were no private boundaries. It would perhaps be more accurate to say that the effective possession thinned out according to the diminishing readiness of the inmates to challenge other cultivators, in proportion to the distance from the homestead, for the question of title, strictly speaking, did not arise until the question of use became a matter of dispute. If the act of starting cultivation passed unchallenged, the cultivator had established his title to the land; if not, the title would be decided by the outcome of the ensuing dispute.

Thus the act of building came to assume great significance in Gusii land law. The building of a hut, even without cultivation, was considered tantamount to an assertion of right to cultivate the land around and in front; the title would be strongest in the land nearest to the hut, and would thin out with increasing distance. Accordingly, at the time we did our fieldwork, it was regarded as an offense to build a hut near someone else's boundary, even if the boundary was not actually violated, because the act suggested that the hut builder's title was or soon would be strong in the very place that his neighbor's was weak. Many Gusii lawsuits have been filed with the charge that "building near my boundary" is an act of encroachment.

The nucleus of the consolidated farm might be any one of the three scattered resources of the family—its homestead, its arable, its pasture. Some families were content with claiming, for their own exclusive cultivation and pasture, land near their existing homesteads. But others built new homesteads (e.g., for newly married sons) at distant plots where hitherto they had exercised only cultivation rights. And others sent one or more sons out onto what had been the common pastures, to start new homesteads and cultivation there. This last tactic resulted in the final individualization of the common clan bush land, and in the disappearance of cattle posts. Most Gusii think that the government deliberately put down the cattle-post system for political reasons, that is, because it mistrusted concentrations of armed Gusii warriors. (District records reveal that officials did regard cattle posts as breeding grounds of idleness and as hideouts for criminals.) But settlement on the clan bush might soon have spelled their end in any event.

In theory, clan bush land was "common" in the sense of being equally open to all members of the community, but in practice cattle posts served to protect the special claims of certain neighborhood communities in particular areas of clan bush. With the cattle posts gone, there was no more such protection, and as a result the newest neighborhood communities, those created on former common pasture during the land rush, developed a very mixed character in lineage terms. The mixture contrasts markedly with the lineage homogeneity that characterizes most old settlements, and also to some extent the older type of offshoot settlements centered on former cattle posts.

When recalling the rush to settle on clan bush, Gusii eyewitnesses emphasized that "at first people only cultivated there, without building, but afterward they both cultivated and built." It is clear that the main impulse, at first, was simply to accommodate growing families with the arable plots they needed in increasing numbers. Homestead building followed, not necessarily because of an objection to the distances involved—the old common-field system had also involved distances—but because of the significance of hut building as a symbol of dominion or effective possession. Without building, cultivation on the clan bush was less protected even than the most distant common-field strips in the old settlement areas. Those had at least been defended against outsiders by the common interest of the neighborhood group as a whole; and within the group the individual's right to the particular plot had been endorsed by the witness of neighbors, all cultivation being carried on in full view of the whole group. But the new clan-bush cultivations, which were well out of sight, seemed to demand that somebody live on the spot to safeguard people's rights. Accordingly a newly married son, or perhaps a son or a group of sons with their mother, would be sent to build somewhere on the clan bush. In effect, the cattle posts, which had once stood sentinel for the communal interests of neighborhoods, were being replaced by splinter homesteads standing sentinel for the interests of particular families. Dominion, or possession, was still the effective principle, but the unit was smaller. The individualization of the clan bush still was no more legal than the consolidation of farms in the old settlements had been.

Common fields, consisting of a number of contiguous plots under uniform cultivation, may still be seen in Gusii country. Although outwardly resembling the old common fields, they rest on different legal and social concepts. The idea of the old common field was that members of a neighborhood community would cultivate side by side on any land they chose, within their territory, every member being expected to participate because he belonged to the community and every outsider being excluded because he did not. The modern so-called common field, by contrast, involves a concept of temporary borrowing and lending. The whole field falls (as all Gusii land now does) within the sphere of one person's own homestead land, his egeita, and the other cultivators are held to have borrowed their plots from this homestead owner. There is an expectation of reciprocity: if X lends plots to Y and Z this year, he hopes they will lend him plots another year, or perhaps even now. (Simultaneous mutual lending makes sense because different crops are grown at the same time.) But it is only a moral expectation, not a firm right. And many people now stay outside the common-field system altogether. Even those who do lend may choose to whom they lend; nowadays they often lend to extraclan kin of their own (such as married daughters), as well as or instead of neighborhood people. Furthermore, the borrower has no fixed right to return to the plot at the next cultivation season, but only a hope or moral expectation. His only fixed legal right is that he cannot be turned off the land until he has harvested his standing crop.

Lawsuits without Law

The appeal to law began to enter the picture in the second stage of the revolution in land tenure, that is, the drive to have the newly consolidated farms legally demarcated and the boundaries legally protected. Eventually this development caused the hardening of farms into what we shall call estates. The vernacular word "egeita" does not discriminate between farm and estate; there is no precise equivalent for the latter. Perhaps the nearest vernacular equivalent lies in the saying that "nowadays land has become etugo."

By the late 1940's the legal and social concepts of estate ownership had become partly, but not fully, standardized. A farmer, for example, would claim complete and exclusive rights within his own homestead farm, and would sue, in the native tribunals, anyone who proposed either to cultivate, to graze, or to build on any part of it. Another farmer would be linked in more complex relationships with his neighbors on one or more sides; from one neighbor he would tolerate encroachments of certain kinds, from others he would not. One farmer could point to exact boundaries on all sides, either in terms of natural objects (streams, trees, stones) or of specially planted hedges. Another would be vague about the boundary on one or more sides—"we have not settled it yet." But Gusii law certainly admitted the principle of protecting the estate, even if it did not yet specify, as a uniform rule, precisely in what sense the land must "belong to" the family occupying the homestead, or how it must be marked off.

Most Gusii stock phrases for farms at different stages of hardening into estates referred either to "boundaries" or to "dividing." The Gusii would speak of "having made permanent boundaries," or "boundaries that are not permanent yet," or "boundaries on this side only"; of "agreeing on the boundaries ourselves" or "having the elders settle the boundaries"; of "dividing the land," or "waiting to divide it," or "not dividing it, for we are all on good terms." The concept of "estate," though not directly reflected in the vernacular, is necessary to reduce these phenomena to order. By "estate" we mean any block of land, whether including one or more *ebieta* (homestead farms), which is externally defended on all sides by authoritative boundaries, and not internally divided by any authoritative boundary. We define "authoritative boundaries" as boundaries that the occupants have had explicitly asserted by legal process and therefore have a right to maintain against any form of encroachment or challenge. As a form of demarcation between neighbors, the authoritative boundary is an alternative to the old-style buffer strip or no-man's-land, or the mere fading out of title by undefined degrees. It stands for protection by law as against dominion.

Within perhaps ten years from the completion of consolidation, the whole of Gusii country was divided into estates with definite boundaries. If a farmer had had all his own boundaries authoritatively defined, he had a single-farm estate. Where two or more neighbors had "not yet divided" or "not yet settled our boundaries," there was a multiple-farm estate. In the latter the plots might be partly interspersed, each farmer cultivating some land on one side of the estate and some on the other side. But this visible sign of a multiple-farm estate was not always present; the real test lay in what kind of action was taken, and by whom, in a dispute over rights to building, cultivation, or grazing. The authoritative boundaries of an estate were shown up by resistance to challenge; on a multiple-farm estate, resistance would be offered collectively by all the farmers within it. If readjustments were matters of purely internal agreement instead of recourse to law, the farms concerned were regarded as still internal to an estate.

Neither farm nor estate was a permanently stable unit; on the contrary, both were stages in an ongoing process. Single farms had turned into estates as, under pressure of land scarcity, men felt more and more need to defend their family's land by authoritative boundaries. But single-farm estates tended to turn into multiple-farm estates (i.e., divide into farms internally) as more sons grew up and needed separate cultivation areas for their wives, areas that could no longer be found on the former clan bush. In turn, these separate farms, linked in one estate so long as the brothers remained on good terms, often hardened into separate small estates later on.

How did it happen that, before the existence of substantive law about estates, people frequently had recourse to legal processes to define estate boundaries? The point at which an indefinite boundary hardened into an authoritative one was recognizable through the outbreak of conflict, marking resistance to proposed encroachment. A man sends one of his wives to cultivate at a given place not far from his homestead, or one of his sons to build there, hoping that the neighbors on that side will do nothing. Instead, the neighbor protests that he has the same patch in mind for his own wife or son. One of the parties then goes to the local etureti elder. The etureti judgment is that the boundary should run along such-and-such a line. One party, perhaps feeling dissatisfied, takes the case up to the native tribunal, where the boundary suggested by the etureti is either confirmed or modified But in any event the crucial fact has been established by the initial recourse to etureti elders: the conflicting parties wish to regard their farms as separate estates, or parts of separate estates, divided by an authoritative boundary.

Boundary definition was prompted by disputes over land that no one farmer had hitherto claimed by the act of taking it into use, just as earlier territorial disputes between clans or neighborhoods arose over land that neither side had previously used. So long as the borderland remains no-man's-land, both parties are content, but as soon as X makes a move, Y fears for his own future expansion. To let X get away with it now would be tantamount to conceding him a permanent right and permitting him to block the line of advance which Y might need in the future, even if he does not need it now.

Clans fought with spears, and neighborhood groups with sticks, but neither weapon is suitable for neighbor families disputing a patch of land between their farms. If argument proved useless (as it probably did) they went to the elders; that is, they started a lawsuit. From this point of view we may, in a sense, regard the initial lawsuits over boundaries as a substitute for fighting. As lawsuits without substantive law, they were open trials of strength with no possible decision by precise legal rules. The principle of dominion smiles equally on both contestants. The result is a large body of tribunal records in which only laconic statements like these appear: "A claims this *shamba* [patch of land] from B. B denies. Judgment: the boundary runs from north to south, the boundary marks being so-and-so." Or, "We order it divided in the middle." Hundreds of such records may be found in the tribunal files, records that do not even hint at any reasons underlying the judgments; they present a marked contrast to the long and explicitly argued records of cattle cases. The reason for their disappointing taciturnity is clear when we realize that the real function of this kind of case was to restore peace merely by having a boundary where none had been before. Once drawn and witnessed, the boundary would be protected by law, but its initial drawing was guided by nothing more than convenience and equity, based on topography and the apparent needs of the two parties.

Indeed, up to the late 1940's, the Gusii still regarded the acquisition and retention of land as a contest of strength between groups, but with the difference that the groups were smaller (families) and the channels were legal. Everyone was constantly on the lookout for action on the part of his neighbors which could be interpreted as encroachment or challenge, to be resisted at law. "He has been cultivating on my land"; "He is building on my boundary" (or even "near my boundary"); "He sent his wife to sow where my wife had dug"; "He has been cutting down trees on my side"—such stock complaints, laid before elders or tribunals, reflected the same attitudes as formerly prevailed in political territorial disputes between clans or neighborhoods: constant vigilance and fear of being forestalled, the interplay of aggressive and defensive considerations.

Just before 1950 some of the legal concepts surrounding the estate and the authoritative boundary were still new enough to be fluid, particularly in regard to rights *in absentia*. If a man left his estate the neighbors on both sides would have an acknowledged right to borrow his land in order to grow and harvest crops there (cf. the right to use the absentee's plot on the old common field). But elders did not agree as to whether or not, or when, borrowing would turn into firm right by possession. Some tended to emphasize the legal right of the absentee regardless of his physical absence; the idea may be found in some tribunal judgments. Others, probably the majority, emphasized the impossibility of protecting absentee rights indefinitely. They felt that right would die away little by little in proportion to the length of absence: "If he comes back after a year or two, he should get it all. After four years, perhaps half. After six years, a smaller piece. After ten years, he should not get anything back." (Differing figures are suggested.) Similar cases seemed to be decided differently by different elders.

Another element of uncertainty was introduced by bribery, which was quite prevalent in all litigation, but particularly so in land cases. The interplay of local factions and influences was also a factor. Recourse to bribery, factionalism, or intrigue was itself a form of self-help, facilitated by the fact that land law, unlike cattle law, had not yet crystallized at all points. The most effective weapon was still to have support in the neighborhood.

Land Law and Cattle Law

THE CONTRACT PRINCIPLE

The legal declaration of family land boundaries, as just described, may be compared with the traditional procedure for concluding a bridewealth contract. Gusii bridewealth law, elaborate as it was, had always left plenty of room for bargaining between the two families of affines. The willingness to contract a marriage alliance at all, the identity of the girl, the quality of the beasts, the size and the number of the customary gifts which in principle must accompany them, the manner of delivery—all were matters for negotiation, often long and hard, in which each family tried to use its strength and cleverness to beat the other. But once the bargain had been struck, the trial of strength was over. This point was signalized by the customary ceremony called "agreement," at which many witnesses from both sides would be present, including the marriage go-between as a neutral third party. From then on the law protected the contract, with all its details, and failure to fulfill any of the numerous and continuing obligations (e.g., to replace beasts that died without progeny) was a matter for judicial process.

Similarly, in the establishment of authoritative boundaries between neighbor families, the seal of law was sought for an arrangement that grew out of a trial of strength between the families. A contract, negotiated on political lines—a trial of strength—is being legally ratified. Some publicity is essential: the bridewealth agreement requires the formal ceremony with all its witnesses; the land agreement requires the formal visit of the etureti elder who draws the boundary in public. The witness of neighbors confirms the agreement as to where the boundary shall run, and each party has a legal right, backed by both the elders and the community, to insist on fulfillment in every particular.

THE PATRIMONIAL CONCEPT

The consolidated farm, or estate, is family land. The competitors who carve out their respective homestead lands, and go to law to have the boundaries authoritatively defined, are the homestead heads, each concerned with providing for his own wives and sons and his sons' wives. We now have to consider the inheritance of land by, and its division among, members of a family. In contrast with interfamily division, intrafamily division is regulated by hard and fast law which is derived directly from the much older body of law about cattle patrimony.

The Gusii saying that "land has become etugo" again deserves careful consideration. "Etugo" refers primarily to cattle, but in a special sense; cattle are etugo only in relation to the human families or kin groups that claim them as property. The kin group with which etugo is most specifically associated is the "house" (*enyomba*), that is, a group composed of one mother and her children, and potentially the descendants of those children in the male line. The etugo of the house is its wealth, not wealth in general, but wealth in "cattle and children," as the Gusii say. The word is from the same root as the verb "to rear" (*ogotuga*), and the Gusii give this association a twofold meaning.

Cattle are necessary for rearing the family, providing them with such essentials as milk, meat, and hides; and cattle are reared themselves, that is, they increase naturally, as families do. Goats, sheep, and fowls may also be counted as etugo, but not grain, chattels, or money. The two basic ideas—sustenance and natural increase—are linked in the concept of continuity; the house and the herd each survive as an ongoing group.

Etugo, in the sense of livestock, has always been safeguarded for the house by an elaborate system of legal rules. It is inalienable from the house except for the proper purpose of increasing the human strength of the house. Marriage cattle brought in by the daughters of the house, for instance, or natural increase of those cattle, cannot be used in marriage by the sons of a cohouse without special permission, and, more important, without an acknowledgment of debt, which will be legally binding until the borrowing house has repaid the lending house, even if it be a generation or two later. The proper distribution of etugo within the family and the lineage, including the system of inheritance, is no less serious a matter than the interaffinal cattle transactions, and is regulated by no less massive a body of law; competing claims by half brothers are as familiar a cause of litigation as those by father and son-in-law.

What then is meant by saying that "land has become etugo"? Land is of course necessary for the sustenance of the family, and is associated in a certain sense with natural increase; but there is no novelty in this concept, whereas the Gusii are quite clear that "formerly land was not etugo." The meaning is twofold: (1) land, being relatively scarce, seems more precious than before; (2) being so regarded, land becomes more and more tied to the kinds of groups—the house and the family—with which Gusii have always associated the ownership of wealth. It is a proper object of competition, both between families and between fellow houses or fellow members of one house. It is part of the patrimony or personal heritage. Law must protect every man's right to patrimonial land, much as it has protected his right to patrimonial cattle.

In the Gusii law of property, notably of bridewealth, the interplay between the agnatic principle and that of house property[9] is such that it is generally impossible to define the extent of anybody's rights without reference to both father and mother. The agnatic principle is supreme insofar as the Gusii entirely repudiate the idea of vesting property in any bilateral kin group other than the elementary family itself; patrimony is always and unequivocally vested in the *egesaku* (patrilineal descent group), and may be inherited only by agnates. But the house principle which tempers the agnatic principle is also very firmly conceived, the rights of each elementary family within the compound being determined in the main by birth, and not being subject to material alteration even by the authority of the paterfamilias. Thus, all Gusii property rights may be reduced to the formula, "From the father but through the mother."

If the traditional cattle patrimony of a house is conceived primarily as the bridewealth brought in by the daughters, its present land patrimony is conceived as the holding of the mother—the land allotted specifically to her within the family egeita. The traditional Gusii pattern is that a newly married woman at first simply helps to cultivate the plots of her husband's mother (or of his senior wife), having as yet no separate household of her own. But within a few years either her husband should move with her to a new and separate homestead, or she should be allotted special plots of her own at the original homestead, for she must, as a mature married woman, become responsible for feeding her own household. The totality of a wife's own plots is her "holding"; in former times it would have consisted of scattered common-field plots, but today it comprises plots scattered through the family egeita, or perhaps concentrated at one side of it. It includes the fallow plots to which the wife will return, as well as those she now has under cultivation. (*De jure* attribution and responsibility are not affected by the day-to-day labor cooperation that homestead wives frequently undertake among themselves.)

In modern land law, the holding of a woman has become the birthright of her sons. A man may say, "This is where my father built and where my mother cultivated," or, in other words, "This is, or is part of, my mother's holding within my father's homestead land," with the implication that he is stating an absolute and incontrovertible claim. Any boundary dispute in which this principle can be invoked is no longer a lawsuit without law; the question is one of fact only.

All the full brothers have theoretically equal claims in their mother's holding (as also in the cattle patrimony of the house). Although the eldest may claim the right to choose first, none can be denied the right to build and cultivate if he wishes, and to make provision for each of his wives. If the house dies out, the inheritance passes to cohouses, following the same definite pattern that is enjoined for cattle patrimony.[10]

So long as people could hive off to virgin clan bush, the mother's holding was, so to speak, only a last line of defense. With the clan bush nearly all gone, it often became of primary importance. Today it may be vitally important to men who are forced to return home after a period as dwellers in another clan community.

How are holdings delimited? The paterfamilias has the main say during his lifetime. It is his responsibility "to show each wife on which side she may cultivate," or, if readjustment is needed, "to take land little by little from one wife and give it to another"; similarly he is "to show each son the place to build" when the son has a wife of his own. The authority of the paterfamilias is, however, subject to two limitations. First, he must always respect the house property principle. He may not authorize a son by one wife to set up house and cultivation on the holding of another wife, except with the full consent of all concerned, and even then it is regarded as a temporary "loan" (as also with loans of cattle). Second, he must see that there is, or eventually will be, provision for all his wives and all his sons alike, on a reasonably equal basis. No son may be permanently disinherited, for his birthright is stronger than paternal authority (as also with cattle birthright).

The death of either parent has an important bearing on the process by which farms harden into estates. The father's death crystallizes the holding of each of his wives into a legally unalterable unit. It removes the only person who was competent to enforce changes in the holding boundaries. The mother's death, on the other hand, first makes possible full individualization as among her sons, for, "While mother is alive, sons cannot divide her land," and "All the land belongs to mother; it is she who gives permission for her sons to build on it and for her sons' wives to cultivate on it." These are semistereotyped formulations which any Gusii will readily endorse. It follows, then, that so long as either parent remains alive, sons cannot establish individual estates in the full sense. The son's farm may or may not have become fully separate as a working unit, but whether it has or not, he cannot assert boundaries in his own right, or appeal to judicial elders about them.

Two reasons may be suggested to explain why Gusii law does not recognize final, authoritative boundaries between the adjoining farms of father and son, or the holdings of mother and daughter-in-law, until after the death of both father and mother. First, the principle of parental authority is at stake. Authoritative boundaries result from disputes; the neighbors who "are all on good terms" are those who "have not divided the land." While the parents are alive, there should be no disputes in the family; if there are, settlement should be made by the paterfamilias himself. He does not need, or cannot tolerate, a third party adjudicating among his sons, or between them and himself. Second, the house, and the compound family, are conceived dynamically; there is always a possibility of increase. However old the father may be, he could still marry another wife and add another house to his egesaku; however old the mother, she could increase her house by "buying" another child or another daughter-in-law. (Even a woman without a son may formally buy a daughter-in-law and grandchildren, using cattle of her house.) Therefore the rights of each child, during the lifetime of either parent, are presumptive rather than apparent. To negotiate a hard-and-fast division before the parents' death would mean disregarding the birthright due to possible future members of the group, their theoretically equal and inalienable shares.

Nowadays practically all estate-holding groups consist of close agnates, but it is not safe to make any further generalization. An estate-holding group composed of father and son(s), for instance, is formed when a son marries during his father's lifetime and is given a separate farm at one side of the parental farm, perhaps because there is no vacant clan bush. A group composed of full brothers results when the father predeceases the mother; the brothers are sons who "cannot divide the land because mother is alive." But these types, though common, are by no means the only groups that occupy multiple-farm estates. After the death of both parents has removed the impediment to establishing firm boundaries, some brothers are inclined to do so; others, however, do not do so "because we are all on good terms." In the next generation the heirs of the brothers who were all on good terms may or may not continue on the same amicable footing. Thus the estate-holding group may, but need not, come to include some members who are related to other members as paternal nephews, paternal uncles, or ortho-cousins.

There is a law entitling every man to stay alongside his brothers, "where father built and mother cultivated," but no law compels him to do so; no legal or structural rule determines which kin within the possible degrees are actually to remain within the estate-holding group, and which are to find land elsewhere on former clan bush, or to go away to be dwellers (*abamenyi*) with cognatic or affinal kin in another clan. Nor does any law, except for the restraint imposed by the life of a common parent, determine who will and who will not contract out of the former estate-holding group by asserting that his present farm boundaries are authoritative boundaries.

Clearly the estate-holding group is not a structural unit but, in Raymond Firth's sense, an organizational one. Gusii land law protects estates as such; it does not attach them to fixed groups of kin as such.

Birthright by Descent: Clanspeople and Dwellers

Through all the changes that have been described, the principle of clan land remained intact. Land within the clan area could never be permanently alienated, but could temporarily be used by dwellers who possessed certain rights.

The clan community, the group that occupies and exploits a clan land, always comprises a majority of true clanspeople and a minority of dwellers. The clansmen claim direct descent from the eponymous founder of the (patrilineally defined) clan; the clanswomen are their wives and unmarried daughters. (Daughters "marry out"; they are recruited into their husbands' clans at marriage.) A "dweller" is a man settled in the territory of a clan other than that to which he properly belongs by virtue of his descent. His proper clan allegiance, by descent, is not annulled, and theoretically can never be annulled, by the fact of his residence in another community; it remains manifest in his clan name and the field of exogamy which is entailed.[11]

A dweller generally establishes himself, in the first instance, near the homestead of some affinal or cognatic relative who allows him to build on vacant land. The arrangement is a personal one between kinsmen, though implicitly sanctioned by the rest of the community. Once the dweller has established his homestead, he becomes a full member of the local community in the sense that he enters into the cooperative organization of the neighborhood and is expected to give his loyalty to the clan when occasion arises. In former times his sons would live in the cattle posts together with the sons of clansmen proper, and his cattle would be herded together with theirs. And, so long as clan bush land was available, there seems to have been no doubt that dwellers were as much entitled to take it in for new cultivation as real clan members.

At the same time the dweller's different origin is constantly brought home by the fact that he is free to "marry his neighbors," and that he is not surrounded by close agnates in whose funeral rites he will join, but has funeral obligations to other people who die far away. There is among Gusii a strong feeling that dwellers must not be allowed to rival in numbers and strength the host clan among whom they have settled. Preponderance of true clansmen is secured, not by limiting the number of dwellers accepted, but by limiting the length of their stay and the absoluteness of their landrights, as expressed in a set of semiproverbial prohibitions with magico-religious sanctions: "A daughter must not grow gray hair at the place of her father"; "A sister's child [*omoigwa*] must not be buried at BoMame [place of its mother's people]"; or "A man must not be buried among his sister's children" nor "at the place of his in-laws." In other words, the only nonclansmen with whom a Gusii could normally hope to find refuge—affines and cognates related to him through a female link—are defined as people among whom he should not die or be buried: "If an in-law or a sister's child is buried at our place, his lineage will become many and ours will die out."

These ideas, still current in the 1940's, were then being invoked in legal contexts. They were being interpreted as extending to the host's whole clan; for example, "places of mother's people" was being taken to mean "clan land of mother's people." [12] The bodies of dwellers who died among their hosts were carried home long distances to be buried in the land of the clan to which they belonged by descent.

The host did not have to wait for death to get rid of an unwanted dweller; by invoking the "gray hair" rules, he could justify sending away a family of affines or cognates which seemed to have been there too long. If, for instance, a dweller made himself unpopular by quarreling, or by failing to cooperate or to return hospitality, he might be requested to leave. In similar circumstances a true clansman could, if he wished, leave by his own free will, but nobody could force him to leave unless his offense reached criminal proportions (e.g., witchcraft). This distinction always existed, but land scarcity gave it a new importance and a new legal precision. As all vacant land within the clan community's borders became an object of competition, with all fathers wondering where they could send their sons to build, the clansman-dweller opposition came into sharper focus. The dweller was expected to go to the end of the queue. He was a member of the political corporation and of the neighborhood community, but he was not in the same full sense a member of the landholding corporation.

Land scarcity sharpened the pressure put on dwellers to choose between two alternatives: (1) to go home; or (2) if they wanted to stay, to merge themselves with the host clan by concocting a more or less fictitious line of common agnatic descent. There was no third way to be reasonably sure of being allowed a place for one's children to build. Accordingly there took place, in the late 1920's, a population movement of considerable proportions, in which individuals, families, and even whole lineages took part. It was a movement of dwellers going home.

A comparable process of sorting out "born members" from "outsiders" also was going on at a lower level, in relation to the component lineages of clans. As competition for land increased, the tendency was for lineage ties to be asserted more and more strongly. This situation had a direct bearing on land litigation. We found that in ordinary boundary disputes between neighboring homesteads, the fees required for lodging a case at a native tribunal might have been raised by a collection within a whole lineage group. Thus, in a case where the disputants were of different four-generation lineages *amaiga,* the lineage of the plaintiff raised the fees. Nobody objected to paying his share; in the words of one contributor, "I gave two shillings myself, because all of us wanted that land." Another case between disputants of different amaiga, after going through several stages of appeal, was finally dismissed at provincial headquarters on the ground that neither party had a valid claim to the disputed plot. It was perfectly true that the individuals concerned had much weaker claims than some of their respective kin. To them, however, it was not a dispute between themselves so much as a dispute between amaiga. The two litigants, both being literate, were the persons deemed most suitable by each side for presenting a case in court.

Land cases that seemed to be concerned with individual holdings could in this way bring into play the latent solidarity of lineage or clan house, or subclan or clan, according to the context (i.e., according to the lineage relationship between the parties). Thus the remark that "BoNyando and BoMwanda [clans] are quarreling over land" meant no more than that individuals on the border were disputing the boundaries of their respective homesteads, but the remark was made to us, with evident interest, by a BoNyando man from two miles away who had no conceivable concern in the matter.

Conclusions

It is a function of any developing system of land tenure, in conditions of shortage, to adjust the competing interests of different groups or categories of people. The developing law may follow, emphasize, and exacerbate lines of opposition which are already clear in the society, as, for example, between nobles and commoners. Or it may, by introducing novel principles, create new groups or categories and new oppositions, as, for example, between efficient producers who have been able to amass land and inefficient ones who find themselves dispossessed.

Where the colonial power, as in Kenya, specifically proposed that land law develop along customary lines without upsetting customary social structure, one would expect that, as it developed, it would merely underline existing oppositions. But these oppositions might also make it difficult to find out what the customary practice actually was. Each group might be inclined to paint the olden days in the colors most favorable to its own sectional interests. This tendency may explain much of the controversy over the Kikuyu land question, Kenya's *cause célèbre* of the 1930's and 1940's. The content of traditional Kikuyu land law was much disputed; the copious literature on the subject reveals a notable failure to recognize the ideological basis of many versions put forward by Kikuyu informants. We are told, for instance, that the Kikuyu disagreed among themselves as to whether or not the principle of land sale was part of their customary law, and, if it was, whether sale was to be interpreted as redeemable or irredeemable, and so on. This circumstance takes on a new importance when we consider the different sectional interests that were involved by the time of the inquiry; certain Kikuyu, including chiefs and tribunal elders, had already acquired large acreages through purchase.

In the Gusii case there were few, if any, particular sectional interests to shape the development of law or color the picture of traditional custom, as the social structure was pronouncedly segmentary, with the lines of division vertical rather than horizontal. Distinctions between have and have-not—for example, owner versus tenant, squatter, or landless man—did not exist in principle as absolute personal statuses. Men played the temporary role of dweller (*omomenyi*) without losing their permanent birthright among their own clansmen. Thus, although there were always dwellers, no one group or class of people were dwellers in perpetuity, and no permanent sectional opposition of interests developed.

The real lines of opposition in Gusii society, the lines of segmentation, were drawn around patrimonial and territorial interests on the principle that every corporate group of lineage type, every family, every individual, was entitled to a portion, and that ideally all portions should be more or less equal, that is, scaled to average needs. Fighting on the one hand, and legal process on the other, were the media in which this principle was to work itself out. Both offered checks to anyone who tried to increase his own portion at the expense of others. Bridewealth law, the model for cattle law, specifically opposed progressive personal aggrandizement. If chance endowed a man with many daughters or sisters, and therefore with many marriage cattle, the law required him to apportion the cattle among his sons, or lend them to other family members in need, instead of taking more and more wives to himself. If chance made one girl more sought after than another, the bridewealth rate—the basic number of cattle paid, not counting their quality, or the accompanying customary gifts—was nevertheless exactly the same in principle for both.[13]

The Gusii ideology was in this respect fundamentally egalitarian, as well as fundamentally competitive. The tendency for the land law to shape itself along the lines of "fair shares for all" is illustrated in an exception that proves the rule. In one Gusii area, at the time of our fieldwork, the government-appointed chief followed an unusually authoritarian pattern. He became unpopular with his people on many accounts, but one of the bitterest complaints was that he "took land away from other men" to increase his own coffee plantations or the farms of his henchmen. In Gusii social thinking there is no precedent for the important man whose importance is reflected in controlling land on a large scale.

The material presented here has provided illustration for two familiar problems of historical and sociological jurisprudence: (1) the relation between changes in custom and changes in law; and (2) the relation between legal developments and principles or ideas manifest in a given society. In regard to the former, we have seen how economic and demographic pressures caused changes away from the customary mode of agrarian organization, and how these *de facto* changes subsequently became the basis for new land law, upheld in the courts. As to the latter, we have seen that legislators or authorities gave little direct guidance to the development of Gusii land law. The law was formed partly on principles that the people themselves were able to formulate explicitly, and partly on more general principles, underlying these, which were implicit in the social structure as a whole. Under the first heading come the rules of cattle law; under the second, the observer can isolate what we have called the dominion principle, and also the egalitarian ethos as expressed in Gusii modes of competition.

4.

JUSTICE AND JUDGMENT AMONG THE SOUTHERN IBO UNDER COLONIAL RULE

by Daryll Forde

The indigenous sources of justice and judgment among the noncentralized peoples of Eastern Nigeria, in whose societies segmentary kin grouping was the dominant mode of interaction and political organization at all levels, reflect the highly segmented character of their society and the number of independent sources of influence and authority.

There is a considerable body of descriptive material and some analysis concerning the southern Ibo which exemplify the diversity of indigenous institutions and the scale of social groups concerned in determining and enforcing legal rules.[1] From these it is possible to establish the main features of the political system, the principles of justice, and the modes of enforcement which were operative at the end of the nineteenth century, before the institutions and ordinances of the Nigerian Protectorate administration were introduced. Many elements of these systems continued to be politically and, more especially, judicially effective after other legal institutions had been introduced by the Nigerian government. They have continued either as informal courts within the smaller social groups, such as minor lineages, or as officially unrecognized parallel sources of judgment to which, in certain cases, there has been recourse in preference to the courts established by the Nigerian administration.

In this paper I attempt to analyze for the southern Ibo, as they have been described from various communities in Owerri Province, the essential character of the indigenous courts, the categorization of offenses, and the modes of compensation and penality they sought to enforce. I also consider some of the problems inherent in the attempt to integrate such local units of law enforcement into a wider judicial system under conditions imposed by the new external political authority, the govern-

[1] For notes to chapter 4, see page 248.

ment of Nigeria, which refused recognition to some offenses or categorized them differently, while also proscribing some traditional penalties and introducing new ones.

Indigenous Social Organization

The basic feature of the traditional organization of the southern Ibo has been a polysegmentary structure of localized patrilineal kin groups. Settlement is dispersed, but small clusters of neighboring compounds are intimately associated as the households of a dozen or so closely related patrikinsmen tracing their descent from an ancestor a few generations back. These small groups are successively incorporated into wider groups as segments of larger territorial units corresponding to lineages (*umu-nna*, children of the father) of wider span. Characteristically, four or even five levels of more inclusive grouping are recognized with respect to the exercise and transmission of land, exogamy and intermarriage, and other rights, as well as the authority of elders in the settlement of internal disputes. The units of settlement in this widening range have been severally referred to in the literature as hamlets, villages (communes), and village groups (towns). Traditions of common patrilineal descent from even more remote ancestors also relate still wider groups, referred to as "clans" in government reports. But these and, a fortiori, the still larger groupings of communities, more closely related in speech and having other cultural features in common, had no political unity.

The unity and the segmentation of the groups are expressed in genealogies which name the ancestors of component groups of decreasing size and narrower leadership span as sons, grandsons, great-grandsons, and so on, of the founder of the whole group. Thus the Umueke "village" described by M. M. Green,[2] which consisted of some three hundred people in the households of seventy patrilineally related men (themselves grouped into several sublineages), is one of more than a dozen similar villages whose founders were held to be sons of two brothers whose father, Abaja, was the ancestor of all the thousand or so men of the Abaja "village group." The men of the other neighboring village groups were held to be descended from brothers of Abaja, and together they all constituted the "tribe" descended from their father, Ehime.

But the frequent displacement of individuals and small groups through migration to join maternal kin or affines, or to seek refuge, frequently complicated the composition of villages and major lineages. Although the descendants of strangers were commonly distinguished as separate lineages, the strength of the doctrine of common descent as the norm for ordering relations among component groups of a community often led to their *de facto* incorporation in a major lineage to which rules of exogamy applied. In many local communities there were also small separate and dependent lineages of servile status, descended from persons acquired by capture or purchase as domestic slaves (*ohu*) or for dedication to the cult of a protective spirit (*osu*). These lineages appear to have been politically and juridically dependent on other lineages for their representation and protection.

Ritual and moral authority for the assertion of customary rights and duties in each recognized major lineage is vested in its *okpara*, usually its oldest freeborn member, whose status and powers derive from the ancestor of the group and are visibly symbolized in the *ofo* staff he carries. And the oldest male member of the smaller component lineages at each successive level of segmentation is the authority and the spokesman for the more recent ancestor of that group. The title "okpara" is usually given only to heads of major lineages constituting the first order of segmentation of a community, usually a village, who form the omnicompetent council of the community. But the character and the sources of the authority of the elders of component segments are similar within their lineages, and they assemble as a major lineage council to consider issues arising within it. The principle of succession by seniority of age implies that succession to eldership of the larger lineage groups is not vested in any one of its component units.

Thus, at each level of lineage grouping, the senior elder presides over a council of household heads or component lineage elders and other representatives at which the substance of any allegation or dispute is thrashed out and any appropriate restitution, compensation, or penalty is declared. The judgment can be enforced on the authority of the body of elders concerned—the *ndi oha*—speaking in the name of the ancestors. The agency of enforcement varies according to the nature of the offense, the span of the group, and the roles assigned to age-grades and associations in the community. The largest unit for the orderly settlement of disputes in this manner is rarely larger than a village group of a thousand or so households, and some are considerably smaller. In such a unit interlineage cohesion is considerable, and the observance of the moral norms of the community, as given by the ancestors, is reinforced by a local cult of Ala, the earth spirit, and sometimes of other tutelary spirits. The shrine of Ala, or other guardian spirit of the community, is in the custody of a priest whose declarations of the spirit's anger against, and of the need for expiations of, peacebreaking, bloodshed, incest, adultery, and other abominations reinforce the judgments of the ndi oha concerning the guilt of offenders and the remedies to be applied.

At the village-group level there is frequently a dual, or sometimes triple, division of the total community for public tasks which also provides a means of enforcing justice. The division, which is not at any given time directly involved through one or more of its members as a possible culprit, self-righteously insists on and seeks to enforce the customary norms applicable to a dispute or an offense. To maintain an effective demographic balance among these territorially discrete divisions, genealogical relations between lineages are sometimes overridden and a lineage is transferred from one division to another, the genealogy being eventually recast accordingly. These demographically more or less equal groups within a community are often distinguished by recurrent conventional names, such as Ama versus Owerri and Ikenga versus Ihite.

Thus, the population of a village group is successively segmented into territorial divisions which are defined in terms of the dogma and ritual of patrilineal descent. Each territorial unit is in principle a unit of cooperation, internal regulation, and external opposition at its level. But the size and the territorial limits of the units may be changed to maintain balance among them. In addition to efforts toward its own self-regulation by the internal judgment of disputes and punishment of offenses, each unit defends customary rights and proper conduct against any shortcomings of the others. Within the system as a whole, the basic units that combine and divide in this manner are minor lineages of ten to fifty adult patrikinsmen, claiming a common ancestor five or more generations ago. Judgment in settling disputes, compensating for wrongs and deciding on punishments and expiatory offerings for offenses, is in principle the responsibility of the elder of the group concerned. This group may range from a single minor lineage to the whole community, according to the character of the alleged offense and the lineage affiliations of those involved. An elder is in principle responsible to other lineages and to the community for restitution and expiation concerning any offenses committed by members of his lineage.

But all were not equal in southern Ibo society. At any level some lineages were large, prosperous, cohesive, and well led, while others were small or poor or ineffective. Some individuals were recognized as endowed with powerful personalities and outstanding ability. The destiny accorded to others was less remarkable, if not unfortunate. Disparities of wealth and personal influence were regarded as the validation of the personal right of a "big man" (*onye uku*) or a "leader" (*onye ise*) to speak with authority concerning public affairs at all levels of kin and local grouping. Even within a small lineage the elder might lack personal influence, while a more junior man had by his drive and capacity achieved effective leadership of the group. Thus the "truth" that might be arrived at in the hearing of a dispute or the judgment of an alleged offense would depend in considerable measure on the standing and the strength of the individuals and kin groups that were involved. Within a minor lineage the effective authority in settling disputes among its members, and in awarding effective rights to the use of land and other resources, might be in the hands of a man of energy who had secured a substantial following, sometimes in opposition to the elder, who usually acquiesced in his demands and decisions. Such a man might also organize his lineage in the successful appropriation of land claimed but not effectively held by an adjacent lineage of more remote patrikinsmen, securing if necessary a favorable decision from the elders of the wider lineage to which both belonged. He might be able to go further and, by means of a combination of rewards and intimidations, build up his authority over several minor lineages, and even achieve recognized leadership of the whole of a large village group. Thus decisions both in civil disputes concerning, for example, boundaries of lands controlled or held by component groups or payments of debts, and in accusations concerning "abominable" offenses, such as homicide or incest, could depend on the influence of wealthy men with large followings, who might be ranged against one another or be able to secure a favorable judgment at the expense of weaker and more isolated persons and groups.

As the several levels of assemblage of the elders of lineage and territorial groups constituted a series of courts of widening span of jurisdiction, with some increasing specialization of competence, the categorization of legal rights and obligations, on the one hand, and of public delicts on the other, is relative to the social groups involved and thus implies jurisdictions at different levels. In principle, every minor lineage was entitled to participate in the hearing and the judgment of any case that concerned its members or the community at large, and the elder, as its ritual head, represented it formally in the adjudicating body for any grouping of which it formed a part. Issues concerning persons or groups within a small lineage which did not involve public offenses such as homicide, incest (sexual relations with a woman of the lineage or with a member's wife), or theft on the farms, were properly settled within the lineage without reference to external authority. But reports of judgments that violated custom in the wider community could become the grounds for charges against the lineage's elder.

Disputes and accusations that were the concern of a lineage of wider span, up to and including the entire local community or village group, were the subject of public hearings in which the okpara of the lineages concerned sat by seniority, sanctioned the proceedings by the deposition of their ancestral ofo staffs, and, in some cases, in conjunction with a priest of a local cult, announced through the senior elder the judgment arrived at. But the elders could and often did, either formally or informally, delegate both the investigation and the judgment of cases to junior men who commanded a following in their lineages. And one or more of the age-sets of middle-aged men were in some cases the effective court of inquiry, as well as subsequent agents of enforcement. Moreover, when disputes involved persons of different lineages, or when a lineage was seeking to defend a member against an allegation of public delict, advocacy and arbitration were often taken out of the hands of the okpara by an onye ise.

It is important to stress that the hearing of cases most frequently took the form of a demand by one lineage for restitution from or punishment of another. Thus the hearing, at which any member of the group embracing the lineages was free to attend and to intervene as a witness or advocate, frequently engaged the lineages in a competitive struggle to exonerate, on the one hand, and on the other to secure justice for their respective members. The effects of such partisanship were mitigated by the participation of elders of other lineages within the group which were not directly involved in the particular case. Arrival at a just settlement and the punishment of public offenders largely depended on their attachment to the social norm concerned, and their anxiety lest supernatural retribution fall on the group as a whole, including themselves, for failure to secure the expiation of offenses. Although the body of lineage elders brought together in connection with a case was in principle united as the ritual embodiment of the succession of ancestors through whom the group as a whole was itself a united body of kinsmen, and although outwardly they collectively sought to preserve this unity, they were often engaged in an internal struggle among themselves concerning the validity of evidence for, or the gravity of, the wrongs committed by those accused.

While all allegations of public offenses were to be brought for judgment before a council of elders, private wrongs could be, and frequently were, settled by securing the personal arbitration of a "big man." Such men built up their reputation for authoritative judgment, and increased their wealth from fees obtained in this way. Within a village consisting of a single major lineage, both parties usually recognized the same big man who was himself sensitive to local opinion. And when, as in most matrimonial disputes and claims for repayment of debts, the parties were from different local groups and major lineages, the complainant could enlist the support of the big man of his group in his request for a favorable judgment by the leader of the other party's community. The interest of big men of neighboring communities in maintaining good relations to their mutual benefit appears generally to have been effective in securing fair settlements of such claims as between persons of different groups.

The bringing of charges, the raising of issues, the impartiality of the hearings, and the propriety of judgments could be affected by marked disparities in economic and political power. In village groups that had come within one or more of the long-established spheres of external trade with the coast or the interior, access to markets had provided a basis for leadership in fields that transcended lineage boundaries and interests. Successful organizers of trading and raiding, who commanded supplies of weapons and trade goods, were often able not only to dominate their own lineages and villages, but to establish relations of patronage over other quasi-client lineages and communities. An informally centralized political organization of this kind might, in favorable circumstances, be maintained over more than one lifetime through the selection and training of sons and other kinsmen as henchmen and successors.

In such conditions, and in a manner not unfamiliar in other societies, both the moral norms and the machinery of justice tended to be modified in the interests of the perpetuation and development of these miniature autocracies. The forms of the moots presided over by a bench of lineage elders might be preserved, but decisions as to whether or not an alleged offense should be brought before them, which witnesses should testify, what compensation or penalties should be awarded and how thoroughly they should be enforced, often depended on the interests or the policies of the big man in a village, a village group, or a wider district as expressed through open or covert directions to the lineage heads and others. The situation could, moreover, be still more complex if two or more such men were competing for power and prestige in the same village group. The elders' courts might then become a major arena for the weakening of opponents and the demonstration of the dominance of one as against another.

The action taken with regard to offenses by persons living in another village or village group depended on the existing state of their mutual external relations, the extent to which a sense of solidarity and *de facto* political leadership by one or more big men existed. The settlement of private wrongs could, as noted above, often be secured through the influence of the big men of the communities concerned. Killing, assault, abduction of women, and thefts of food supplies or livestock by people of another community justified armed retaliation and demanded the threat of it unless compensation was forthcoming. Whether or not a feud developed between the communities, and, if so, how long it persisted, similarly depended on the state of their relations. Usually, it seems, especially if both were of the same linguistic or cultural subgroup, the limitations and the precautions imposed on daily life by the insecurity resulting from a feud with a neighboring community led both sides to accept, and even to solicit, the intervention of a third neutral community whose elders, cult priests, or political bosses undertook to arbitrate the original dispute, to confirm any losses in killed, injured, and abducted on either side, and to prescribe compensations to restore the balance. The latter might include the handing over of men to be executed or sold to slavers, or of women to be taken as wives and assimilated.

The Native Court System and the Warrant Chiefs

With the establishment of the Protectorate of Nigeria in 1900, pacification and administration by British officials of the hinterland of the coast to the east of the Niger Delta began. A network of government stations with police posts, linked by secure tracks and telegraph lines, was extended over southern Ibo country in the half-dozen years that followed. The initial administrative effort sought to establish and maintain minimal law and order, together with expanding facilities for peaceful trade and, in particular, for a greater and more regular evacuation of palm produce to the coast. For the latter there was a long-established overseas market, and export trade alone could yield the income from which the Ibo themselves and the administration could finance the development of basic services and a higher standard of living.

To this end, a number of hitherto autonomous village groups were brought together into all-purpose administrative units designated as native court areas. These units were formed on the basis of such knowledge of the cultural affinities and political relations of the local groups as could be gained from inquiries at public assemblies and interviews with those who came forward to make terms, as they saw it, with the white officials and their police escorts, who were proscribing fighting and offering a larger and more peaceful future. Each recognized community was invited to designate a chief who would sit in rotation as a member of the bench of the area court, would also inform and instruct his community concerning the ordinances and other requirements of the Nigerian administration, and would undertake to see them observed and carried out. In recognition of their status, these spokesmen and intermediaries were given a hat, a staff, and a written warrant authorizing them to give judgment when summoned to sit in the area court, insignia from which their official title as "warrant chiefs" derived.

As suggested by the foregoing sketch of the indigenous structure of authority and adjudication in and between Ibo communities, the men who came or were put forward varied widely in their local status and in their comprehension of the functions intended for them. One chief was usually appointed to represent each village group. The chiefs ranged in capacity and outlook from experienced, conscientious local leaders through cynical bosses to nonentities put forward as a supposed screen against the unpredictable demands of the administration. Senior okpara of the senior village, who presided at elders' courts, were commonly self-excluded by their age and ritual positions. Where there was an outstanding local leader—the big man of a large lineage in an influential village already in command of the strings of power and influence in his area—there was little question so long as he had some appreciation of the shape of things to come, and did not make the mistake of nominating a junior relative in the belief that he should sup with a long spoon. But if there was competition for influence, or if the village group had little unity, the selection of a warrant chief was often subject to misconceptions on the part of confused, if not apprehensive, councils of elders and the briefly visiting administrators.

As most of the southern Ibo village groups were small and the population was dispersed, the number of local leaders in a given area was correspondingly large. Those who secured appointments as warrant chiefs were given a newfound authority and influence over previously autonomous neighboring communities. The leaders of the latter, quick to resent this authority, later became sources of opposition to the warrant chief and of complaints against him to the administration.

A court clerk was attached to each court area to organize and record its activities. As there were at this period among the southern Ibo few literate persons with any experience of the working of the administration, and as any such were often held too subject to local pressures, court clerks were for the most part outsiders who had been clerks in coast stations under the old consular regime. As such they could not fail to be regarded as the resident agents of the new administration. A court clerk might claim to know only too dogmatically, and sometimes, in the event, mistakenly, what government required of the warrant chiefs and the people, but he appeared to have the power of affecting the recurrent interventions, requests, and decisions of the administrator at his headquarters. Hence, needless to say, the effectiveness of the warrant chiefs so far as matters of interest to the Nigerian government were concerned, and their own comprehension of their duties and powers, depended very largely on the capacity and the advice of the clerk.

A generation ago, not least among those who sincerely sought better things for Africans, but made their appraisals without local experience of the physical obstacles and the limited resources available in the first period of administration of this densely peopled but hitherto unorganized area, the warrant chiefs in Iboland were commonly regarded as an example of administrative obtuseness, ignorance, and even indifference which met its just reward in outbreaks that began with the women's riots in Aba in 1929. This facile view was neither supported nor refuted by debate as to whether the area courts of warrant chiefs were a manifestation of Direct or Indirect Rule. It ignored strong internal demands, as well as external pressures, to move toward the integration of a turbulent and unorganized region in a wider economic and political world.

The new powers, opportunities, and privileges afforded by the offices of warrant chief and court clerk, protected by the Nigerian administration and recognized under its ordinances, were sometimes abused by strategically placed and unscrupulous manipulators of the new politico-legal situation. No doubt some chiefs and clerks came to be detested for intimidations and extortions by many of the people whom they were supposed to represent, people who could often find no effective means for making their grievances known to the remote European officials of the administration. Warrant chiefs were no doubt sometimes believed to have established an alliance with the administration for the exploitation of the community. At times, too, a court clerk, an alien but almost the only person able to speak directly in English to administrative officers, seeking to ensure his own position and betterment, would discover ways of intimidating and misleading the warrant chiefs of his court area to his own supposed advantage. Through his control of the means of official communication, his retinue of official messengers, and his apparent ability to summon police into the area, a court clerk could in the initial phase enjoy both the appearance and the substance of personal power.

But the rapacious warrant chief and the intriguing or tyrannical court clerk who condoned or even instigated crimes, and extorted wealth for their own advantage and aggrandizement, were rare exceptions in most areas, according to the recollections of both British officials and the people themselves. This is not to underestimate the growing pains and the individual misfortunes and hardships of this first phase in which there were prohibitions on accusations of sorcery, orders for the apprehension of anyone chargeable with homicide and his eventual trial before an alien High Court judge and hanging in a distant prison, or instructions to a warrant chief that, for reasons not locally apparent, he should mobilize the men of his community to build or repair a section of roadway before the next rains or provide labor for government buildings. The new regime offered opportunities for the ambitious and the crafty to exploit new regulations for their advantage and to pay off old scores. But against these injustices must be set a deeply welcomed increase of security for persons and goods, and enhanced facilities for securing larger and more regular incomes from produce and labor, which brought superior tools and new medicines, luxuries, and means of display.

A just view has probably been given by an administrator and anthropologist who worked among the southern Ibo toward the end of this phase, and who has more recently surveyed its later development:

> The system functioned reasonably well where each local community had its own Warrant Chief, but there were areas . . . where local conditions did not permit this . . . [and] the sudden introduction of taxation in 1928 [intended to provide resources for the further development of southern Nigeria comparable to those being obtained in the north] at a period when the world oil markets were turning from boom to slump conditions produced a revolt . . . in the areas most hit by this fall in prices [which] were also the areas in which the Warrant Chief system had become most unpopular. The commission of enquiry which followed concentrated mainly upon the political rather than the economic causes of those riots.[3]

Indigenous Judicial Procedures

We have, however, to confine ourselves here to outstanding features in the changing pattern of law and administration which developed in this phase. Previously, in the autonomous communities, the elders' court of a village or a village group had come together only for serious matters, that is, those in which a wide span of kinsfolk were concerned. It did so at the request of a complainant and his supporters, including his own minor lineage head or a local leader to whom he and his close kin were attached. The court also assembled on its own initiative if it had become notorious that an abomination—a serious public delict—had been committed, an offense that demanded expiation and punishment in the interests of the material and mystical security of the community. In the former instance, offerings of palm wine, meat, or currency were made openly, and more or less equally by both sides, to enlist and reward the concern and fair judgment of the court. The lineage heads would co-opt others with special knowledge or prestige, such as cult priests and political leaders, to sit and retire with them to consider the case. When direct evidence of disinterested witnesses was lacking, ordeals were administered to test or sanction the veracity of accusers and defendants. A court rarely had formal control of agents of enforcement of its decisions. But senior men acting collectively, whether formally organized as an age-set or as "junior elders," were entitled by custom to secure compliance, where necessary, by depredations on the goods of the kin and neighbors of any person judged guilty who was recalcitrant in complying with the orders for expiation, compensation, or restitution.

Allegations of offenses which were believed to expose the community to grave, if often ill-defined, misfortunes as punitive reactions of ancestral and tutelary spirits brought pressure for a hearing before the court, whose members might often be divided by their respective attachments to and interests in the persons or the groups concerned. Persons likely to be informed could be compelled as witnesses, on oath if necessary, to declare what they knew.

Some cases were treated as both private wrongs and public offenses in that compensation or restitution to the injured parties was combined with penalties and ritual payments to assuage the anger of the spirits. The severity of penalties reflected the gradation of interest in social relations, the relative importance of different categories of property characteristic of largely closed and self-subsistent economies, and the stress on deterrence where the protection of goods and the identification of offenders were difficult. The last was reflected in particular in the greater severity of penalties on offenders caught *in flagrante delicto*. The social status of an offender also affected the sentence, most noticeably in the tacit right of a notable, such as the head of a strong lineage, a cult priest, or a diviner, to offer a substitute in relevant cases for execution or for sale into slavery, or to provide a woman for marriage into the group that had suffered injury.

In homicide cases where the killer and the victim were men of the same major lineage, questions of intention and provocation were often secondary considerations, and expiation was the dominant principle. The offense was regarded as fratricide requiring the elimination of the offender. Unless he had exceptional influence, a man would be ordered to hang himself or be driven into exile. The killing of a man from another major lineage and village, even within the same village group, was a grave private wrong, but the entire minor lineage of the offender was held responsible for restitution. Here the circumstances were material. If the killing was held to be murderous, the handing over for execution of the offender, or of a substitute if the offender was of high standing, was demanded by the injured lineage. When it could be held that the killing was unintended, the elders of the village group would approve the handing over of a young man to be incorporated into the injured lineage, or of a young woman to be married into and bear sons to the lineage. If such compensation was refused, the injured, unless in an exceptionally weak position, would resort to feud and, in any subsequent settlement, would demand compensation for the original offense. And in all such cases expiation by the offender and his lineage through offerings at the Ala (earth spirit) shrine of the whole community was ordered as essential to its protection.

Punishment of theft depended on the mode and the object of the stealing. Petty thieving in the compounds by women and unimportant men was punished on a first occasion by shaming; the offender was tied up in public to be ridiculed and degraded by the kin and neighbors of the victimized. Those found guilty of persistent theft, and, in particular, of theft of crops from farms and the unguarded yam barns on farming paths, lost the protection of their close kin who connived at their abduction, by the lineage which they had injured, for handing over to a slave dealer. Debtors who persistently evaded demands for repayment were said to be similarly treated in some instances. But even flagrant misappropriation of the goods of others by powerful men and their followers—phrased as retaliation for insults—might go unpunished.

There is little evidence of witchcraft accusations or punishment among the southern Ibo, but sorcery by persons of other villages was feared and challenged. Regarded as equivalent to direct physical injury, it required the same compensation as assault and homicide, and ordeals were resorted to as a means of testing accusations and declarations of innocence.

Judgments concerning sexual offenses appear to have closely reflected the social status of the parties and of those who had rights in them. Sexual relations within a minor lineage and adultery with the wife of a minor lineage kinsman were sins that required, when they came to public knowledge, costly expiation on behalf of the lineage as well as the killing of the offenders. Adultery with the wife of a distant lineage kinsman, usually within the village group, had to be expiated, and was also subject, as was adultery outside the lineage, to the payment of damages. But in the latter instance the relative strength of the lineages involved and the status of the offender could affect the bringing of a case before the court, as well as the penalty and compensation awarded.

Effects of New Judicial Procedures

The focus of judicial authority, procedures in the hearings, the categorization of cases, and the penalties attached to offenses were all affected in considerable but varying degree by the establishment, recognition, and supervision of the new area courts with a bench of warrant chiefs. Disputes and offenses that had previously been dealt with within smaller groups had, in principle, to come before the area court. The external authorization of the area court and of its judgments encouraged the reference to it of disputes and offenses that would previously have been dealt with by the elders of component segments. The unit of jurisdiction was often changed. Usually it corresponded to at least the largest grouping for which traditional elders' courts assembled, but it might be wider; to foster greater cohesion and to make administrative control feasible, one court area often linked together two or more previously autonomous communities. And although this policy, under favorable conditions, fostered the growing together of small groups required by the new technical and economic conditions, the judgments of the courts and the new forms of penalty they could impose were a frequent source of resentment.

Prison sentences for assaults deprived the injured of the compensation they traditionally expected, and often came to be seen as a means of escape and even of reward through good food for the violent. Punishment for accusation, as opposed to the practice of sorcery, reversed the order of traditional legal values whereby sickness and misfortune afforded occasions for exposing and punishing those who had long been suspected of malevolence. The replacement of the indigenous doctrine of the collective responsibility of the men of a lineage for the good behavior of its members and for compensation of wrongs done by any one of them, by the Western doctrine of individual and personal responsibility for offenses, weakened the power of the kin groups both to protect and to discipline their members. On the other hand, it was recognized by many Ibo themselves as fostering a process of social individualization which was needed to take advantage of new opportunities in the growing exchange sector of the economy.

More drastic was the removal from the jurisdiction of the area courts to magistrates and High Court judges of offenses categorized as felonious under Nigerian law. Charges of murder and of sorcery accusation were outstanding among these. The geographical and psychological remoteness of a court presided over by a judge who was both sociologically and culturally external to the community lent the court an arbitrary and dangerous character. However patient and conscientious the hearings, witnesses seem often to have felt insecure. Evidence was likely to be incomplete, and its comprehension and interpretation were difficult. In sorcery cases, as noted above, the initial assumptions and criteria of the hearing and the judgment appeared to turn indigenous judicial logic upside down. Early reactions, needless to say, were attempts at concealment, conspiracies of silence, and the translation of wrongs into charges that did not expose the complainants to external jurisdiction. On the other hand, it came to be realized that the magistrate's court could be used as a weapon in internal conflicts if charges before it could be trumped up by the audacious and the unscrupulous.

The resort to "big men" for judgment and arbitration of private claims continued under the system of area courts. Indeed, the members of the courts expected such cases to be heard in their own communities in the first instance, and might send complainants back to seek a local settlement if they had not already attempted to do so. The warrant chiefs were in a strong position for the hearing of such cases in the communities they represented, for they could secure enforcement of their decision through a subsequent judgment in the area court if the matter was not initially settled in accordance with it. It was not infrequently a complaint of other leading men that the warrant chiefs came to monopolize such hearings, and to amass wealth at the expense of others through the fees they received.

At the same time it must be recognized that the Nigerian courts soon had a real and positive effect in affording protection against local tyranny and in curbing violent attack and retaliation between peoples of traditionally hostile communities. It made movement of individuals and groups into and between different communities more secure.

The court clerk who received and transmitted communications from and to the divisional office over which the district officer presided, and who was both required and privileged to issue summonses and to record in his own summary version the findings, awards, and sentences of the court, was, as has been said, in a key position with regard to the bringing forward of cases and the determination of judgments on them. In addition to this exceptional standing and power as the unique and literate local agent of the new administration, he was usually a stranger with no close ties in the communities, and hence not subject to its sanctions. The warrant chiefs whom he was intended to serve could exercise no corporate control, for they might number as many as a hundred in any one area and never come together as a body. They were called to sit in the area court, in rotation as individuals, for only a month every year or so. Under these conditions the clerk had strong incentives to be authoritarian, and felt a great temptation to exploit the situation to his advantage, both materially and in prestige. It was not until considerable experience had been gained both by the people and by administrative officers, and until literacy had increased to the point where direct communication between them became more effective and local men could serve as clerks, that the likelihood of effective protest against any arbitrary action sanctioned the powers of the clerks.

The area courts were designed to serve as large a cluster of local communities as thought practicable, having regard to some homogeneity of custom. At the same time, in order to secure wide participation and representation, an attempt was made to appoint warrant chiefs from as many as possible of the numerous discrete local groups. There were thus too many warrant chiefs to sit together as a body gaining collective experience and authority, and they remained, except for their several and brief periodical sessions on the bench, largely isolated channels of communication from the administration. The individuals initially selected for appointment after brief public hearings and local inquiries were usually men of locally recognized standing and leadership. Usually they were not senior lineage elders or cult priests, who rarely sought or were considered suitable for appointment, but were often leading men of large and more influential lineages, already accustomed to taking the lead in the actual running of an elders' council or of activities in the community and in bargaining on its behalf in external relations. Many such men wore their warrant chiefs' caps as well-deserved recognition of the trust of the majority in their community, tempering the new code judiciously in handling the disputes and the offenses of their fellows.

But there were occasions when a warrant chief, formerly of modest status, saw an opportunity, under the protection of this new external political power and through the manipulation of its powerful punitive sanctions, to build up his own personal following and humble hitherto independent people of other lineages or other communities which had come under his *de facto* jurisdiction. The opportunities offered by the innovations in the avenues to power were by no means always lost on ambitious or previously less dominant individuals and groups. A warrant chief's appointment was virtually permanent unless he gravely offended in the eyes of the administration, for the office was regarded as a quasi-indigenous one; apparently there were no generally effective means whereby the community could secure removal for incapacity or abuses. There might be very little local control, for example, over the actions of the chief who could secure support from the clerk and the district officer and was able to ignore or to flout local opinion.

In the provision of a relevant and evenhanded justice, the main weakness of the system of area courts with warrant chiefs was that it could not be kept under close supervision, and that abuses could not be discovered by the handful of British administrative officers who also had to keep the peace, see that roads were built and kept open, and protect and encourage means of increasing production and trade. Far from being Direct Rule, in the sense that warrent chiefs and area courts became the subservient tools of an authoritarian administration, this early system was highly indirect in its delegation of authority to organize, legislate for, and control through its courts the daily lives of the people in a changing economic situation. Its defects seem to have lain in the intermittent and insufficiently searching nature of inquiry into and supervision of the activities of warrant chiefs and their courts.

We may guess that in 1928 few district officers had any close knowledge of how the warrant chiefs under their supervision were reacting to and interpreting to their communities the decision of the Nigerian government to require an annual tax payment of all able-bodied adult men. By hindsight it can be appreciated that a tax of a few shillings, coming at a time when the price of palm oil was steadily dwindling, was seen, by chiefs and people alike, as a threat to their money incomes, which had increased at first and on which they had come to rely. One can understand, too, why some were tempted to impose the obligation of paying the tax on women, who had embarked successfully in petty trading. After the Aba riots and the Nigerian government's recognition of the unfortunate timing of its overdue taxation legislation for southern Nigeria, there was a decade of inquiry and reorganization of local government in the eastern provinces. Much was learned concerning the lineage organization and traditional roles of lineage elders. Judicial and executive functions were separated in principle. Court membership was revised and enlarged to accommodate lineage structure, and court areas were adjusted where incompatible groups had been put together. But, as G. I. Jones has observed, "Despite this exhaustive . . . reorganization (distinguished officially as the 'Native Administration' system) and the less intensive but no less thorough reorganization which preceded the introduction of the [still more recent] Local Government system which replaced the Native Administration system after the second world war, there has been surprisingly little alteration of the divisional and Native Court boundaries originally established under the native [area] court system."[4] Nor was the personnel of the bench in the new courts permanently changed. Although in some areas all the former warrant chiefs were removed and new members were appointed to the Native Administration courts, many of the former, against whom there had been loud protests of high-handed conduct, were renominated as court members within a few years. But, as their continuance in office depended on the support of their own people, they had taken pains to regain the people's confidence. The fields of jurisdiction of the courts also remained substantially the same. The Native Administration district courts of the thirties and forties in southern Iboland were gazetted as Grade D courts, with similarly limited competence from which homicide and other serious crimes were excluded, and with sentences restricted to short terms of imprisonment. The award of damages in civil cases was similarly limited and cases involving non-natives of the district were reserved to the magistrate's court. Court clerks functioned in much the same manner as before, although now they were more frequently natives of the district, a situation that could, of course, be a mixed blessing. The widening of the field from which the bench was drawn together, with the restriction of its authority to strictly judicial matters, seems to have increased both the responsibility and the influence of the clerk.

The generally successful working of the Native Administration courts—in that their jurisdiction was widely respected and accepted by the people of the district and that covert and unofficial parallel sources of judgment and penalty dwindled—is in fact an indication that the intentions and the machinery of the earlier attempt to provide a local judicial system were not so much amiss as has often been suggested. Had the means been found at the outset for more regular supervision and for the replacement of court members, judicial abuses (which do not seem in any event to have been the burden of resentment) would have been few. It appears rather that a more serious defect of the initial and pioneer period of local administration lay in the delegation of executive as well as judicial powers to one and the same warrant chief. But formally this policy was consistent with Ibo tradition, in which the elder of a lineage or an assembly of elders was in principle omnicompetent, as were in practice the big men who had unofficially dominated affairs in some communities. But the elders, as we have seen, often accepted *de facto* delegations of their executive powers and could not, unless they were wealthy and personally dominant themselves, curb manipulations by wealthy and dominant individuals who could build up a following. One might be tempted to suggest that had more external resources in men and money been made available for the pacification and unification of Iboland, it would have been wiser from the start to have instituted systems of local courts and councils, both of which should have been well provided with firm but patient external guidance. To estimate how the okpara and the onye uku would then have sorted out their respective memberships and fields of authority would be an interesting exercise in hypothetical social anthropology.

5.

A TRADITIONAL LEGAL SYSTEM: THE KUBA*

by Jan Vansina

The Kuba consist of a group of culturally different tribes, numbering about 70,000 persons, united in a single kingdom. They dwell between the rivers Kasai, Sankuru, and Lulua in the former Kasai Province of the Republic of Congo. They are matrilineal, organized in shallow three- or four-generation-deep matrilineages. The localized cores of these lineages consist of a few elderly men and women, for marriage is virilocal and males live with their fathers until the latter die. Then the men move to the residences of their mothers' brothers. Several lineages form a clan. The number of members belonging to a clan may vary from ten or twenty to several hundred, with a mode of less than fifty.

A village, the smallest political unit, consists of several clan sections, that is, the localized cores of the lineages and dependents. There is no dominant lineage in the village, and its headman, usually the oldest man in the community, may be drawn from any section. The headman represents the village but has little authority. The community is governed by a council made up of the heads of all the clan sections and by *mbeem* and *mbyeeng*, officials who represent the two sides of the village, for villages are built on two sides of a long street. These and other less important village officials are appointed for life by the village council, and no position is hereditary in any sense.

Villages are organized into chiefdoms. There is a special clan in every chiefdom from which chiefs may be elected. This clan may be different from one chiefdom to another. Chiefs are elected from available candidates by a council of electors. There are nine, or a multiple

*Field data were collected in the period 1953-1956, but not specifically for a study of Kuba law. More than a hundred cases from courts, and good descriptions of the poison oracle, are available, but there is little material on moots. The ethnographic present, used throughout, refers roughly to 1890. Later innovations are specifically indicated.

of nine, seats per council, and every seat is hereditary in a different electoral clan. But every elector is chosen from among the available men of such a clan by the other members of the council. This council elects chiefs, may depose ruling chiefs, and has to be consulted on the most important political decisions to be made by the chiefdom, such as questions of peace and war. Besides this council there is another council, *makaang* or *mbok ilaam*, composed of the ten or so highest titleholders and of the chief, which functions as a day-to-day administrative and legislative body. Some titleholders are nominated by the chief and some have to be chosen by the chief from one or more clans in which the title is vested, after approval of the other main titleholders. In the field of law the chiefdom is the highest political unit. Conflicts between chiefdoms are settled by war or through diplomatic arbitration, but there is no court system at a higher level than the chiefdom.

Chiefdoms may be linked informally together in clusters when they share common chiefly and common electoral clans. Clusters may be linked together informally when they belong to common tribes, that is, when there is public recognition by their neighbors and by themselves that they share a common culture, different from that of the neighbors. Above these informal levels the chiefdoms are all united in a single kingdom.

The kingdom is ruled by the Bushoong, a centrally located tribe organized in a single chiefdom. It is the largest in the country and dominates the others by military means. The Bushoong chief is automatically the king of the Kuba. He alone has the title *nyim*, king. The central institutions of the kingdom are those of the Bushoong chiefdom, whose organization is a little more elaborate than that of other chiefdoms. There are nine provinces headed by four provincial chiefs who reside in the capital, and the provinces are subdivided into districts which comprise a few villages each. The council of electors, *ibaam*, consists of two halves, each with nine members. The council, mbok ilaam, is the equivalent of the makaang in other chiefdoms. There exists, however, still another council for day-to-day affairs, the *ishyaaml*. Mbok ilaam convenes only when there is a conflict between the ishyaaml and the king. Finally, a fourth council, *ibaanc*, holds public sessions. It meets only in the event of a national emergency. Membership in the different councils is arranged as follows: in ibaam the titleholders are drawn from the electoral clans and cannot sit on any other council, with the exception of the president of the more important half, the *mbyeemy*. The ishyaaml is composed of the four provincial chiefs whose titles are vested in a number of electoral clans:

the mbeem and the mbyeeng of the capital, who must be respectively a son and a grandson of former kings; the *kikaam*, or highest-ranking titleholder, who must be at the same time a king's son and belong to an electoral clan; and, if they want to be present, the mbyeemy, the *katyeeng* and the *mbaan* of the capital (the female counterparts of mbeem and mbyeeng), and the *mwaaddy*, the oldest living son of a king. Mbok ilaam includes all the members of ishyaaml, the king, and a handful of other titleholders. Ibaanc includes all the hundred or so titleholders (see table 1).

The links between the Bushoong chiefdom and the others are, from an institutional point of view, only the following. Every other chiefdom has a representative, *ibwoon*, at the capital, who serves as intermediary between the king and the chiefdom and is responsible for the annual payment of tribute by the chiefdom. Every chiefdom gives a wife to the king, and she may also act as go-between. These institutions are indicative of the true relations between the Bushoong chiefdom and the others, which are quasi-diplomatic relations. Every chiefdom is autonomous internally and externally except for the payment of annual tribute and the rule that when it elects a new chief, he has to be acknowledged by the king, who cannot refuse to do so. Moreover, from a more descriptive point of view, it is clear that chiefdoms heeded royal commands or paid tribute only when they felt threatened by the royal army. This situation explains why it is that one has to speak about a single kingdom, but still has to regard the system, from the point of view of law, as multicentric, with interchiefdom relations regulated, not by law, but by war or arbitration. This is, of course, true if one accepts a definition of law as peaceful decision making in a unicentric power system.[1]

The Judicial System

The judicial system consists of two different systems, the moots and the courts, and of three levels, the lineage or clan, the village, and the chiefdom. Cases that do not involve murder or rebellion may be settled at the lower levels, but all cases of bloodshed are likely to come to the chiefdom. The courts are located at the chiefdom level; the moots, at the other levels.

A moot[2] is an assembly of neighbors (village) and kinsmen (lineage or clan) who decide disputes. Moots are different from courts in that

[1] For notes to chapter 5, see page 248.

TABLE 1

STRUCTURE OF THE KUBA KINGDOM

Territorial grouping	Titleholders	Formal structures
Bushoong Chiefdom		
Village	Headman; *mbeem; mbyeeng*	Council (*malaang*): headman; *mbeem; mbyeeng*; heads of all clan sections
District	Headman	None
Province	Headman	None
Capital	*Mbeem*; *mbyeeng*	None
Chiefdom	King; all titleholders	Coronation Council (*ibaam*): 9 + 9 = 18 representatives of 18 electoral clans (*mimbaangt*) Council of Seven (*ishyaaml*): *kikaam, mbeem, mbyeeng* of capital; 4 provincial chiefs (*mbyeemy*) Council (*mbok ilaam*): *ishyaaml*; king; 4 or 5 more titleholders Council (*ibaanc*): king; all titleholders Courts: panel of titleholders Court of appeal (1): *mbaang*; panel of titleholders Court of appeal (2): *kikaam*; panel of titleholders Court of appeal (3): *mbyeemy*; 9 elector clans; king
Other chiefdoms and clusters of chiefdoms		
Village	[1]	[1]
Chiefdom	Chief; all titleholders	Coronation Council (*ibaam*): 9 or multiple of 9 representatives of same number of elector clans (*mimbaangt*) Council (*makaang*): chief; *kikaam, mbeem, mbyeeng* of chief's residence; 4 or 5 highest titles Council (*ibaanc*): chief; all titleholders Courts[1]
Cluster	All chiefs chosen from same clan share electoral clans but not electoral councils	None
Kingdom	King; deputies of other chiefdoms (*ibwoon, meshoosh, paangl*)	None

[1] Same as in Bushoong Chiefdom.

they have no fixed membership. Decisions cannot be enforced, and the aim is arbitration rather than dispensation of justice. In the lineage or clan assemblies all older men, and occasionally even youngsters and women, participate in the discussions. In the village all the older men sit on the moot; in the single case that was carefully investigated, one of the younger men was the most active member of the group. A sign that this is not a village council meeting is that the proceedings are public and that all sit together on one side of the village plaza, except the accuser and the accused who face the moot. There are no spectators; there are only participants. The counterpart of the village level at the capital is the compound, *laan*. Here again disputes are settled by the members of the compound or the compounds if there is a quarrel involving two compounds. In addition, the parties invite older men, known for their wisdom, the *bangol a moot*, to help in the moot. These are men from any place in or out of the capital; many are judges on the courts but sit here in a private capacity. Moots attempt to reconcile the parties involved in a conflict and, therefore, try not to attribute all the blame to any single party. They are judiciary institutions, but, as they do not come to legal decisions, they are not here considered further.[3]

The courts, ibaanc, have a complex structure based on the title system. The basic significance of most titles has to do with the judiciary systems, except for the highest titles which play a prominent role in the council system as well. Every case in court is heard by a panel of judges, chosen because of their particular competence to hear that case. Each title carries with it a particular field of jurisdiction. The system is set out in table 2, which reveals that jurisdiction is determined by the personal status, the residential status, and professional role of the litigants, and by the type of conflict. Panels are chosen so that the largest possible number of background facts about the litigants and the case can be known to the judges. No knowledge is irrelevant in Kuba courts, and out-of-court knowledge is considered very desirable.

From the basic court, appeals (*abaan laan*, to climb a compound) to a similar court headed by the titleholder *baang* may be made. From that court, appeal may be made to a similar one presided over by the kikaam, and from there to a supreme court. The latter, consisting of the more important half of the council of electors, is presided over by the mbyeemy. The king assists but does not preside; his only supreme right is to grant a stay of execution.

The personnel of the courts is the same as the personnel of the councils, but the courts themselves are different. The distinction between the judiciary and other organs of government thus reflected is not common elsewhere.[4]

TABLE 2

JURISDICTION OF BUSHOONG TITLEHOLDERS[1]

Title	Competence
	Territorial
cikl	3 provinces
ipaancl	2 provinces
nyimishoong	1 province
nyaang	1 province
nyoom	1 province (acting for queen mother)
mbeem	left half of capital
mbyeeng	right half of capital
mbaan (woman)	left half of capital for women only
katyeeng (woman)	right half of capital for women only
	By personal status
cikl	royal lineage
nyoom	royal lineage only for adultery
nyimishol	royal lineage in matters of fishing ponds only
mwaaddy	children and grandchildren of kings
nce iyol abaan	children and grandchildren of kings when bloodshed is involved
tataam	wives of the king in the harem
men mbweengy	wives of the king in capital but out of harem
nyibit, nyibit ldiing, nce iyol a nkong	royal slaves (also used as policemen)
pok ibaan	children of royal slaves
pashdy muyesh	twins
	Professional
nyibin	sculptors, blacksmiths, weavers
tancoon	blacksmiths, iron miners
mandoong	milliners
nyim angwoonc	weavers
nyim lakul	leatherworkers
ngaan angom	musicians
ncyeem	singers
mwep ngom	drummers
maloom	saltmakers, artificial fishing ponds
makaan	traders, trade matters
nyimishek	technicians of the poison oracle
kikaam	titleholders
	By type of conflict
kikaam	debts, court of appeal from baang
baang	marriage affairs, especially adultery, appeal
nyibyeem	theft
nyim bayeeng	attempt at murder through use of magic
nyim balk	involuntary homicide
nyim ashim	suicide
nyim (king)	murder, rebellion, last appeal
iyol nce, iyol bukel, iyol, shesh, sheshesh	injuries
nyibit	injuries inflicted with a weapon of war

[1] All titles of substitutes and sub-substitutes have been omitted.

Procedural Law in the Court

A case is introduced by one of the disputing parties. He brings his complaint to any judge in the capital, who directs him to a competent judge. The party deposits a payment of 700 cowries[5] for the formal lodging of the complaint. Through informal consultation the judge then forms a panel. In cases where a public authority has been flouted, the responsible political official, a village headman, for instance, lodges the complaint. When the day of hearing is set, usually a few days after reception of the complaint, the judges send somebody to notify the defendant. The messenger may be the child of one of the judges or *nyim shapdy*, a special messenger. The messengers must be well treated in the villages, for courts can hold villages in contempt. The courts of appeal have their own means of summoning the defendant: baang sends the *iyol abaang*; kikaam and the supreme court have the summons announced on the main square of the capital by the town crier. Anybody who meets the accused is under obligation to notify him. When an accused person refuses to answer the summons, he is fined and arrested either by his covillagers or by slaves of the king or the chief, who form the police force. He is then bound and put in the stocks at the jail in the kikaam's compound. The stocks are used only for preventive detention of this sort. Any person may arrest any other *in flagrante delicto*, a fact that often leads to fights. A wise man notifies the two village policemen who exist in every village.

Before the session of the court opens, the accused pays 700 cowries to the panel, and the 1,400 cowries of both parties is divided among the judges. This amount constitutes their salary. Both parties, one after the other, then tell the facts, the plaintiff being the first speaker. At this stage they may be interrupted only by judges or spectators who want to elucidate one or another detail. Eyewitnesses or character witnesses are then called in and are cross-examined by the judges, who also cross-examine the parties. Usually the statements of the parties and the testimony of the witnesses elicit the facts to the satisfaction of the judges. The latter, in any event, have a general knowledge of the facts, having heard about the matter through gossip at the capital or through inquiries made beforehand by the provincial chief. Sometimes, however, the facts are not clear and there are no witnesses. The accused may then propose to swear an oath (*ndokl*). He says that he is innocent, invokes the Creator God as a witness, and steps over a leopard skin, the symbol of political authority. If he lies, he should die on the spot. But the oath is rarely used, for it is believed that the Creator punishes those who swear for trifles. I believe that the judges feel that swearing an oath is taking the matter out of court. A milder oath also exists, but it is considered no more than an emphatic form of speech.

After the evidence is heard and the facts are elicited to the satisfaction of the judges, they withdraw to deliberate. They must reach a unanimous verdict. After doing so, they emerge and proceed to the announcement of the verdict, which is introduced by the following formula:

> The king doesn't walk with a bow
> the collecting of conflicts, the verdicts of the cases.
> The black genette eats the white termites
> Be not afraid of the grass the genette carries
> The old animal of the councilors of the supreme court
> when he proceeds to decide cases, he doesn't like protests.
> Above the thieves, the leopard of the witches
> the spoon of the porridge
> is the instrument which probes the depths of the fire.
> It dawns at the chasm which begets the hills
> at the world which begets the living.
> The river of trade bears the weak ones.
> It becomes daylight at Mbeky Butwiim
> at Makum maNyaang
> at the king who stares intently at the verdicts
> at Mboom Kol Mishumn.

The formula means:

> The king is in court to
> settle the conflicts.
> The king destroys the criminals
> the innocents must not be afraid.
> The king in the supreme court
> does not stand for protests against the verdicts.
> Despite the thieves, the king
> can find the culprits.
> It dawns at the king's who creates the world
> who creates all the living beings.
> The king protects the weak.
> It dawns at the famous capitals
> at the king's capital when he holds his court.

The formula is given in full because it is typical of Kuba thought. It emphasizes that the court holds its authority from the king, and that the king has authority by virtue of divine kingship. It reminds the guilty parties that justice will find them out, and the innocent parties that they are protected by the king. It reminds all that verdicts should not be questioned. It expresses the Kuba philosophy of law, and stresses that fundamentally the law has equity. It is guaranteed by the powers of the king, but the equity of the king himself is guaranteed by the supreme court.

The verdict announced by one of the judges designates explicitly who lost the case and inflicts a fine on the loser, half of which goes to the kikaam and half to the king. It sets the amount of a payment to be made by the loser to the winner in compensation for the harm done. Punishment never includes terms in jail or corporal punishment. The loser may appeal, failing which he must carry out the sentence. If he does not, he will be arrested by the slaves of the king and put in the stocks. If he cannot pay, he must leave some of his personal belongings in pawn with the court, which will deposit them in the house of one of the judges.

This whole description of the court is valid for precolonial times, but since then a few changes have been made. There are only a small number of judges who are recognized by the judicial authorities. The panel system still functions, but the judges take turns and decide all cases, irrespective of their nature, so long as they fall within the category labeled "civil" by the Congo Code. Cases that are labeled "criminal" are also handled if they do not involve murder or attempted murder. Under the colonial regime, all cases involving Europeans were outside the competence of the courts in Kuba land, but all cases dealing with non-Kuba (other than Europeans) living on Kuba land were dealt with by the Kuba. Little or nothing has changed in procedural law, except that nowadays the messengers are policemen of the regular police force. Sentencing to a term in jail, and the practice of making the parties pay for the administrative costs of the case, have come into usage. But, for the rest, very little has changed. The procedural law dealing with injuries or death has, however, practically disappeared, and I have had to reconstruct it from accounts by older titleholders.

When the conflict entails injuries, the wounded party is brought to the chief policeman of the capital, the iyol. He starts proceedings by setting himself on an inverted mortar (a symbol of military authority), and asks from the defendant a small sum which he uses to buy a meal. He eats (the symbolism of the meal remains somewhat unclear), and then informs the king about the case. If the small sum is refused, the defendant is taken into preventive custody. Then the usual court procedure is followed, but the final penalty consists of a fine which is not divided between kikaam and king, but goes to the king only. The penalty includes compensation as well as the fine. Compensation consists of a serf woman, who must be either a serf woman or a woman of the lineage of the culprit.

In a case of murder the king is notified and the responsible territorial official is ordered to bring the culprit in without delay. If the man resists arrest, he is killed by the slaves of the king without further trial.

Otherwise he is placed under guard of the *nyibit*, the commander of the army. The case is tried by the supreme court at night. When the verdict is given, the usual formula is omitted as the court gives it in the presence of the king. There is no delegation of judicial powers. The king then confirms the judgment. When he does so, the mbeem and the mbyeeng of the capital beg him to spare the life of the culprit. The king may turn down their appeal. If he does not, the condemned person becomes a royal slave and, as likely as not, is put in the village from which *nkukuun* (slaves to be sacrificed at the death of the king) will be chosen. The nkukuun are always criminals condemned to death, but spared previous execution. If the appeal is turned down and stay of execution not granted, special officers among the king's slaves take the culprit home so that he can bid his farewells. They leave him there, coming back a little later to ask ceremonially for him. They address their demand to the head of the settlement in which the man lives, and use symbolic objects and gestures signifying royal power and the death sentence. The man is ceremonially given up. What happens next is unclear. It is said that the murderer is allowed to inebriate himself on palm wine and then is urged to hang himself in the forest. What happens if the criminal refuses to do so is also unclear. In all cases of murder the lineage of the criminal has to pay a person—this time not a serf woman, but a slave—to the king. The power over life and death has been taken away from the Kuba since the period 1910-1916, which explains why the recollections are vague.

The procedure in the case of murder illustrates a cardinal point in the Kuba conception of kingship and chiefship. The king and the chief are the only persons who hold rights over life and death; they hold them because kingship and chiefship exist by divine right. Kingship and chiefship are responsible for the general fertility of the country, and the king holds this right because it has been given in so many words and by symbolic ceremonial to him at his accession. One of the formulas then used stresses that "the head of the criminal belongs to the king." In practice, a murderer who resists arrest is killed, and his head has to be brought to the king.

The same procedure illustrates the concept that royal authority, although it is supreme, has to be checked. The trial is held by a court that the king does not lead, although he is present. The only court that can hold a murder trial is the election council; that is why the more important half of the council sits as a court. The same holds true for the other chiefdoms, where that council or part of that council also acts as a court in murder trials.

Appeals may be made by any of the parties involved in a case. The party who appeals must first pay 150 cowries to the lower court so that it will desist from acting in the case. The procedure at all higher courts is similar. Appeals are discouraged, however, because sentences tend to become heavier. The usual sentence for any case coming to the supreme court is reduction into slavery of the whole lineage of the loser, or the payment of a very large amount of goods to the king or the chief. The latter penalty has the same effect, for, in order to pay the fine, the condemned person would have to sell several relatives into slavery or at least pawn his matrilineal womenfolk as serf women. At this level no compensation is ever paid to the winner. The Kuba feel, therefore, that one who does appeal to the supreme court must be motivated by hatred. Moreover, the court may turn down any appeal on the grounds that the case is too trivial and was handled correctly in the lower court.

Procedural law shows two further characteristics: first, some form of symbolic ceremonialism is used; second, the graver the offense, the more the symbolism that is attached to the ceremonial. In this way the social meaning of what is happening is made clear to all. The symbolism used always stresses in part that law is dispensed by the political system and its head, the king or the chief. Procedural law also shows that there are two types of cases: those that involve bloodshed and those that do not. These types are distinguished in the following discussion of substantive law.

Substantive Law

CASES WITHOUT BLOODSHED

The Kuba court may deal with any conflict that arises in society, with the exception of particular situations to be discussed later. The composition of the court varies with the type of case, and some cases are reserved to the courts of appeal. The baang hears all matters pertaining to marriage, in the first instance, and the kikaam hears all cases of debts. The types of cases heard by a modern court and their relative frequency are best illustrated by listing the cases from the *chefferie* court that succeeded to the court of first instance in the Bushoong chiefdom (see table 3). Table 3 reveals two important facts. First, the present so-called customary law is distorted in terms of modern Congolese law, based on the Code Napoléon. Some of the listings under both civil and criminal headings are odd, which explains why reports from scribes or collections from legal journals are often almost useless. Second, most of the cases deal with marriage problems (adultery, marriage, divorce, bridewealth), with claims on goods (debts, pledges, bridewealth, loans), and with violence in word or deed (insults, threats, assault, slander). Marriage problems total 51.5 percent of the cases; claims on goods, 52.5 percent; and violence, 40.5 percent. (Overlap between categories explains the total of 144.5 percent.) In fact, violence seems to be generally an expression of conflict, not of the grounds of conflict, and it may safely be said that most cases involve either marriage or the transfer of goods. This is even more true of the pre-colonial period, when a number of cases listed in table 3 would not have existed (e.g., modern administration, drunkenness). We might

TABLE 3

CASES HANDLED BY A "CHEFFERIE" COURT OF THE KUBA, MAY, 1952–MAY, 1953

Civil cases		Criminal cases	
Subject	Number	Subject	Number
Debt	84	Theft	21
Loan	13	Adultery	62
Sharing	18	Insults	35
Bridewealth	38	Disobeying a chief	16
Kingship	3	Threats	17
Marriage	40	Assaults	74
Pawning	30	Modern administration	17
Fields	6	Drunkenness	1
Inheritance	23	Slander	3
Divorce	30	Accidental arson	4
Fishing	6	Contempt of court	4
Guardianship	1	Fraud	13
Nkaan (initiation)	1		
Hunt	3		
Others	13		

Total number of cases = 318

expect, therefore, that most substantive law deals with these matters.

The Kuba view on substantive law is reflected in their division of cases by types and in the assignment of special judges to special types. Debts come immediately to the kikaam's court, and marriage affairs go to the baang. The number of appeals is therefore limited, and the first court tends to hand out the final judgment. In addition to these two, there are only two judges for cases not involving bloodshed: one for thefts and one for attempted murder by the use of charm. And as a transfer of goods is involved in the case of theft, the kikaam might be called in even at the first trial.

The Kuba, be they judges or not, have no code of substantive law, nor do they come up with a discussion of precedents on points of substantive law. If one asked a Kuba man about a specific problem, he would be likely to state that such and such is an offense and that the penalty is so and so. Moreover, the chances are that the man in the street and the judge would do about as well in solving the problem and indicating what rules were involved in the solution. On the whole, the Kuba do not give the impression that they are interested in legal matters. In any event, by following cases brought before the court and by questioning in terms of hypothetical trials, one can derive a number of rules of substantive law. It is impossible to set all of them forth in a brief paper. Furthermore, the notation and the order of presentation of such rules would imply a serious distortion of the legal notions held by the Kuba. In fact, one quickly discovers that the legal norms—that is, the rules explicitly stated by the Kuba—are social norms, and nothing more than the usual social norms for the regulation of behavior which are implied by the institutions concerned in the case.[6] The following instances illustrate this fact.

Instance no. 1. The younger brother steals a wife.—X accused Y of adultery with his wife. X and Y were full paternal parallel cousins, and Y was the elder brother of X. Y answered, "Certainly X is my younger brother. Therefore I could not possibly take his wife. But he is wicked [*ipaangt,* a technical term] for his wife was first mine. X was a messenger for a European firm and lured my wife away. I had to abandon her because my younger brother had married her. Why, on top of all this, does he accuse me now?" The judges found out that X had worked for a European firm and that his wife had been Y's. They did not even deliberate, but handed a verdict of innocence to Y and had X pay the costs of the trial. One judge scowled, "You knew, X, from the villagers that the girl was the wife of your elder brother. Why have you married her in turn?"

The interest of the case lies in the fact that it arose as a case of adultery, but as soon as it became known that the younger brother took the wife of the older one, that aspect crowded out the matter of adultery. The norms involved are that elder brothers, even classificatory ones, may never have sexual intercourse with the wives of younger brothers, whereas the latter may banter with the wives of their elders and inherit them after the death of the elder brothers. To steal a wife of an elder brother puts the latter in a position where he has to divorce her. It is wicked because it is the illicit exploitation of a norm of behavior to one's unfair advantage. Once it was established that X had acted in full knowledge, he lost the case. The legal reason as written in the court's register would be that the accusation was not proven. The real reason was, of course, the behavior of X.

Other cases in which such general norms of behavior apply are legion. For instance, in one case a man accused another of slander because the latter had hinted that the plaintiff had put poison in his food. The case was dismissed because the defendant had not asked the plaintiff to settle the matter by the poison ordeal, which was the proper thing to do, even though use of the ordeal had been forbidden by the European administration thirty years before. In another case a father accused his son of having wounded him. The boy was not even allowed to speak, but was sent to jail "until the wound healed," and then only would the case be tried. In another case a father simply asked to have his son jailed because the latter did not obey him. The son was promptly jailed. The cultural norm in these cases was the expected behavior of a son toward his father. As deviance from the norm had been serious, punishment was inflicted even without full investigation.

When two norms of behavior conflict, the judgment may be more difficult.

Instance no. 2. The careless wife.—A sued his wife B. He said that he had cultivated his cornfield, but, when harvesting time came, his wife had not harvested and the corn had been destroyed by bush pigs. B explained that she had left her home to assist her pregnant daughter. One judge asked her in wonder, "Why did you, a woman, go to live elsewhere when the crops were ripe in the forest?" The woman was condemned but not fined.

The norms involved are clear: a woman shall reap the harvest planted by her husband and a woman shall assist her pregnant daughter. When the two conflicted, the judges felt that the first duty was more imperative than the second. But, realizing that there was some choice possible between the norms, they did not fine the woman, although they may have refrained from doing so in order not to endanger the marriage.

A curious aspect of these norms is that they cover the amount of compensation to be paid if a norm is breached. In cases of adultery, where the breach is very clear, the penalties are as follows. An adulterer pays 300 cowries as a fine, and a compensation of one *mapel* (man's dancing cloth, worth 20 dollars) and one *ikul* (man's knife, worth 1 dollar) to the wronged husband. If a woman introduces a complaint, the adulteress pays one *ncak* (woman's dancing cloth, worth about 10 to 15 dollars). If the plaintiff is a king's child, the amounts are doubled. If the defendant is a king's child, no compensation is paid. Three cases judged in 1954 adhered to these penalties, replacing the customary 300 cowries with 300 francs and adding a month in jail in all cases. Other instances may easily be cited. In case of theft, the stolen goods must be returned, but no other compensation is given. In cases of beating without bloodshed, the compensation is 600 cowries. In cases of attempted murder with the use of charms, it is 3,000 cowries. (In practice, this sentence would often mean that the culprit would have to pawn a woman as a serf woman in order to raise that much money.)

These tariffs are not organized in a system and therefore do not form a penal code. The norms they sanction are social norms, not legal ones. The Kuba have not defined any institution in legal terms as distinct from common opinion about what an institution is about. In our society we have redefined every institution in law, and all our social norms have been carefully translated into legal norms, which are based on the definitions made by the law. In fact, our lawyers have created a second world, in which any functioning element of the society casts its shadow and has its counterpart. The Kuba have no writing and they have no lawyers. Their law uses the institutions and their norms, and the penalties for breaking norms as they come, without systematizing or redefining. One might say that in our society law has duplicated and permeated society. One might say just as well that in Kuba society the social norms have taken the place of the field of law. They function as legal norms, but they are social norms. As there are no legal norms, the social norms have built up a set of tariffs because society demands that man should have at least some expectation as to the consequences of any behavior, even antisocial behavior.

If this reasoning is accepted, it becomes understandable that the content of substantive law is no less than the totality of the institutions of the society and that the law does not construct a "reasonable man,"[7] but that all institutions have role expectations that must be observed by the participants in the institution.

CASES WITH BLOODSHED

There is a distinction between cases involving bloodshed and others, as is evident from the description of procedural law. The distinction does not overlap with Western notions of criminal and civil law, as may be illustrated by the following type of case. When orders from a political authority other than the king have been transgressed, the complaints are lodged by the authorities involved. When the case is decided against the accused, compensation is awarded on a personal basis to the authority who introduced the matter, as if he were simply an ordinary plaintiff. Such a case does not involve bloodshed, yet it might very well be criminal in Western eyes.

The serious concern shown by the Kuba political structures about the settlement of conflicts involving violence is revealed by the special procedures and symbolic ceremonials that are used. The concern is also clear from the types of cases assigned to special types of judges. As against four specialists for cases without bloodshed, which constitute the large majority of all cases that come to the courts, five are found for five types of cases involving bloodshed. Distinctions are made among involuntary homicide, suicide—an involuntary homicide by the relatives of the deceased—simple injuries, injuries inflicted by a weapon of war, and murder. In the last three instances, where accident is excluded and intent seems clear, the offense must be reported at once to the king or to the chief of the chiefdom, and the procedure is of a special type. In all instances, compensation involves a human being and is paid, not to the wronged party, but to the head of the chiefdom.

Substantive law with regard to cases without bloodshed was said to be based, not on a corpus juris, but on social norms of the relevant institutions. Cases of violence have in common that they are a breach of a fundamental political norm and that peace should be maintained, and also, of the norm in a case of murder, that only a king or a chief can take a life. It is because a fundamental political norm is broken that cases of bloodshed are distinguished from the others. The fact that such cases are a threat to the political system explains why the reaction is so dramatic, why the specialized judges are all military officers when intent of bloodshed can be shown, why the king or the chief has to be notified, why the procedure moves more rapidly than usual, and so on.

It is characteristic of the Kuba political system that the use of physical force is strictly limited to the political authorities, excluding self-help under practically any circumstance. The Kuba have gone further in this respect than many other African states, including even the interlacustrine kingdoms, where feuds are still allowed provided the kings have given their permission to the lineage of the victim. But Kuba political structure has to react vigorously, for the spirit of the feud—the principle of a life for a life—is not dead. It is still applied between clans in connection with poison ordeals, and in the institution of serf women whose transfer is usually a transfer of lives and life potentialities. The principle is present in law as well; when a murderer has been executed, his group still has to hand over a person to compensate for the victim. But that person is not given to the group of the victim, but to the king or the head of the chiefdom, the representative of the whole political structure.

In recent times most instances of bloodshed have not been tried in

Kuba courts, and it is not possible to obtain detailed evidence on earlier cases. But the norms still exist, and so do the tariffs for breaches of different norms. In a case of suicide, as also in involuntary homicide, the surviving relatives had to pay nine slaves. When blood was shed with or without a weapon of war, a serf woman was paid to the king along with bells, lances, swords (note the symbolism; these are weapons of war or symbols of military authority), and cloth in large amount, which probably meant that the culprit would have to pawn several girls of his lineage as serf women. If somebody wounded a person for the second time, the offense was tantamount to murder. In a case of murder, a slave was paid to the king or the chief if the murderer was executed. If not, it could happen that the murderer and his whole immediate lineage were condemned to slavery. These tariffs entail two sorts of judgment: compensation, which has to be a life; and penalty, which may be death, payment in goods or slaves, or enslavement. The fact that compensation and penalty are directed toward the same authority obscures the distinction between them at first glance, but the distinction is relevant to Kuba law as a whole.

Law and the Poison Ordeal

The legal institutions described so far cannot cope with accusations of witchcraft, which are made very frequently. Yet no moot, no court, will accept them. The proper technique is to ask for a poison ordeal. The accused drinks poison; if he dies he is guilty, and if he survives he is innocent. Normally the head of the clan of the victim—often the clan of the suspected witch as well—makes a public accusation and asks the suspect to drink poison. A village headman may do the same with regard to suspects in his village, but he may not accuse dependents (slaves, serf women, spouses married into the village) without the permission of their masters; if they drank poison, they would take it in their villages of origin. If the suspect does not belong to the clan of the victim, the head of the victim's clan asks the head of the suspect's clan to submit his man to the ordeal. The request is almost never refused, but, if the man is innocent, compensation must be given by the victim's clan, either by payment of 200–400 cowries or, as is often done, by having one of their men take the poison. This is the closest the Kuba ever come to a feud, and they recognize that such cases may create permanent hatred between some clans.

After the accusation is formally voiced, the accused person agrees to take the poison. If he should refuse, the poison would be slipped into his food or drink anyway. Many suspects themselves cheerfully ask to drink the poison so as to clear their names. The ordeal itself is a complete ritual performed by a specialist. It is supposed to be directed supernaturally by the Creator God and the nature spirits.

Why do the Kuba courts not take control over the administration of the ordeal? Matters of life and death are matters of kingship and chiefship, and they are vital to the political structure. And by far the most numerous accusations of murder concern witchcraft. Yet the courts do not act. The Kuba recognize that in a way the poison ordeal is a legal instrument; in the myth that supports the institution, the ordeal is invented by a man named Justice. After his death, long ago, the courts used to administer the preliminary ordeal leading to the poison ordeal, if no witnesses were available and an oath had been taken. But later the ordeal developed in its present form and became restricted to accusations of witchcraft. The courts withdrew completely from this field. It is tempting, but untenable, to hold that the courts are not concerned with witchcraft because the alleged crime is supernatural and cannot be established by natural means. The use of black magic is forbidden, and action is taken in court when accusations of this nature arise. That no material evidence can be offered in cases of witchcraft should not necessarily stop the courts, for, when there are no witnesses and there is no evidence, the defendant takes an oath which the court accepts as evidence.

In fact, alongside the moots and the courts, the poison ordeal may be considered the third major institution of the Kuba legal system. It might be argued that the poison ordeal is not administered by the courts partly because of the large number of cases that arise, which would have justified the creation of a special court to deal with the problem. But the nature of the ordeal is such that the whole community in which the drama of witchcraft has unfolded itself plays a part in the drama, in a way not unlike the participation of the whole village in a moot. This community encompasses all persons who are interested in the case, and none of those who are not. The latter circumstance suggests that cases of witchcraft are not seen as affecting the whole large political community, and can be dealt with by an institution like the moot at the village level. That the ordeal has to be impartial, and not a condemnation, is clear from the type of crime—it cannot be traced—and from the type of judging body—no person could condemn a fellow villager or clansman and not disrupt the fabric of social relations in the village. The condemnation is not given by the villagers; it comes from above, and nobody but the dying witch can be blamed for it.

The Upper Limits of the Legal System

A number of conflicts cannot be solved by law, as law has been defined. These are conflicts between the king or the head of a chiefdom and one of his subjects, and conflicts between chiefdoms. The king is outside the law. He is immune. No case is known of a king ever being brought before a court. And a king who feels he has been wronged may ignore the legal machinery completely, and act on his own. For instance, in 1921 a man was supposed to have committed adultery with one of the ruling king's wives. The king kept him chained for months, and only after long pleading did the titleholders obtain his release. Scores of instances are known in which kings have killed paramours of their wives and tortured their wives. Nobody ever interferes. Gossip has it, and it has been substantiated in some instances, that kings who dislike certain key titleholders have them poisoned. In a well-known case the king went out at night and himself set fire to the house of a man he disliked, though the man had committed no wrong the king could complain about. Yet, even for actions like these, the king is still immune from the law, as are chiefs in their chiefdoms. If kings kill too many people, however, they themselves are killed, not through a process of law, but by the national charm. If chiefs kill too many people, they are pushed out of office and sometimes are killed by their electors or by a mob.

The Kuba say that the king is immune because the authority of king and chiefs is supreme. This authority, to be maintained, must be backed not only by the prestige derived from wealth and title but by the possibility of physical action against rebels. The king or the chief is the symbol of the kingdom or of the chiefdom. Nobody can engage in a conflict with either of them and be "right," for the conflict would be against the kingdom or the chiefdom. Also, nobody can admit that a court would find against a king or a chief, since it finds in the name of the king and its authority derives from the king. In fact, kings and chiefs are immune simply because they are at the apex of the political structure, and law is a function of that structure just as the courts are a structural part of it.

Law cannot solve conflict between chiefdoms because the Kuba kingdom is a multicentric power system. The Bushoong dominate the other chiefdoms militarily, but every chiefdom remains a power system. If its power is not very inferior to that of the Bushoong, as is true of the Ngongo, the chiefdom is practically independent; if its power is puny compared with that of the Bushoong, the chiefdom becomes almost a supplementary province, as is true of the Bulaang. But there is no machinery to unite all the chiefdoms for the purpose of the exercise of the law. The limit of the legal system and of law is set at a lower territorial level than the upper limit of the total political system, the kingdom. Therefore, conflicts between chiefdoms lead either to war or to arbitration by an outside chief, who is asked to act by the warring chiefs. The arbitrator is often the king, mainly because he has the biggest army. Arbitration does not aim at finding a guilty party, but at reconciling the factions without putting the blame on anybody. If war then does not solve conflict, a form of diplomacy does.

Besides the conflicts mentioned, another type of breach of behavior, incest, falls outside the scope of the law. A logical explanation would be that, as both parties are guilty, there could be no plaintiff and therefore no action by moot, court, or ordeal. But the Kuba say that incest falls outside judicial action because the offense is punished automatically by the Creator God, who inflicts lepra on the culprits. Very few cases of incest are actually known. The one recent case, in 1953, was involuntary incest, and the man hanged himself to escape public scorn as soon as he discovered it. So few cases seem to occur, and they are kept so secret for fear of public ostracism, that it is largely hypothetical speculation to question further why the courts do not handle these matters.

The Nature of Kuba Law

The legal system of the Kuba is part of their political structure. Titleholders have other tasks besides their legal duties. The limitations of the legal system, and the special care taken in cases involving bloodshed, make the point. If a generalization is possible, and I think it is, we might say that wherever political systems are different, legal systems are different too. Traditional societies in Africa might have centralized political systems with a monarchy, as the Kuba have, or they might have such systems without a monarchy. There might be segmentary lineage systems, age-grade organizations, simple village organizations, and all sorts of intermediate types between these major ones. Moreover, different variants of Muslim law were accepted in differing degrees in West and East Africa. In short, one might justifiably expect a wide variety of traditional legal systems; the Kuba system is only one of them.

I have said that Kuba law has no corpus juris, and that the norms of the law are those of the institutions concerned. There is no code and there is no case law, for Kuba law does not use precedents, nor does it compare cases to deduce legal analogies. This feature the Kuba probably have in common with a great many African systems, such as the

Tiv, the Lozi, and the Rwanda,[8] irrespective of the political system of which the law is a part. Kuba law is thus very different from any European legal system, and to try to define it in terms of European legal concepts is like trying to fit a Bantu grammar into a Latin model of grammatical categories, something that actually was done until descriptive linguistics taught us better.[9] Insofar as possible, Kuba law should be analyzed on its own terms. One can analyze it on a broad basis by examining the existence and the use of legal vocabulary, by investigating the legal formulas, if there are more than one, and by exploring the structural and institutional features of the system itself.

As suggested above, the formula states that the process of law is based on equity and rooted in the political authority, chieftainship or kingship. An examination of the most important legal terms—maybe nearly all the specific terms there are—shows more clearly what law means to the Kuba. There is no term for "law" itself, but there is one for general custom, the mores: *iya*. The word *look*, meaning the capacity to listen, the ability to judge, justice ("justice" being semantically equivalent to "the ability to give a good judgment") is derived from the verbal *wook*, to listen. The idea of justice is thus tied pretty closely to the court or the moot, where parties may present cases. The process of law itself is most often referred to by the name of the court, ibaanc, and the judges are the "chiefs of ibaanc." As in the English word "court," the notion "ibaanc" covers a plaza, a judicial court, and sometimes the entourage of a king or a chief. In addition, the Kuba word also means the great council that meets on the plaza. A "case" is *matyeen*, "things looked at, things scrutinized"; the connection with a court is evident. All other technical terms found so far deal with a case in court, and all of them are only half technical in the sense that they may be used with other meanings in nonlegal situations. *Waabwaak* normally means "you fell," but in a court it means "you lost the case." The terminology shows that judges "overcome" cases by "looking intently" at them, and that parties are "elevated" or they "fall." The whole vocabulary, then, shows few exclusively legal terms and even few technical terms, which supports the theory about the absence of a corpus of legal norms.

The sources of Kuba law are the norms of behavior existing in the society, and they change as rapidly as it does. But there are also statutes and orders, which in time become norms. *Nkyeenc* are orders given by the king, probably without consultation with his councils, and *shyaang* are statutes given after proper consultation with the councils. Instances of such statutes are legion. In 1953 the king forbade dancing and singing during the night within the borders of the capital. A recently formed witch-finding cult was flourishing, and had just started to hold nightly shows. When many people complained about the noise, the king's order was promulgated. About 1910 a new charm had made its way, and was being used to kill one's enemies. So many people died that the king had to forbid the possession of such a charm under penalty of death. The two instances cited exemplify adaptations to changes in the society. But sometimes statutes initiate changes, or favor change, in certain directions. Oral history has it that around 1680 a king proclaimed special prerogatives for royal children in matters of marriage, bridewealth, and adultery. The statute aimed at enhancing the status of such persons, and later history shows that their status was indeed improved shortly afterward. The two sources of Kuba law, social norm and statute, may be expected in all African monarchies, and indeed are fairly typical for them. For example, in Rwanda and Loziland the situation is essentially similar. But statutes as a source of law cannot be expected outside the monarchies, for there would be no supreme authority to proclaim the edicts.

The main divisions of Kuba law, indicated above, follow logically from the absence of codex and the differences in laws of procedure between cases involving bloodshed and cases without bloodshed. In contrast with the moot, the legal procedure in court is not merely a process of arbitration. Courts are institutionally defined as to membership and competence, moots only vaguely so; courts can coerce, moots cannot; and, most important, a court has to designate clearly who is the loser, and has to fine him. That is, a court may blame one party for this, another for that, but it holds one party responsible for breach of the peace and the creation of conflict. Poison ordeals are like courts in all these respects except that the culprit is not designated by man; the judge, being supernatural, is in fact absent. The active part played by the spectators, however, brings the ordeal close to the moot.

In court decisions, two forms of action are clearly involved. The first is restoration of the former situation if at all possible (e.g., a thief hands the stolen goods back, but pays no further compensation), or new action by the guilty party (e.g., the payment of mapel and ikul to atone for adultery). What the atonement shall be is often determined by the norms of the institution involved. This type of legal action is very close to the type proposed in a moot. In fact, cases are known in which an adulterer simply paid mapel and ikul to the wronged husband, even without calling a moot. In this action of the court, its decision can be accepted by all involved because it conforms so strictly to known norms. The second action of the court has to do with the situation of conflict itself, the responsibility for conflict. Somebody is held responsible and must be penalized. The fine goes to the political structure which has been injured by the existence of conflict. The distinction between compensation and penalty is clear in cases not involving bloodshed, but it applies also to cases with bloodshed, as shown above. The difference between cases of bloodshed and others is simply that in the former instance compensation goes to the political authority, and not to a private plaintiff. The distinction between the moot and the poison ordeal in this respect is simply that the moot imposes no penalty, restoration being the only aim, whereas in the ordeal compensation is absent, the penalty being the only aim.

6.

REASONABLENESS AND RESPONSIBILITY IN THE LAW OF SEGMENTARY SOCIETIES

by Max Gluckman

I have been given a brief for this paper which asks me to examine one problem of law in segmentary societies,[1] and not those in African states of the type I have myself studied. I rely, therefore, on the excellent material collected by others on law in segmentary societies, and subject it to some reanalysis which I hope does not distort it unduly. But I shall not always be able to give detailed references, as on many fundamental points I have to build up my own analysis from information scattered in many isolated references through a variety of books, references that have to be marshaled to the solution of juristic problems. My brief continues by asking me to consider the rights and obligations that inhere in membership in different corporate groups, the methods of dealing with conflicts, the maintenance of routine order, and the application of the conception of "the reasonable man" in societies that superficially might appear to be without such a concept.[2] I am thus asked to focus on modes of ratiocination, rather than on legal procedures or political processes.

I take this as a compliment because, while the idea of the prudent or the reasonable man has long been accepted in Western law, and in studies of early European law, it has not been well reported in studies of tribal law. In writing my own book, *The Judicial Process among the Barotse of Northern Rhodesia* (1955), I was struck by the dominating presence of the reasonable man in all Barotse court trials. He was the standard figure against which, both in cross-examination and in judgment, the councilors assessed the behavior of the disputing parties. Every departure from the conventions and modes of behavior expected of a reasonable man was treated by judges as a possible indication that the defaulter was likely to be guilty of a more serious breach of rule. Hence even items of etiquette, which were in themselves not sanc-

[1] For notes to chapter 6, see page 249.

tioned at law, were used to attack the party's ostensibly reasonable story, and then were seriously weighed in giving judgment. But because Barotse society, despite its highly organized system of courts, is mainly organized in kinship relationships and political relationships serving multifarious purposes, Barotse judges do not work only with a general picture of a reasonable man or woman. Disputes coming before them often involve persons who are permanently interrelated in established status pairings, set within a larger complex of status relationships. The Barotse judges have standardized pictures of reasonable incumbents of each of the social positions included in this complex. That is, they think of a reasonable husband, a reasonable wife, a reasonable father, mother, maternal uncle, nephew, relative-in-law, or a reasonable councilor or headman, and a reasonable underling. As it is characteristic of tribal societies that each social relationship is differentiated within the general context of kinship by highly specific conventions, modes of etiquette, and taboos—in short, by custom[3]—the idea of the reasonable incumbent of a social position contains also the implication that he or she abides by this custom. Deviation from custom, while not always strictly punished, may therefore be at least evidence of graver default. I drew attention at the time to the similarity of this concept to the conceptions and the expectations of roles that have become the core of sociological and social anthropological analyses. The idea of the reasonable and customary incumbent of a social position is the indigenous view of a role as it is handled in the course of trial. In fact, I demonstrated that among the Barotse the crux of many disputes is the judgment whether the party sued has or has not acted as a reasonable husband, or wife, or father, or uncle, or son, or nephew, or in-law, or lord, or underling.

The concept of reasonableness here involves another standard. The Barotse see their reasonable man (*mutu yangana*, a person of sense) as contained in an upright man (*mutu yalukile*, a straight or upright person). I was able to show through actual trials that the judges hold before people, as well as before themselves, the model of an upright man, who is generous beyond the demands of the law. The court does not enforce these higher standards; it demands only what it defines as reasonable standards of fulfillment, as Western courts do. The standards of the upright man are the measure of morality; those of the reasonable man are the measure of forensic or legal compulsion. Assessment of this leeway is often the main problem that faces the judges. They have to determine what they can reasonably expect a person in a specific status to do for the relative who prosecutes him, in terms of his wealth, strength, age, and the balance of obligations he owes to all his lords and relatives. Thus the judges are measuring separate standards of fulfillment of specific duties to a wife, a father, a father-in-law, and so forth; and these standards have been changing as Barotseland has been drawn into the new economy and polity of Northern Rhodesia. The term "reasonable" is therefore highly flexible. This flexibility allows the court to adapt rules of law—such as the rules that a husband must take reasonable care of his wife and that an underling must render reasonable duties to his overlord—to the new situation in which the Barotse live.

It therefore seemed to me that the concept of the reasonable man must exist in all systems of law; and I made bold to say so in my book. Professor E. Adamson Hoebel, who besides carrying out (partly with that leading jurist Karl N. Llewellyn) important studies on North American Indian law, has also done much to focus the interest of anthropologists on juristically formulated problems, has recently stated that my presumption was unwarranted. In a review of my own book, and of those of Howell on Nuer law[4] and Bohannan on Tiv law,[5] Hoebel states that the idea of the reasonable man is not found in many tribal systems, and does not exist in Soviet law.[6] I have therefore welcomed this opportunity to examine whether the idea does exist in some selected African segmentary societies, and, if I can establish that it does, how it influences processes of social control in the absence of courts. It does seem that when colonial authorities have established courts in these segmentary societies in Africa, the courts begin to operate with the idea of a reasonable man.[7] For example, Howell reports that it is customary among the Nuer for bridewealth cattle to be returned to a widower whose dead wife had not fulfilled her "procreative obligations," though the wife's family could claim certain deductions. Nuer regard "this procedure as logical and correct," though Howell says it is doubtful that it was followed in the past. The effect of refund of bridewealth is to dissolve the marriage. The husband may not want the marriage to end, perhaps because the wife gave birth to sufficient children. Her family may then assist him by giving him cattle to feed the children, or to enable him to marry again so that there would "again 'be a mother in the home.' " There is usually no dispute over these payments, but, if the issue does come to court, the court enforces payment: "The court will begin by saying to the wife's family that it is customary to give [cattle to feed the children] in such circumstances and that the husband is in the right: . . . 'he has a right.' " Howell then adds: "They are taking as a criterion what a reasonable Nuer may be expected to do in similar circumstances, and will call upon the wife's family to conform to that criterion."[8]

This use of the phrase "reasonable man" does not in my opinion bring much evidence to bear upon the query raised by Hoebel, for the phrase "what a reasonable Nuer may be expected to do in similar circumstances" adds little to the statement that such a payment is now customary. But Howell's earlier discussion of the same legal problem suggests that this claim by a widower is newly developed out of the conception of how a reasonable mother's brother behaves to his sister's children; in recognizing this claim the court "is expressing public opinion, which feels that a reasonable man will in certain circumstances assist his brother-in-law and his sister's sons."[9] He reports differences of opinion among the Nuer chiefs, appointed by the government, at a meeting in 1945 on this point; we may therefore say that new law does seem in this instance to have arisen out of a general conception of recognition of reasonable obligations to certain kin.

I have found only one other use of "reasonable," in the sense in which I used the word, in Howell's manual. Kai son of Bithou married

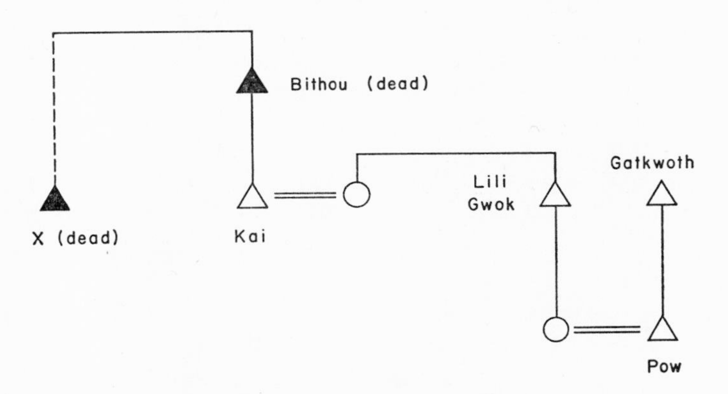

Lili Gwok's sister. A man called Pow, son of Gatkwoth, then married Lili's daughter. Previously Pow's father Gatkwoth had killed a close agnatic kinsman of Kai's (X). Kai then claimed dissolution of the marriage on the ground that there was "blood between them." On appeal the court was divided.

> The minority were of the opinion that dissolution was essential; the majority ruled that, since compensation had been paid for the act of homicide and the feud settled by the leopard-skin chief, no bar to marriage existed. It will be noted that Lili's family are not involved in the feud, and Kai's contention is that Lili, by marrying his daughter into a family who are concerned [in a feud with him], has brought himself within the range of the impediment. At the same time Gatkwoth was the actual killer of X, not merely an agnatic kinsman of the killer, which intensifies the feeling of indignation.

Howell adds that "in this particular case, it is doubtful whether Kai wanted a divorce merely because of these circumstances, or whether the 'blood between them' provided a reasonable excuse for a divorce which he desired for other reasons."[10]

It is clear from my remarks on Howell's other uses of the word "reasonable" that I am not proposing to hunt out such examples, and then argue that they indicate that the conception exists among the Nuer. Howell was mainly concerned to state Nuer substantive legal propositions, and dealt to only a limited extent with processes of reasoning by Nuer to a conclusion. But I think we can extract from this case points bearing on our present problems. Howell presumably takes the case from a court record, and he does not give the full arguments of the minority and the majority of judges. Nor does he tell us on what evidence he considers that Kai took the new marriage as a reasonable excuse for a divorce he wanted on other grounds; presumably Howell is implying that the husband needed a reasonable excuse in order to get the support of the court for return of his marriage cattle. But we may at least look at the implicit argument of Kai and the minority of judges who supported him, as well as the argument of the majority of judges who opposed him, in terms of how they must argue to discuss such a contention. Kai seems to me to argue that no reasonable brother-in-law contracts a marriage for his daughter with the son of a man who killed a close agnate of his full sister's husband. Such a marriage makes him simultaneously brother-in-law and father-in-law to two enemies; and it means that the children of his sister look on their mother's brother's uterine grandchildren as enemies. In short, if there is any conception of how a reasonable incumbent of a status behaves toward his relatives, it must lie in the formulation of arguments balancing obligations to a series of these relatives. The minority seem to have accepted that in these circumstances dissolution was inevitable, and presumably they did not look at what Kai's other motives may have been. The majority apparently felt that, since compensation had been paid, a reasonable brother-in-law could not be expected to avoid marrying his daughter thus. And it is clear from the very structure of Nuer society, as I show below, that there must have been frequent crises of this sort when a feud threatened a marriage. Hence, when Howell tells us that "for this reason [which?] it is safe to conclude that although the existence of a feud is considered a serious bar to marriage, the action taken in such circumstances depends largely on the actual relationship in the kinship structure . . . of husband and wife to the killer and the killed," he summarizes the effect of the court decision, but he does not give the process by which the judges arrived at their respective decisions. And it is in this process of judicial analysis, and settlement of a verdict, that I believe the conception of the reasonable man is important.

If we use the idea of "reasonableness" in analyzing a legal system, in practice we do so in several different contexts. First, there is the whole question of how you measure fulfillment of obligation demanded in general terms from one person to another. And here, I suspect, all societies have to have the measure of reasonableness—what a reasonable incumbent of a particular social position must do. This obligation is obscured to some extent by the fact that tribal societies have so many fixed and definite payments of gifts, and observances of conventions, between relatives and in-laws. When you marry, you have to give certain definite payments to make a woman your wife; among the Nuer there is a minimum number of cattle that have to be transferred. This cannot be evaded. How much more is it reasonable to expect a man of particular wealth to proffer, without so reducing his herd that he cannot support his wife and any children borne by her? Must her kin take reasonable note of this position? If a man's cattle die and he appeals to his wife's kin for cattle to support their uterine nephews and nieces, will they discuss with him what is reasonably due from them, as against the support he might get from his agnatic kin? The problem emerges more clearly if we look at obligations such as that a man must contribute reasonably to the support of his agnates, and of his in-laws, and of his maternal kin, and of his age-mates. How is he to balance, out of his relative poverty, the distribution of his products in terms of these several obligations? Do these various relatives assess—as Barotse judges would do—what he can do for each, in terms of the balance of his means against his total commitments? Could he go to his father-in-law and say, "I am sorry I cannot bring you meat as I would like, because I have had to help my brother's son"? Or are the claims of the father-in-law a strict and absolute liability? It is on these kinds of problems that we need information. Howell tells us that "disputes over small items of property never appear before the courts."[11] As Evans-Pritchard stresses how the Nuer's material poverty gave a high emotional and symbolic value to all property,[12] dealings with property by a man must be an important measure of how deeply he feels the appropriate sentiments to his various relations, and how far he meets his obligations to them. And poverty means allocation, which must surely be measured by reasonable standards. We do not have this material on the Nuer because Howell in practice does not deal with the maintenance of relations within groups of agnatic kin, or the day-to-day relations between in-laws. His book is in fact an account of the substantive law of homicide and injury, of the establishment and dissolution of marriages, of the legitimacy of children as between father's and mother's lineages' rights, of violation of rights in women, and, more briefly, of property rights, inheritance, trade, and loans.

In my Storrs Lectures at the Yale Law School on Barotse jurisprudence,[13] I argued that all tribal systems of law have certain common ideas which can be referred to their common economic and social structure. These same ideas are found in early European law. But here we are concerned with processes of settlement of disputes; these vary, and reports on them are very inadequate. If my Barotse and Zulu experience is any guide, the measure of observance of reasonable standards in fulfilling obligations must raise critical problems for the Nuer; dealings with agnates, maternal kin, and in-laws have to be adjusted to a man's means. And in this respect I am sure that every society must have such criteria. I could demonstrate, possibly against Hoebel's contention, that this kind of reasonableness is present in the fine study he made of Comanche law,[14] and the epoch-marking study he and Llewellyn made of Cheyenne law.[15] Indeed, early in this paper I used the word "leeway" to define the measure of reasonableness in the sense I am now discussing, because of a pregnant passage in *The Cheyenne Way*:

> It will be noted . . . that deviations from any of these lines of standard are of two main kinds: some deviations are rebuked; others are not. Indeed, one phenomenon of law, as of institutions in general, which has received altogether too little attention save in relation to bills of rights and the due process cause, is the two *ranges of leeway* of man's conduct which are a part of any legal or social system—the range of permissible leeway, and the range of actively protected leeway. For the kind and degree of permissible variation, invention, experiment, and "play" are as important a part of any institutional scheme as the kind, degree, and direction of its canalizing or organizing of behavior.[16]

Earlier Llewellyn and Hoebel speak of "right ways" against which action is measured.[17] I consider that it is implicit in these statements that there must be a measure of permissible leeway against these "right ways"; this measure must be determined by reasonable standards for the society concerned. The sheer economic problem compels this policy, for every man is set choices in directing his scarce resources to multiple ends, all enforced on him by varied obligations to different relatives.

I have worked through a large number of studies of tribal law, and it seems to me that of all students looking at the law of segmentary societies, Barton has grasped this problem best. He does so in his studies of two Philippines segmentary societies: *Ifugao Law* (1919) and *The Kalingas* (1948). In the former (pp. 12-13), Barton emphasizes that certain things are "rather *arbitrarily* forbidden"—I shall shortly discuss these rules in relation to the idea of reasonableness—and gives examples of such Ifugao rules. He then states that "a small part of Ifugao law consists even yet of taboos that are arbitrary and, except in essence, unreasonable. But the greater part has advanced far beyond this stage, and is on a firm and reasonable basis of justice." Presumably he is judging here by Ifugao standards, and not by his own, though he does not clearly say so. He is here referring to the inherent logic of the system of Ifugao law, a problem of tribal law to which I shall also later return. But his main awareness of the problem of reasonableness I can show by a series of citations. Among many grounds for divorce are the continued failure of the father of either of the spouses to deliver the fields called for in the marriage contract "when the couple has reached a reasonable age"; unreasonable jealousy; failure on the part of one spouse or of his or her family to meet obligations; continued laziness or shiftlessness of one of the spouses (p. 31). He does not state how failure to meet obligations, or shiftlessness and laziness, are measured, but the tenor of his account is that reasonable standards are set. We are told (p. 42), for example, that if an owner abandons a rice field for however long a period of time, another man may take it up provided the owner does not intervene. Then if the other clears the field, repairs the dikes, levels the terraces, tills and plants, he is entitled to use the field for the same number of years as it was abandoned. Thereafter it reverts to the possession of the owner. Should the owner wish to reclaim the field earlier he must repurchase possession. But if in similar circumstances the field is made in privately owned forest lands from which timber has long been cut, the owner can demand payment for the land when he proves his title. "But he may not take advantage of the labor that the other has spent on the land . . . to demand exorbitant payment"—and what is exorbitant payment but unreasonable payment?

Among the Ifugao these settlements are all negotiated by go-betweens unrelated to both parties. Barton does not recite in detail the words and actions of go-betweens in specific cases, but he gives us (p. 94) a graphic description of how a go-between operates: "To the end of peaceful settlement he exhausts every art of Ifugao diplomacy. He wheedles, coaxes, flatters, threatens, drives, scolds, insinuates. He beats down the demands of the plaintiff or prosecution, and bolsters up the proposals of the defendants until a point is reached at which the parties may compromise." If either party will not listen, the go-between may threaten symbolically to throw his armed support to the other side; and since he is neutral in relationship to both this threat may be decisive. The compromise can be only at a point that the go-between considers to be reasonable adjustment. This is made clear in

Barton's discussion of the transfer of fields by the *ibuy* ceremony. Many payments have to be made to transfer land, and "at any time before the *ibuy* ceremonial which forever transfers the field, the seller may demand a payment or *all* the payments, except the fees to the witnesses and his kin. He may do this as a matter of malice, or he may do it as a matter of necessity. He sends a go-between, to demand payment. The go-between and the buyer arrange a reasonable time—usually not less than ten days—within which the payment is to be made" (p. 49).

If we put this description together with various other statements about how go-betweens act, it is clear that they are always striving to get agreement based on a reasonable standard. And Barton, unlike most other ethnographers, continually poses problems in terms of degrees. Two umpires, appointed to distribute equitably the property of spouses on divorce, may take as their fee "any odd articles of personal property," but "they may not carry this appropriation for themselves too far" (p. 33). That is, they must be reasonable. After a divorce, the parent who cares for a child must care for that child's property and use it only to meet "legitimate obligations" *(ibid.)*. How is "legitimate" assessed? In another context, children are obliged to provide food and clothing and secular and religious care for their parents, as well as to provide requisites for a funeral feast in accordance with the station of a dead parent (p. 38). All these provisions give rise to the need to assess performance or station, and hence to measurement by reasonable standards.

I have drawn thus on Barton because he is exceptional among ethnographers in emphasizing continually that performance has to be measured in what may be variable social circumstances, and that therefore, by implication at least, reasonable standards are set up, and are argued for by the go-betweens. It is this conception of reasonable standards which is of such critical importance in Western law. And precisely because of the limitations that Howell put on the area of law he covered in his book, these problems did not arise for him.

The problem of reasonableness also did not arise for Howell because he dealt mainly with types of disputes in which liability tends to be strict or absolute, namely, the payment of dues at marriage, to legitimize children, to compensate for injury, and, above all, for the operation of rules of vengeance. These dues are required on set scales, without variation. But the obligation to take vengeance for the murder of one's kinsman, or injury to a kinsman, among the Nuer brings up sharply other aspects of the doctrine of reasonableness: recognition of intention to kill as against killing by negligence or accident, questions of responsibility and liability, problems of proof, and provisions for restitution or punishment. In almost every society that demands that a killing be avenged or compensated for to the kin of the deceased, the demand is set in the context of particular social relationships. These relationships stand between groups that are defined as distinct vengeance groupings, thus implying an absolute or strict liability for any aggressive action by one against another. This problem is covered by Evans-Pritchard's[18] and Howell's discussions of the structural relativity of Nuer law. It has also been well discussed by Nadel in his study of Nuba law, under the rubric of "the social range" of offenses.[19]

Howell constantly emphasizes that the purpose of the compensation payment after homicide among the Nuer is to "restore the equilibrium" between the groups of killer and killed.[20] A killing, even if it is unintentional or accidental, disturbs the balance of blood—the debt—between the groups, and has to be redressed, since the social description of the groups is that they take vengeance upon each other for all killings. To do so is part of their rights against each other. We have, of course, to think of a particular killing in these societies not as an individual offense, but as one of a series of offenses occurring over a long period of time. Each offense is relative to its context of social relations, and the chances of securing redress for a wrong in the absence of a governmental organization depend on the social relations between offender and injured. If a killer is a member of a Nuer tribe other than that of his victim, the victim's kin are unlikely to secure compensation. Theoretically it is due, but as the parties live far apart there is no pressure on them to reach a compromise, in which the one will offer and the other accept compensation. If the two vengeance groups live sufficiently close together for them to reach a *modus vivendi*, so that they may go about their business in some peace, various social mechanisms and pressures induce a compromise.[21] But if a killing occurs within a vengeance group itself, the payment of blood money has to be made by the very people who are due to receive it. No redress is then possible, and the killing may be regarded as a sin subject only to ritual or religious sanctions. Hence in dealing with these systems we must recognize that there is a close connection between liability and views of intention. When absolute liability is enforced in terms of the social relationship between the parties, intention is presumed to be malicious. This presumption is reasonable from the fact that the groups stand in a feuding relationship with one another. In terms of the problems of this paper, we might say, perhaps at a stretch, that the reasonable member of one feuding group intends to kill members of the other group.

This statement may be stretching the concept too far, but I do not think that it is. Unfortunately most ethnographers have not looked at these wrongs in these terms. But again we may get some help from Barton. This time I cite a case from his study of the Kalingas. Kalinga constabulary turned out to deal with a disturbance. They ran from their barracks with fixed bayonets. The way was steep, and one constable slipped and slid back into the bayonet of another and was wounded in the leg. The pact holders of the native towns of the two constables conferred and decided that the wounding was accidental. A year later the injurer was discharged and returned home. He became drunk at a feast where the pact holder of the wounded man's group was also present; he began to boast that he had wounded a man of that group—and where was his kinsman whom the pact holder had wounded in retaliation? The pact holder became incensed and made a speech declaring that the injurer should be excluded from the pact, whereupon a heated quarrel arose during which the pact holder wounded the other in the head. The relatives of the wounded man then decided that if the injurer was boasting of having wounded their man, the case could not have been one of accident.[22]

We need not be surprised at this conclusion of the kin of the wounded man. What is striking is that the constable who had wounded the other clearly by accident himself later treated the accident as if it had been a deliberate attack, launched in the line of duty within the feuding relationship of the two groups, and from which he could take credit. That is, regarding himself as a dutiful member of his group, he took credit from an accidental wounding of an enemy, within the tale of debts of this kind between their two groups. And if an accidental injurer thus boasts of his offense, it is even more probable that the offended group, after agreeing that an offense was palliated because it was accidental, and therefore they could accept compensation, is likely to reopen the score and maintain that the injury was deliberate. There are many records from feuding societies which report this reopening of apparently compromised offenses.

The enforcement of absolute liability in these circumstances does not always mean a presumption of malicious intention. Peristiany recorded a long-standing feud between two Pokot clans in East Africa. Their district was attacked at night by another tribe, and during the fighting a member of one clan fired an arrow at the enemy and killed a fellow tribesman of the other clan. His clansmen and he admitted their liability to pay recompense, but thought that the payment should be substantially reduced because the killing occurred in mutual defense of their country. Neutral elders also urged that this suggestion was equitable and reasonable, but the deceased's clansmen insisted on a full payment and obtained it. This demand so embittered relations between the clans that apparently this record of a feud was the fullest one that Peristiany was given sixty years later; the killer's clansmen constantly tried to get even and brought suit whenever any of them was injured in any way connected with the greedy clan. For example, they claimed compensation when one of their members was killed falling from a tree belonging to a member of the other clan.[23] This case shows that even when absolute liability is enforced by the letter of the law, it may be accompanied by a reasonable adjustment of claims to meet mitigating circumstances. (I am indeed prepared to affirm that behind this intransigence in the Pokot case there lay some previous deep grievance.)

Howell gives rich detail to illuminate how mitigating circumstances affect Nuer reduction of absolute liability in these circumstances. Some liability is enforced for every death between separate vengeance groups. If a man is thatching another's house and falls and is killed or seriously injured, the owner must make a purely symbolic payment in bundles of grass and ropes accompanied by appropriate ritual.[24] I consider that symbolic payment is still acknowledgment of liability; and presumably if a man helps a fellow in this work they are closely related. But when killing is with weapons, if it was not intentional the deceased's kin are readier to accept compensation, even if this compensation is not always less than in cases of intentional killing, since fixed dues to various kin have to be met. For instance, killing with a fighting spear signifies deliberation, and in some tribes a homicide with this weapon entailed higher compensation than if it were committed with a fish spear or a stick. The latter weapons seemingly suggested that the killing might have been by chance. According to Howell, "theoretically the question of intention does not enter into the assessment of compensation [after homicide] because the principal object of the payment is to restore the balance [between the groups] which has been disturbed, but Nuer do in fact take it into consideration." Before the Sudan government instituted courts that had some power to enforce peace and payment, Howell adds, there were set scales for compensation for various injuries, but these were in practice a basis on which compromise could be reached. In "unintentional homicide the indignation of the dead man's kin will be less than in cases of intentional killing." Nowadays, in the newly instituted courts, Nuer "chiefs" have held that half the compensation is due after an accidental, as against an intentional, killing.[25] Howell does not state whether killing in self-defense affected compensation. It is worth noting here that the standard payment of blood money was due in all circumstances to the kindreds (differently constituted) of deceased in both Anglo-Saxon and Welsh law, but if killing was intentional an additional payment was due to the nearest blood relatives.

Seemingly, among the Nuer, the issue of guilt for a particular killing was unlikely to arise. It was a heinous breach of moral duty for a man to conceal that he had killed another, for killing set up a spiritual barrier between the two sets of kin. For example, if they ate together illness would assail them. The killer himself had to be cleansed from his spilling of blood.[26] Hence there was no problem of fixing guilt. This "ritual detection" of bloodguilt is reported from diverse parts of the world. But one would like information of the kind that Barton provides on how the Nuer were convinced that their kinsman had been slain by accident, or how the Nuer convicted another of adultery with a wife. Barton records for the Ifugao that for conviction for adultery there must be either a confession, or "evidence that the accused wilfully and intentionally placed themselves in such a position or circumstances that the crime would be presumed by any reasonable person to have been consummated."[27]

I emphasize again, therefore, that if it is clarifying to analyze the operation of law in these situations in terms of reasonable standards, reasonable proof, and ultimately the reasonable man, we must realize that offenses cannot be seen apart from the context of specific social relations. It is this element that gives such high importance to the arbitrary taboos and conventions which Barton placed outside the ambit of reasonableness, except of their own essence, in Ifugao law. As I stated in summarizing Barotse law, it is an important characteristic of societies in which there is little functional differentiation among the roles of persons as they interact with one another, that convention and taboo indicate and demarcate different roles, either roles of several others in relation to one person, or roles held by that one person himself. Observance of these conventions and taboos may, therefore, be strictly enjoined, and breach imposes absolute liability of the kind I have been discussing in connection with vengeance. If a person commits this kind of offense, he or she must pay compensation to the person wronged; the question of intention is irrelevant. It is presumed that the offender intended the offense, or he would not have committed it.[28]

I have gone at some length into these specific relationships because they bring out that the juristic and social conception of "the reasonable man" is based on certain presumptions about motivations. The objective circumstances of a killing included attention to the specific relations of groups with a history of feud; from these circumstances it could reasonably be deduced that the killing was intended. The psychology involved is an ethical and legalistic psychology, including in itself the norms appropriate to the relationships involved. It deals with legal imputation of motive irrespective of a person's actual motives. Hence the first reasonable presumption is of full guilt, which need not be proved, but which may be rebutted to establish mitigation, but still does not then avoid liability.

When mitigation is established, even though it does not discharge liability, the injured party is readier to accept compensation and not insist on blood for blood. Among the Nuer, the structure of vengeance groups excludes the possibility of maintaining a feud in a closely settled district. Elsewhere[29] I have discussed the manner in which the pressure of threat of vengeance in such a situation itself brings about a settlement. The Nuer vengeance group is in fact scattered through several communities. Owing to the rules of exogamy each member of the group (except for full siblings) has a different set of maternal kin, and a different set of in-laws, from his fellows. It is therefore likely that a killing will dislocate relationships of at least some members of the two vengeance groups. There will be some who cannot eat with their mother's kin, or even their own wives, under the taboo that prevents avengers and wrongdoers from eating together until the appropriate payment and sacrifice, in earnest of blood compensation, have been made. These persons will press their kin to accept compensation; and it seems unlikely that they will alternatively dissolve their marriages, though Howell as cited gives one example. The division of loyalties which is set up in this way by conflicting allegiances among the members of the group demanding vengeance thus brings pressure on other members to accept compensation. Further pressure is also exerted by the very fact that they live close together and must reach some adjustment if they are to go about their business in relative security. This last pressure is symbolized by the Nuer ritual mediator, the "man of the earth" or leopard-skin chief, who represents the unity and the power of the land. He it is who spiritually cleanses a killer from blood, and holds the killer in sanctuary while he tries to negotiate a settlement. The kin of the deceased have by custom to exhibit what Howell calls "a conventional vindictiveness," in which they demand blood for blood, and reject cattle for the blood of their kinsman. They continue to exhibit this conventional vindictiveness even after the man of the earth has brought the two parties together, and perhaps separated them by drawing a line with his hoe on the ground. Eventually the mediator could compel them to accept compensation by threatening to curse them by the land, so that they should not prosper. This circumstance enabled the dead man's kin to accept, "without great shame," the mediator's pressure not to insist on the debt of blood for blood.[30] Here the other relevant factor was that "in the case of unintentional homicide the indignation of the dead man's kin will be less than in cases of intentional killing." On the other hand, their indignation would be stronger if the killing had been from ambush, and not in fair fight, though no extra payment was exacted for this offense against Nuer ideas of chivalry.[31]

It would clearly be most useful if we had detailed reports of the actual negotiations carried out by the man of the earth, and of the process of discussion among the two groups of kin. Presumably neither Howell nor Evans-Pritchard was able to collect these data. But one would like to know what kind of proof was required to rebut the presumption that a killing was deliberate, and not accidental. How did the various members within the dead man's group argue among themselves, with those desiring peace cajoling the more recalcitrant to accept compensation? What precisely were the arguments used by the mediator, and how were they framed? Here again demands for reasonable proof, and stress on reasonable standards, may have come to the fore. It is important to note that both Evans-Pritchard and Howell report that when Nuer are adjusting grievances, they take into account the "justice" of the case. Evans-Pritchard writes that when a dispute is being settled, five points are important: ". . . (1) the desire of the disputants to settle their dispute, (2) the sanctity of the chief's [man of the earth's] person and his traditional role of mediator, (3) full and free discussion leading to a high measure of agreement between all present, (4) the feeling that a man can give way to the chief and elders without loss of dignity where he would not have given way to his opponent, and (5) recognition by the losing party of the justice of the other side's case." But he adds that he never saw the method used, and he believed it would be used only rarely, and only between parties who are fairly close neighbors.[32] Howell agrees, but considers that Evans-Pritchard underestimated the influence of the ritual mediator. For a man to be recalcitrant when he was in the wrong was difficult, because a wrongdoer had to win the support of his kin, and they were influenced by considerations of justice.[33] Evans-Pritchard also makes much of this. Detailed records of debates of this kind, like detailed records of trials before courts, are essential to solve the problems set here. Unfortunately, in the one fully recorded debate of this kind, reported from the Mazabuka Tonga of Northern Rhodesia by Elizabeth Colson, none of these questions arose. Guilt was obvious and admitted; hence, though the case shows beautifully what kinds of pressures act in these situations on the parties,[34] we get few further data on the problems of this paper.

Data on the doctrine of reasonableness and the reasonable man are thus scarce for these segmentary societies, but the logic of situations of disputes still inclines me to believe they must be present. In fact, only Howell on the Nuer and Bohannan on the Tiv have dealt with them; Bohannan heard my lectures on the theme at Oxford in 1947-48 before he went to study the Tiv, and Howell looked at my first drafts for my book before he wrote his account of the Nuer. Thus I may have influenced their interpretations. Certainly Nadel did not deal with the problem in his searching analysis of Nuba law, and, after my book was published, he more or less stated that the doctrine could not be operated in the absence of courts.[35] It would be too complicated for me, in a short paper, to reanalyze the Nuba material. Philip Mayer (who has had legal training) tells me that the idea is present among the Gusii. But as Bohannan has considered the problem, I examine his analysis in detail. His rich and graphic case material seems to indicate definitely that Tiv courts, instituted by the British, operate with these doctrines. What happened before these courts were established is not clear.

Bohannan writes:

> Professor Gluckman has used the notion of "the reasonable man" liberally in his analysis of Lozi [Barotse] law. The Tiv have similar concepts which are useful in analysis.
>
> A man who calls a *jir* [case] well, presenting history in a concise and orderly manner, is said to be a "man who knows things." . . . This phrase, indeed, is used of any person who is well versed in Tiv custom and belief, and who governs his external life according to the standards of propriety compatible with such custom and belief. A man who cannot tell a connected story, or who constantly makes errors in calling and pleading his case, is a "man who doesn't know things" . . . or even—if he is particularly inept—a *bumenor*. This latter word comes from the verb *bume* (not to be confused with *bum*, to swear); "to be unreasonable" is about as good a translation as any. A person who through ignorance, neglect or wilfulness fails to act in accordance with those customs to which Tiv attach moral value is said to *bume*. The foolish or unreasonable act in itself is *ibumegh*.

To beat one's wife is reasonable, but only a *bumenor* beats his wife until she cannot work. "A man 'who knows things' may try to sleep with as many girls as possible, but only a *bumenor* commits incest, and incest is the greatest *ibumegh*." So, too, stealing from distant lineages, though wrong, is reasonable for a man who knows things; a *bumenor* steals at home. Bohannan then discusses reasonableness of actions. Unreasonable or wrongful acts are committed by ignorance, by accident, or by willful going against custom. It is in terms of these ideas that "the 'reasonableness' of a man's actions is judged by Tiv judges and laymen. The 'reasonable man'—he who knows things—is the one who follows custom, who has 'character,' and does not act wilfully against the norms to which Tiv subscribe."[36]

Bohannan thus describes the reasonable man of the Tiv mainly in reference to pleadings, and only occasionally does he refer to the doctrine in his record of cases. But some cases in fact focus on questions of the reasonable behavior appropriate to the incumbent of a particular social position, though most of his cases are much simpler than those I reported from the Barotse. For instance, we are told of a woman who repeatedly brought silly complaints as grounds for a divorce, and was told to go home with her husband and be "a sensible woman."[37] Similar cases, though in reverse, are cited in which women, or their guardians, sue husbands on grounds that the husband has not attained what I would call reasonable standards in caring for them, by giving them adequate sexual attention leading to birth of children, adequate clothing, and adequate farmland with adequate help in working it.[38] In most of the cases cited, divorce was not granted, as when a woman admitted that her husband was in all these respects good, but said she did not like him (Case 39),[39] or when a woman brought such a complaint but was confounded by her husband's statement that she had been caught in adultery (Case 42).[40] In one case, a wife's guardian was summoned by her husband because the guardian had allowed her to commit adultery. It was proved that the husband beat and ill-treated the woman and her four children, of whom at least the last two were not begotten by him; but it was held that the wife was entitled to get children if her husband failed to give her these. In fact, such an action is "not adultery," but bearing children for her husband. The husband was admonished for being neither a good husband nor a good son-in-law, and was required to pay a conciliatory gift to his father-in-law for bringing an unwarranted suit against him (Case 31).[41] Here apparently the wife did not ask for divorce. But divorce was granted in a suit when the wife's guardian had taken away his ward from her husband who did not pay attention to her, dress her properly, or provide her with adequate farms, since the guardian was prepared to refund the marriage payment. But he had to establish that there were grounds for divorce, in departure from reasonable and customary standards—"reasonable and customary standards" being my interpolation (Case 36).[42] Finally, grounds for divorce are that the husband has tried by charms to hold his wife fast and prevent her straying; in one case cited the woman was successful in her plea, when she alleged that her husband had cut her nail parings and hair to form a charm when she was sleeping (Case 45).[43] Divorce from a leprous husband seems automatic (Case 43).[44]

Few of the cases tried in courts (discussed in Bohannan's report) involve kinsmen and the detail of their relations with the women married into their group, and with their in-laws. It was in these cases that I found the setting up of the standard of the reasonable incumbent of a social position to be most complex among the Barotse. It is not clear whether or not the complexity among Tiv exists because, when cases involving husbands and wives, and wives' guardians, come to court, the court goes straight to the issues without bothering much about details, or because Bohannan has given shortened versions of the evidence and cross-examination, though he stresses the importance of cross-examination.[45] Bohannan tells me that, although cross-examination is detailed, judgments are not full expositions of evidence and grounds for decisions, as they are among the Barotse and the southern Bantu. The judges state briefly what Tiv believe to be the "correct solution," which exists for every case. But the complex assessment of evidence is manifest in what he calls "moots," which are inquiries into the mystical causes of misfortunes, or threatened misfortunes indicated by omens and dreams. These moots deal with the full intricacies of social relationships within joint families. Here rights and duties attach to the incumbents of several interrelated social positions. It is impossible for me in the space I have to disentangle this point from Bohannan's graphic descriptions of these moots, or séances, as I would prefer to call them, since they open with divination. What is clear is that while mystical causes are sought by divination, this procedure is used to indicate the possible fields of disturbance in the group. The structure of those fields of disturbance may be determined by inquiry in a fairly rational manner into the actions of the group's members. Such inquiry is at best quasi-judicial because important persons at a moot are often trying to manipulate the situation to their own advantage. They are not impartial. Thus, in the first moot reported,[46] a man with seventeen wives had sent an adult, unmarried son to bring home from a distance a girl, whom the father had courted, as his eighteenth wife. The girl was already married. The son, with marriage money in his pocket, found another girl whom he married without specifying that it was in the name of his father. He consummated the marriage. When his father found his wife was not a virgin, she said she had had intercourse with his son as she thought the son was her husband. If two men, and especially father and son, have intercourse with the same woman, the situation threatens mystical danger. So the father called a gathering of his lineage. His kinsmen clearly considered it unreasonable—Bohannan says "not a satisfactory state of affairs"—for a man with so many wives to employ an adult unmarried son in such business; the father ought to get his son a wife, rather than the son get one for his father, especially so many-wived a father. The father, a man of strong character, obviously dominated the others, and they spoke tentatively, though one elder said, apparently openly, that "unmarried sons of much-married fathers resent their bachelorhood." But the father overbore them, and they agreed to perform a ceremony ritually to separate son and father's wife. This is what I would call working, though here unsuccessfully, with the model of a reasonable and customary father in relation to his wives as well as his sons.

It is important to note that in discussing the Tiv concept of *inja* (custom), Bohannan does refer it to his description of the reasonable man, which I have cited at length, but he does not apply the conception to the moots.[47] Nor does he bring together observance of custom, ability to act and speak intelligently, living up to reasonable standards, and making a reasonable allocation of women and other resources, in an attempt to elucidate the course of disputes. The complex determination of social relations by these standards is manifest in another moot[48] where a whole series of disturbances are exhibited to flow from unreasonable allocations of women to the men of an agnatic group. I can here cite only that one woman was married to an old man and remained a virgin until her husband's death. She was then inherited by his eldest son, but refused to have anything to do with him because he was a leper. He therefore granted a younger brother access to her. When her leprous husband died, she was given to another brother, and not to the one who had cohabited with her. This decision was against usual practice. The woman herself had said she was shocked when given to the other brother, but, like a good woman, she had left the decision to the elders, and she agreed after some time to have intercourse with him. Then she and her first lover fell into their habitual intercourse. Eventually she got a child; and she argued that it did not matter which of two brothers had begotten a son to the lineage. She had tried to reconcile the two men by persuading them to eat together in friendship, but had been unsuccessful. Out of the course of this moot, and the elders' admonitions and approvals and their interpolations and attempts to settle the threatened split between the full brothers, one can build an analysis of how persons should adjust demands and duties reasonably in terms of approved norms. In another moot the problem is raised in another way, by the insecurity in a lineage of a wife who thought that proper marriage payment had not been given for her.[49]

A number of other cases also indicate that the courts work with, or establish, the reasonable man, specified for a certain social position, to determine issues and facts. Thus a witness to a transaction who is accused of defrauding his principal, and who refuses to swear on a fetish, fails, says Bohannan, to comply with the norms of the role of witness and may therefore be convicted (Case 15).[50] A man who justified wounding another's pig by saying he had warned the owner that the pig was continually foraging in his gardens was convicted for not reporting the matter to the court, as a reasonable man would do (Case 51).[51] A policeman from a distant area who sued a local youth—whose father recused himself from the "bench"—for throwing him off the path was told he should wear a uniform or produce his papers, or else all Tiv would order people out of their way on the pretense that they were police (Case 67).[52] What these cases indicate is that when the issues in dispute are not clearly defined, concepts of reasonableness are bound to come in. But I must stress that all these cases are hearings before judges, who cross-examine and hand down a decision of some kind. And unfortunately the full value, in my opinion, of introducing the concept of the reasonable man is not made apparent, for the process of cross-examination is, I judge, not fully set out by Bohannan. That the conception of the reasonable man is at the core of the judicial process is shown in a few cases, where the record of judges' questionings is published.

In one case a youth was sued for exceeding the privileges of a sister's son's status. A sister's son may take property from his mother's brother. This youth had taken five chickens from the compound of his mother's brother. The owner of the chickens complained that he was not closely related to the youth, and that to take five chickens from a mother's brother who is not a close kinsman is stealing. The youth admitted that he had taken the chickens, but said he had a right, as a sister's son, to do so, and he maintained that he was not stealing. Let us follow the cross-examination. One elder asked him: "On the day that you caught those chickens, to whom did you show them?" The boy said he had shown them to no one, and tried to continue; but the elder pressed on, to ask what he had done with the chickens. The owner interjected that the accused had taken them to sell, which the accused denied. The elder then asked if he had eaten them on the spot, for the sister's son can take chickens thus only to eat them on the spot, or to sacrifice. The verdict, which took a complicated course, was for the plaintiff (Case 26).[53] It was for situations of this kind that I elaborated the manner in which Barotse judges work with the concept of the reasonable and customary man, to destroy the stories told by litigants or witnesses who are lying, but are casting their lies so as to appear to have acted rightly, or to be asserting a right. I stressed the importance of this conception as inherent in the judicial process itself; and I believe that this case alone indicates that full records of Tiv trials would show its importance in their courts. For example, Bohannan reports two other cases (Cases 23[54] and 68[55]) in which a sister's son's rights were protected. But this sister's son had behaved immoderately, secretively, and so on—in short, unreasonably. But it may be significant that the lineages concerned here were possibly at more considerable odds; they were involved in the incident of "drumming the scandal" described elsewhere in the book.[56]

In one of the cases where a sister's sons were upheld in their privileges, a long-settled line descended from a woman was supported in its land claims. Here the court held in effect that it was unreasonable to bring suit after so long a period, and that the land had been given to the defendants. No other proof was required. In a contrasting case, a sister's son had probably stolen cassava and had certainly assaulted a wife of his mother's brother's lineage. He was severely admonished, and warned not to make trouble where he had been granted the privilege of residing. Besides paying damages to the woman, he was fined, and a fine was also levied on the kinsman who harbored him. These fines were in a sense purificatory (Case 26).[57] Reasonable standards for uterine and maternal kin are implicit in all these cases.

One other case exhibits the importance of how the Tiv judges cross-examine by the standard of reasonable behavior. A woman was taking a billy goat and a nanny goat to market. She found it difficult to lead them. Tiring, she entered the compound of a distantly related man, and left the goats with his son, who said he would bring them to market the next day. He did indeed bring the billy goat, but he made excuses about the nanny goat. The woman alleged that he sold this goat several months later. She sued for it and two kids as possible progeny. His defense was that, when she had brought the two goats to his compound, she had asked him to sell only the billy and had placed the nanny to be herded by him. It was sickly and died, having borne no kids. His whole defense, ostensibly reasonable, was demolished by one question: Had he reported to the woman that her goat had died? No? Then he was to pay the goat and one [unborn] kid to the woman, and keep one [unborn] kid as his reward for herding.[58] The court seems here to have found an implied contract.

These last two cases are not complicated, but they indicate that wherever the facts are in dispute, Tiv judges, like Barotse judges, use the conception of what I called the reasonable man as a means to break down a story cast so that it appears to conform with norms, customs, and standards of performance. From this situation, the judges move to assess whether parties have behaved as reasonable incumbents of particular social positions, with their legalistic psychological implications. I suggested in my own study of the Barotse that it was in illuminating this judicial situation that the reasonable and customary incumbent of a social position was a valuable aspect of our general sociological conception of a status and a role. Reasonable standards come in, as I have indicated, in measuring degrees of fulfillment.

We do not know how the Tiv operated their settlements before the

British established courts. The citations I have given from moots suggest that wherever there was any kind of reasoned inquiry the conception was significant. Bohannan's only statement about the past is that in the old days litigants would go from one elder to another till they got the "correct solution."[59] I would guess that this method applied when kinsmen were quarreling. In such a situation a quasi-judicial inquiry may have taken place. That it did is suggested by the fact that nowadays Tiv do not make the principals to a case swear on a fetish, "for this would take the matter out of the hands of human judges."[60] As the elders make all witnesses who are in any way related to the principals swear by a fetish, but not independent and impartial witnesses, or the litigants themselves, it does seem as if methods of judicial inquiry were at least practiced within groups of a certain size. Meggitt, following my analysis of the Barotse, has indicated that within an Australian tribe still without courts there is an investigation of "the manner in which reasonable occupants of . . . statuses should fulfill the expectations" of their roles, even if the rules are simple and well known.[61] The evidence thus suggests that despite the use of oaths and ordeals, perhaps to a considerable extent as among Kamba and Kikuyu and Chaga, the reasonable man as a juristic model was used in all tribal societies, at least within groups whose elders attempted to achieve adjustments of claims. There is some evidence that when mediators or arbitrators tried to adjust claims between groups standing in a relationship of mutual absolute liability, some standards of reasonable assessment may have been involved. We may definitely say that as soon as courts are established in these societies, they begin to operate with the conception of the reasonable man. It is inherent in the judicial process itself; and I venture to suggest that its indigenous recognition, even in small groups, enables it to be used to achieve rapid adaptation of the law of segmentary societies to modern conditions. For a time it must operate within the confines of indigenous jurisprudential ideas: absolute liability for certain offenses within certain ranges of relations, recognition of transactions only when property of some kind is transferred, failure to enforce executory contracts, rules of *caveat vendor* and not *caveat emptor*, and so on.[62] But my own work in Barotseland, and Epstein's in Northern Rhodesia on urban African courts,[63] as well as that of others, show that "reasonableness," allied to basic ideas of duties and rights, gives further scope for development to meet changing standards. The establishment of a court with power to summon parties and witnesses, and to cross-examine them, is decisive; but everywhere the court is able to use indigenous ideas, so that the law enforced by the court is cast largely in terms of traditional law.

The concept of the reasonable man thus covers several juristic problems. Overall it is the view under legal and ethical examination of the actions of an incumbent of one role as he or she interacts with incumbents of other related roles in a complex of actual circumstances. If the society is undifferentiated, the judges or mediators do not explicitly distinguish, on all occasions, these different juristic applications of the conception, and they may well make the most significant use of the conception in cross-examination. In some societies there may be no explicit working out of the analysis in judgment. The ideas involved are (1) the measurement of standards of fulfillment of specific obligations; (2) the combination of several such standards (degree of performance, observance of etiquette or custom, adherence to rule of law) to assess whether or not a party has fulfilled the demands of his or her role, as the crux and main issue of the case; (3) the use of this model as a technique in cross-examination to destroy an apparently reasonable story; (4) the establishment of proof through demonstration of unreasonable deviation from custom or of failure in degree of performance of obligation; (5) the relation of proof to questions of whether responsibility and liability are strict and absolute in the specific relationship involved, with problems of onus of proof and possibilities of rebutting presumptions of intention; and (6) the whole question of "juristic" views on intention in terms of ethics and law, as against actual motivation.

The persons concerned, parties and mediators or judges, look at the internal consistency among all these attributes of action. In tribal societies, which are undifferentiated, disputes arise in the context of specific relationships involving multifarious commitments between the parties, and between them and others. The concept of the reasonable man is operative in these situations of trial or mediation, and hence it is not broken up into its several constituent elements, as it is in many parts of our own legal system. Our system deals with differentiated and specialized relationships, so that the branches of our law and our processes of trial are specialized. It seems to me that the idea of a reasonable incumbent of a social position will be more developed in systems of multiplex relations, that is, in tribal societies and in familial areas of modern life. Even in our own society, as many jurists, like Cardozo in *The Nature of the Judicial Process,* have shown, the flexibility of "reasonable" enables legal rules to be developed to meet new circumstances and standards. The undifferentiated use of the conception in Africa may well give African law even more flexibility in meeting new situations.

I have had the privilege of discussing this analysis with Professor Bohannan, who authorizes me to state that he accepts all of it except the final point of my argument. He says that the Tiv clearly work, in cross-examination and coming to judgment, with a general conception of a reasonable man, but that it is not explicitly formulated. Hence he does not regard it as a Tiv "folk concept." The problem of why African jurists in some tribes expound the doctrine clearly, and jurists in others do not, is a specific one. It may be connected with the whole question of why in some tribes judgment is not an explicit statement of grounds deduced from the evidence and connected with rules of law; the Barotse do base judgment on evidence and rules of law, as do South African tribes, whereas the Tiv and others do not. Yet, even in the latter tribes, according to my reanalysis of Tiv cases, one cannot understand the judicial process without using the concept.

Hoebel argues that "the reasonable man" did not exist as a working concept in many systems of law. This is a question of fact. I have discussed whether it is found among Tiv and Nuer, and to some extent among Ifugao and Kalinga. But Hoebel also queries the utility of the idea as a tool of analysis; he states that

> as an analytical concept the reasonable man is not an effective tool for the job to be done. The job calls for identification of clusters of behavioral norms (roles) linked to specific statuses, with determination of how much leeway in deviations is permitted without the invocation of legal restraint. This calls for much more particularistic concepts than such a loose and general one as "the reasonable man," which is not by pedigree an analytical concept at all, but a highly specialized folk concept out of Anglo-American practice,[64]

against the use of which Bohannan warns us. Hoebel suggests that the Barotse situation is better covered by the conception of "parental law" developed by Karl N. Llewellyn to handle Pueblo Indian law and applied to the analysis of Soviet law by Berman.[65] But, although this last concept is possibly useful in handling the substantive law which courts enforce, I do not consider that it is able to deal with the problems arising in course of trial which I dealt with in my study of the Barotse judicial process, and have tried to tackle in this essay. If Tiv judges work even implicitly with the concept of the reasonable man in a way such that we cannot understand the process of trial without dealing with it, then it must be analytically useful.

I end with one additional note. I have spoken throughout of "reasonableness" in a limited sense. Reason in another sense exists in the law of segmentary societies, as of states, in Africa in quite another manner: in the logic within the structure of particular institutions, of succession, inheritance, marriage payments, and the like. Each area of law has its internal logic, even if, as in Western law, the premises of law in different areas may be discrepant with one another. Evidence of this logic is marked in both books on which I have been asked to concentrate my analysis. I cite only Nuer rules to avoid confusion of status in agnatic affiliation. If a man seduces an unmarried girl he can legitimize his child by a payment to the girl's agnatic kin; the child is then attached to him and his lineage. If the girl subsequently marries, her husband may compel her kin to return the cattle to her seducer, and he claims the child. The position of a woman's children, determined by who gave marriage cattle for her, must be clear. Similarly, an adulterer is due to pay a ritual cleansing beast to the husband, and some cattle as damages. If a child is born of the adultery, the latter cattle are returned lest they be confused with cattle of legitimation, and the child's agnatic attachment be in doubt.[66] Bohannan brings out clearly this internal logic in Tiv legal propositions. Some laws may appear to be arbitrary, but one anthropological analysis after another has demonstrated that they have a logic whose reason can be made plain to the outsider.

As this essay goes to press, I add a commentary on the same issue as raised by Gulliver in his *Social Control in an African Society: A Study of the Arusha Agricultural Masai of Northern Tanganyika* (1963), a people lacking indigenous courts. Gulliver has recorded in fair detail a number of negotiations toward settlement of disputes outside the courts set up by the British; yet we must note that negotiations could not be broken off by one party in order to resort to force because of the presence of British authorities.

Gulliver considers that the outcome of a dispute was largely determined by the bargaining strength of the parties, the influence of particular situations, and the general social context: "... neither party is willing to agree to a resolution of the dispute to which it is not compelled—and a party is not compelled only by appeals to norms." He states that he found it neither empirically nor analytically "valid to adopt Gluckman's hypothesis of the 'reasonable man,'" even though the Arusha have a more or less explicit concept of reasonable expectations of persons occupying specific roles. He considers that the conception of these expectations can be developed into the idea of the reasonable man only where there are courts deciding impartially by evidence. Here I can say only that Gulliver may be correct about the influence of power in negotiations; but if one examines, in his own records of cases, the processes of ratiocination and the steps toward adjustment, clearly the idea of the reasonable incumbent of a particular social position is crucial, at least in cases involving closely related people. I illustrate this from his longest record (Case 21, pp. 243 f.). I have inserted "reasonable" and "unreasonable" into the narrative.

A father-in-law demanded outstanding cattle from the bridewealth due for his daughter, stressing that he had to have the cattle to pay tax (i.e., he was being reasonable). It was pointed out to the son-in-law that under Arusha custom it was not reasonable to expect to have wife and children without paying cattle. The son-in-law admitted liability but said he could not pay, as he could not afford to because he needed the cattle to feed his children, and his father-in-law should not take the food from his own grandchildren. Note how he raises here the standards of reasonableness in father-in-law and grandfather, as balanced against reasonableness in son-in-law and father. He listed other occasions on which he behaved reasonably. The father-in-law repeated his urgent needs to justify the reasonableness of his claim. He resisted demands by his brother that he take his daughter home; in all matters except this last payment, his son-in-law had been good and reasonable. It was later disclosed that the son-in-law was bargaining to buy a field; the other side asserted this project was unreasonable when he owed debts. He countered that he needed the field to feed his children, who were the plaintiff's grandchildren, and hence from plaintiff's as well as from his point of view his behavior was reasonable.

Lack of space prevents me from giving more of the narrative, which covers three meetings. The arguments show consistent attempts to balance in terms of a series of normative demands, the reasonable needs and requirements of the two related men, joined by common interest in the woman and her children. Each asserts his reasonableness, and admits much about the other's reasonableness in distinct roles, and tries to bring the pressure of norms on the other. Their protagonists mostly operate similarly. A compromise was reached; payment of a male calf immediately was agreed on, in place of an ox, and later of a sheep, in place of a cow.

Lack of space prevents me from referring to other cases, but I suggest that the processes by which "a virtually acceptable resolution of the dispute was made" (Gulliver) clearly involve argument around the idea of the reasonable man and reasonable incumbents of varied positions. In practice, the negotiations proceed along the route of balancing the reasonable needs and obligations of the plaintiff as father-in-law to the defendant, father to defendant's wife, and grandfather to defendant's children, set off against defendant's claim that he can plead for further deferment of payment in view of his attempt reasonably to discharge his obligations to his children, the plaintiff's grandchildren. Defendant sets this plea in the context of his previous faithful discharge of duties in his three relevant roles, as husband, father, and son-in-law—all admitted by the plaintiff. I cannot see how sense can be made of this case without analysis of the manner in which bargaining proceeds around reasonable standards of performance in varied roles, or reasonable standard needs for cattle to pay taxes, procure the means for food, and so forth.

Clearly, as Bohannan commented to me about the Tiv, there is no explicit statement by the Arusha equivalent to the idea of the reasonable man. But the idea influences argument and must be taken into account. That in these tribes, unlike those with indigenous courts such as the Barotse and the Zulu, the steps in argument are not always explicitly stated, raises another problem.

PART III.

ADAPTATION AND DIRECTED CHANGE

7.

THE ADAPTATION OF MUSLIM LAW IN SUB-SAHARAN AFRICA

by J. N. D. Anderson

Introduction

In discussing the adaptation of Islamic law to indigenous legal systems and to European systems in sub-Saharan Africa, I shall confine my attention to those countries south of the Sahara which look to Britain, rather than to France, Belgium, Italy, or Portugal, for their imported law, for only with these territories have I had firsthand acquaintance. I shall therefore be concerned with Nigeria, Ghana, Sierra Leone, and the Gambia in the west, and with Zanzibar, Tanganyika, Kenya, Uganda, Nyasaland, the Sudan, and the former British Somaliland in the east.

Of primary importance is the question: How far, if at all, can Islamic law properly be "adapted," whether by customary law or by legislative enactment? It must be realized that, in the classical doctrine of Islamic jurisprudence, the *sharī'a* law is based exclusively on divine revelation, or on the conscientious attempts of jurists to work out a law firmly founded on such revelation. In the classical theory of Sunnite (or orthodox) Islam, indeed, the law is derived from four main sources: the Koran, as the *ipsissima verba* of the Almighty; the Sunna, or practice of the Prophet (as established by the *aḥādīth* or traditions of what he said, did, and allowed to be done), as also inspired in content, if not in form; the *ijmā'*, or consensus of the jurists, as yet another manifestation of the divine will; and *qiyās*, or the analogical deductions of the jurists from these primary sources, as an earnest attempt to work out the implications of the divine revelation in the form of a legal system.

Obviously this theory leaves little, if any, scope for custom as a source of law. It is true that here (as at certain other points) the classical theory parts company with the historical facts; for Professor Joseph Schacht[1] and others have shown that the customary law and

[1] For notes to chapter 7, see page 251.

administrative practice of the Umayyad era in fact supplied a vast amount of the raw material from which the Islamic law was forged. Customary law certainly provided the basis for a number of the koranic prescriptions, as also the explanation for the strange way in which these prescriptions were, very occasionally, ignored in practice;[2] it represents the origin of many of the rules that are held to rest on the Sunna of the Prophet; it underlies many an instance of alleged *ijmāʿ*; and it has no doubt influenced *qiyās*. Yet the fact remains that in the classical theory the resultant rules of law are not regarded as owing their authority to custom, but to one or another of the four formal sources of the divine law. And it is still more certain that no customary practice that runs counter to the doctrine derived from these sources could today be accepted by this theory as valid.

Although certain maxims that seem to give real recognition to local customs may be quoted from the classical texts, on analysis they amount to little more than principles of interpretation, assessment, and application, rather than sources from which the law is derived. They provide that certain customary provisions may be read into a contract in default of explicit mention, or that a person's behavior, or the amount of a sum of money, may be assessed on the basis of what is regarded as usual; but they do not assert that custom as such can provide a valid source of law. Only occasionally does the recognized doctrine of a later period seem to go further, as in the Mālikite recognition that what the courts have habitually recognized (*ʿamal*) may prevail over what would otherwise be the more authoritative opinion of the jurists, or as in the principle recognized (within strict limits) in more than one school that certain practices for which there was an urgent demand must be accorded a reluctant acceptance.[3] The fact remains, however, that the classical theory, potent though it has certainly been in promoting uniformity, in practice has never succeeded in totally suppressing local customs that run counter to the orthodox doctrines of the law. Often, indeed, such customs are brought within the fold of orthodoxy by their identification with some variant view of the jurists, or by their reconciliation with the requirements of the *sharīʿa* by some legal device (*ḥīla*). But quite often they are simply accepted in practice, however unorthodox they may be in theory. Indeed, we find many examples of such identification or reconciliation in sub-Saharan Africa.

The classical doctrine of Islamic jurisprudence is equally uncompromising on the subject of statute law. In one of the most widely accepted classifications of the jurists, all human actions are, without exception, subsumed under five different categories: things commanded, recommended, left legally indifferent, reprobated, or positively forbidden by Almighty God. In strict theory, only within the category of things classified as legally indifferent by the divine law was any scope left for administrative regulations issued by a human ruler, for he could never make lawful what God had forbidden or prohibit what God had allowed. As a consequence, the administrative decrees that Muslim rulers, like others, regularly promulgated have always had a somewhat equivocal status.

It is, indeed, impossible to discuss Islamic law in any context with clarity or precision without making a clear-cut distinction—not once or twice, but again and again—between the jurisprudential theory of the law and its theological concepts, on the one hand, and the realities of that law, as it has evolved in history and is administered in practice, on the other. The theory is rigid, monolithic, uncompromising; the facts are often much more flexible, syncretic, and equivocal. Over the centuries, it is true, the theory has been forced to make a number of rather grudging concessions to the realities of the contemporary situation; but, for the rest, it has maintained its logical integrity and its resistance to deviation.

It is against this background that we must view the fact that legal reforms, when the Ottoman authorities first became convinced that they were urgently needed, were introduced not as amendments to the *sharīʿa* as such, but rather as new codes supplementing the *sharīʿa*. In this way legislation of Western inspiration, such as the Commercial Code of 1850 and the Penal Code of 1858, was represented as additional, rather than contradictory, to the divine law. What this practice in fact amounted to was, of course, that the divine law was simply put to one side, in matters of commercial law, criminal law, and much else, in favor of alien codes forced upon Muslims, as they would say, by the exigencies of modern life; for at this stage it seemed preferable to most Muslims to preserve the *sharīʿa* intact and inviolate as the ideal law for the Golden Age, even though it was largely disregarded in practice in the workaday world, rather than to allow any profane meddling with its immutable provisions.[4]

It was not very long, however, before this expedient itself proved insufficient, as reforms became urgently needed even in the law of marriage and divorce, a sphere in which, it was felt, the *sharīʿa*, and not Western law, must still prevail. As a consequence, radical reforms in such matters have been effected in recent years throughout a large part of the Muslim world, by means of legislative enactments that are regarded as having a valid basis in the *sharīʿa*.[5]

It is obvious that, from one point of view at least, such reforms represent a complete reversal of the classical theory. Instead of the divine law, as enunciated by the jurists, reducing the scope of human legislation to the point of virtual insignificance, statutory enactments promulgate the divine law. This reversal, in turn, reflects to a considerable extent the triumph of the modern mystique of the sovereignty of the people. Yet it can plausibly be justified as a legitimate manifestation of the ruler's right, under the *sharī'a* itself, to confine and define the jurisdiction of his courts, even to the extent of specifying which of the wide variety of rules sponsored by the great jurists of the past are to be applied. For this principle there is considerable authority (in the texts of the Shāfi'ite and Ḥanafite schools), but its implementation, on any significant scale, necessarily requires a measure of codification. In recent years this principle, reinforced by administrative regulations represented as being complementary, rather than contradictory, to the *sharī'a*, has been stretched to distinctly questionable limits in many Muslim countries. Thus the family law of Islam has been extensively reformed in one after another of the Arab countries.

On occasions, moreover, these two methods of reform—replacement of the *sharī'a* by a statute law of foreign inspiration, and amendment of the *sharī'a* by a variety of expedients—have been combined. Obvious examples may be found in the Egyptian Civil Code of 1948[6] (which has been largely adopted in both Libya and Syria) and the Iraqi Civil Code of 1953; both include provisions, frankly inspired by Western models, which, on occasion at least, are manifestly contrary to the *sharī'a* law as traditionally interpreted, as well as others that represent the codification of principles derived from the *sharī'a* itself.

Islamic Law and Customary Law

The interreaction of Islamic law and customary law in sub-Saharan Africa is bewildering in its variety and complexity, and can best be understood, I think, from a consideration of the way in which Roman-Dutch law developed in northern Europe.[7] The first component of Roman-Dutch law was the Germanic customary law which was indigenous to the area. Then the rediscovered Roman law began to infiltrate, largely through the influence of the Church and the universities. Finally, a day came when the Roman law was officially "received," although it never wholly ousted the indigenous law, but fused with it into a distinct amalgam. This process is very similar, in a number of respects, to what has been happening over the centuries in many parts of sub-Saharan Africa. Everywhere the indigenous customary law originally prevailed. Next, in one place after another, the principles of Islamic law began to spread, through the influence of holy men, merchants, or even slave traders. Finally, in a few places, a Muslim ruler professed to accept and impose the Islamic law in its purity and entirety. Yet Islamic law has never wholly ousted the indigenous law, but either co-exists with it as a separate and distinct system, each being applied in suitable circumstances, or else has fused with it into an amalgam that may be termed "Islamic law" or "native law and custom" according to taste or local practice.

Clearly, then, it is not so much that Islamic law has suffered "adaptation" by the customary law as the other way around; for the usual pattern is that those Africans who embrace Islam gradually adopt more and more Islamic law at the expense of their indigenous systems. Yet this pattern can scarcely be said to be invariable, for in parts of West Africa one gets the impression that certain Islamic practices are the relics of a system that has receded rather than the harbingers of a system that is advancing. But the resulting amalgam of the Islamic and indigenous systems, whether or not it may be appropriately regarded as an "adaptation" of Islamic law, merits the closest attention.

At one extreme is the phenomenon of a tribe that has embraced Islam in large numbers and yet has failed to apply the Islamic law, except in such matters as ritual and diet. For example, the Yao of Nyasaland, Tanganyika, and Northern Rhodesia are much concerned with such questions as the propriety of dancing and feasting in honor of the dead or the lawfulness of eating hippopotamus meat, but regulate matters of marriage, divorce, paternity, and succession in accordance with their customary law alone.[8] Among the Yoruba of Western Nigeria, at a far higher level of civilization, one often finds those who profess Christianity, Islam, or animism united in one family, and religion is regarded, in the Western way, as regulating matters of personal belief rather than legal relationships.[9] It is true, of course, that the customary law of the Yao is matrilineal, and might, therefore, be expected to be more resistant than the law of a patrilineal system to the influence of Islamic principles; yet Islamic law has had a profound effect on the law followed today by the Wa-Digo of Kenya, which is also matrilineal.[10] And one has only to travel northward from the Western Region of Nigeria to find an attitude fundamentally different from that of the Yoruba to the obligations of the *sharī'a*.

It is, in fact, the "holy North" of Nigeria which represents the other extreme. The explanation for the difference probably lies in the fact that Islam reached the west at much the same time as Christianity and Western influence, whereas in the north it was imposed by Muslim rulers long before there were any incursions from the West.[11] In some of the most staunchly Muslim emirates the official attachment to the strictest doctrines of the Mālikite school is carried to such lengths as to suggest that they are the ultimate bastion of orthodoxy. Yet examination reveals that even here the pure doctrine of the books has been greatly diluted by customary practices. A few examples may be of interest.

According to the dominant doctrine of the Mālikite school, a divorced or widowed mother is entitled to the custody (*ḥaḍāna*) of her children, unless she does something to disqualify herself, until boys reach puberty and girls go to their husbands' homes. It is only a variant and weaker opinion that a boy may be claimed by his father or other guardian between five and seven years of age.[12] Yet this is the maximum[13] age for a mother's custody in Northern Nigeria and, indeed, in West Africa as a whole. The reason for the variant opinion is not far to seek, for it coincides with the indigenous customary law much more closely than does the dominant doctrine.[14]

Another example common to West Africa is that a Muslim wife can almost invariably obtain a judicial divorce, whether or not her husband so desires, provided she or her family are able and willing to make a suitable refund of marriage payments.[15] Such a divorce is in effect a *khul'* divorce (i.e., a divorce for a financial consideration provided by the wife), ordered by the court rather than voluntarily accepted by the husband. A forced *khul'* is permissible in the Mālikite law alone, but only on the recommendation of the two arbitrators appointed by the court to investigate cases of marital discord. One factor favoring the greatly extended use of this form of divorce in West Africa is, no doubt, that the courts will not forcibly execute a decree of restitution of conjugal rights (*ṭā'a*) against a recalcitrant wife; but the fundamental reason for the practice lies in the customary law.

Another departure from orthodox Mālikite doctrine may be found in the criterion adopted by the courts in calculating the rate of maintenance due to a deserted or a misused wife. The amount is regularly based, in Northern Nigeria, on the financial position of the husband alone,[16] whereas the Mālikite rule is that it should represent the mean between the financial standing of both parties to the marriage. If, moreover, a wife is left without maintenance by an absent husband, the Nigerian courts normally give her a judicial divorce rather than provide her with maintenance by selling any of her husband's property on which hands can be laid. This practice, again, is directly contrary to the orthodox doctrine.[17]

Efforts to reconcile customary law with Islamic doctrine differ widely from country to country or from community to community; in other words, the constituent elements in the amalgam of Islamic and customary law vary greatly. In parts of Sierra Leone and the Gambia, for instance, a chief who professes Islam frequently does not scruple to marry many more than the four wives permitted by the *sharīʿa*, regarding his children by all these women as equally legitimate. In other areas a halfhearted attempt is made to reconcile an excessive number of wives with the requirements of the *sharīʿa* by the curious, and ineffective, expedient of regarding no more than four of these women as "free" wives and the remainder as "slave" wives. In the more staunchly Muslim areas of Northern Nigeria, however—where it is realized that the *sharīʿa* does not permit more than four wives, whatever their social standing, and that the only further license allowed to a man is to have sexual relations with his slave concubines—the expedient is adopted that a man may have such relations with a girl who would have been his slave had slavery not been abolished, or with a girl "given" to him by the one who would have been her owner. Such girls are, of course, free from all legal restraint, but they are regarded as slave concubines insofar as the legitimate status of any children to whom they may give birth is concerned.[18]

In some countries the Islamic law and the customary law coexist as two distinct systems, each applicable in suitable circumstances. In the former British Somaliland, for example, the *qāḍī*'s court applied the Islamic system, and a different kind of subordinate court administered Somali customary law. Matters of marriage payments and compensation for adultery were governed exclusively by Somali law, and such questions as the essential validity of a marriage or a divorce, or the distribution of a deceased person's estate, were properly determined by the *sharīʿa*. The position was somewhat complicated by the fact that much of the Somali customary law had itself been considerably influenced by the *sharīʿa*, whereas customary practices—such as the exclusion of females from any right to intestate succession (particularly in camels), the prohibition of marriage between cousins, and the drastic curtailment of a divorced or widowed mother's right to the custody of her children—were apt to linger even in spheres properly reserved to the *sharīʿa*.[19]

In Tanganyika and the Protectorate of the Gambia, on the other hand, the same courts regularly apply both Islamic and customary law according to circumstances. The issue depends on the religion of the litigants, the type of case, and the identity (and the knowledge) of the person who holds court. Almost inevitably, therefore, the judgment usually represents a compromise between the two.[20] No one other than a purist, moreover, would deny that this solution is, in many cases, the most equitable one. In matters of procedure a similar compromise is frequently effected between the unfettered liberty of the customary system and the excessively rigid rules of the *sharī'a*. In matters of substantive law, moreover, some courts are prepared to make special adaptations of the customary law in favor of Muslim litigants.

Islamic Law and English Law

The adaptation of Islamic law as a result of its confrontation with English law is chiefly, although by no means exclusively, concerned with statutory enactments. In every territory under discussion the Islamic criminal law, for example, has been largely displaced by a statutory system based fundamentally on the common law[21] of England. In Zanzibar, the Penal Decree of 1934 completely excludes application of the *sharī'a* in matters of crime, and the *qāḍī*'s have no criminal jurisdiction whatsoever, even though the Courts Decree of 1923 declares that "in civil matters the law of Islam is and is hereby declared to be the fundamental law of the Protectorate."[22] Elsewhere the exclusion is not always so complete. In Northern Nigeria, where the Islamic law reigned virtually supreme in the native courts until 1959 (except that the imposition of certain penalties prescribed by the *sharī'a* was precluded by the protecting power), the new Northern Nigerian Penal Code makes certain very limited concessions to Islamic principles. The consumption of alcohol in any quantity whatever, except for medicinal purposes, is punishable for a Muslim, but for no one else; illicit sex relations are punishable when engaged in by anyone whose religious or customary law regards such relations as a criminal offense. In all such instances, moreover, the specifically Islamic penalty of "*haddi* lashing" may be imposed on a Muslim offender.[23] Yet the ways in which the offense may be proved, and some of the penalties that may be imposed, do not by any means conform to the strict requirements of the *sharī'a*. In the former British Somaliland, too, traces of the Islamic criminal law were not wanting.[24]

In Zanzibar, it is expressly declared that the "Muslim law of evidence shall not apply in any court in Zanzibar,"[25] while Section 11 of the Kenya Courts Ordinance of 1931 (which provides that "all courts shall follow the principles of procedure laid down in the Civil Procedure Code and in the Criminal Procedure Code, so far as the same may be applicable and suitable") has been held to exclude the Islamic law of evidence from the Muslim courts of Kenya. Yet in many respects the *qāḍī*'s of both Zanzibar and Kenya regularly follow the Islamic system, for it is the only one they understand and the only one they regard as binding on their consciences.

In regard to contracts and torts there is no such explicit exclusion of the Islamic system. Contracts are still concluded under it in many areas, although much less frequently in some than in others; and in both Zanzibar and Northern Nigeria the Islamic law of tort is occasionally applied. But today contractual relations are everywhere regulated, with ever-increasing frequency, by the imported statute law.

Even in the sphere of family law the scope of the *sharīʿa* has been considerably restricted, whether explicitly or implicitly, by ordinance law. The Christian and civil marriage ordinances enacted in territory after territory, for example, provide ways in which a Muslim may contract a marriage that would be precluded by the *sharīʿa*, and would continue to bind one who had contracted a marriage thereunder even if he subsequently embraced Islam.[26] In some territories adoption ordinances provide a means by which a Muslim can adopt a child, with all that the adoption process involves, in spite of the fact that adoption is unknown to the *sharīʿa*.[27] The consummation of a marriage before the bride has reached a prescribed minimum age is a criminal offense under the law of some of these territories, regardless of the fact that the Islamic law might, on occasion, regard such consummation as allowable.[28] Sometimes legislation regarding the guardianship of children makes the welfare of the child the fundamental criterion, and the child's well-being has been held, in suitable circumstances, to override the relevant Islamic provisions.[29]

Further examples could be adduced if space would permit, but at least a reference to the Natives' Betrothal and Marriage Ordinance of 1928, in the former British Somaliland, is in order. Section 3(1) provides that any "unmarried woman betrothed by her father or guardian shall have the right to register personally . . . her refusal of the betrothal, and in that event her betrothal shall forthwith be terminated," and Section (3)2 specifies that any "widowed or divorced woman shall have the right to register personally . . . her intention to marry contrary to tribal custom." The first of these sections was, of course, designed to restrict the application of Islamic law, as the *sharīʿa* doctrine applicable in Somaliland allowed a father or a father's father to contract his daughter or granddaughter in compulsory marriage whether she liked it or not; the second was intended to give women the right to refuse the levirate marriage of Somali customary law.[30]

Another type of legislative enactment which is relevant to this study may be found in the ordinances that expressly provide for the application of Islamic law within specified limits. The most outstanding examples are, perhaps, the Sudan Mohammedan Law Courts Ordinance of 1902,[31] and the Mohammedan Law Recognition Ordinance of 1905 in the Colony of Bathurst. The latter provides that a "Mohammedan Court" be established to "have jurisdiction in all causes and matters, contentious or uncontentious, between or exclusively affecting Mohammedan natives, relating to civil status, marriage, succession, donations, testaments and guardianship"; that "save in so far as may be prescribed, the procedure and practice of the Court shall be according to the rules of Mohammedan law"; but that the recognition of Mohammedan law "shall not extend beyond the matters specified," and, in particular, shall not extend to the constitution of religious trusts, to civil contracts other than marriage, or to "any criminal or quasi-criminal matter whatever."[32] A somewhat similar scope is accorded to Islamic law in the Gambia Protectorate, under the Native Tribunals Ordinance of 1933.[33]

A much more common example of this kind of legislation may be found in the ordinances regulating matters of Muslim marriage, divorce, and succession. Here there are many differences and some anomalies. The Mohammedan Marriage Ordinance (1905) in Sierra Leone is applicable only in the colony, not in the protectorate. The Marriage and Divorce of Mohammedans Ordinance (1906) in Uganda, unlike similar ordinances elsewhere, includes no provisions about succession. The Marriage of Mohammedans Ordinance (1907) in Ghana applies only to marriages registered thereunder, and very few Muslims do so register their marriages. The Mohammedan Marriage, Divorce, and Succession Ordinance (1920) in Kenya, the Marriage, Divorce, and Succession (Non-Christian Asiatics) Ordinance (1923; amended in 1947) in Tanganyika, and the Asiatics (Marriage, Divorce, and Succession) Ordinance (1929) in Nyasaland do not, by definition, extend to indigenous Muslims. The Mohammedan Marriage and Divorce Ordinance (1941) in the Gambia extends only to the colony, not to the protectorate.[34]

Further examples of relevant legislation may be found in various ordinances in different territories dealing with the abolition of slavery (which commonly include certain interim concessions concerning the legal status of slave concubines and their children)[35] and with the taking of oaths (which often provide a bridge between the Islamic and the English methods of procedure).[36] Such, too, are the Ma'dhun Regulations (1912), the Mohammedan Law Courts Organization and Procedure Regulations (1915), and the Preemption Ordinance (1928) in the Sudan,[37] and the Mohammedan Estates (Benevolent Payments) Ordinance (1918) and the Administration (Small Estates) Amendment Ordinance (1947) in Tanganyika.[38]

The chief point calling for comment in these ordinances, however, is the attempt that has been made, especially in Kenya and Tanganyika, to regulate the circumstances in which the Islamic law and the customary law, respectively, are properly applicable in cases of succession. The Kenya legislation provides that Islamic law shall govern the distribution of an estate only if the deceased (whether male or female) had professed Islam and had either contracted a marriage under Islamic law or was the child of such a marriage. In Tanganyika the criterion is somewhat different. If the deceased was a Swahili, Islamic law is to apply unless the court is convinced, from his statements or manner of life, that he intended otherwise; if the deceased was a member of an African tribe, tribal law is to apply, unless the court is satisfied from his statements or manner of life that he intended the Islamic law to be followed. It is noteworthy that some of these ordinances speak of Mohammedan law as though it were a single, clearly defined system with certain sectarian deviations, and have scant regard for the exceedingly numerous points in which there is no "norm" but the sects and schools all differ among themselves;[39] for although almost all indigenous Muslims in West Africa (and, indeed, in the Sudan) are Mālikites, and the vast majority of those in East Africa are Shāfi'ites, there are also quite large numbers of Ibāḍites in East Africa, and immigrant Muslims may belong to almost any sect or school: Shī'ites of the Zaydī, the Ithnā 'Asharī, and the Ismā'īlī sects (the last named belonging to both the Nizārī and the Musta'lī varieties), as well as Sunnites from each of the four recognized schools.

There are a few examples of legislation aimed at reforming the Islamic law itself as administered by the courts, on the model of similar legislation in Middle Eastern countries. The earliest instance is probably the Wakf Commissioners' Ordinance (1900) in Kenya, but it made no very significant innovation. The Wakf Validating Ordinance, which replaced it in 1951, is considerably more noteworthy, as is also the somewhat similar legislation in Zanzibar.[40] Unfortunately, the wording of these ordinances is far from adequate, and this failing has led to many disputes, and regrettable decisions, in the courts. For a really effective example of legislative reforms in the Islamic law, as applied by the courts, one must turn to a long series of judicial circulars promulgated in the Sudan.[41]

The legislative basis for these circulars is found in Section 8 of the Sudan Mohammedan Law Courts Ordinance (1902; amended in 1961), which provides that "the Grand Kadi may, from time to time, make regulations regulating the decisions, procedure, constitution, jurisdiction, and functions of the Mohammedan Law Courts and other matters connected with such Courts." In accordance with this provision, the Sudan Mohammedan Law Courts Organization and Procedure Regulations were issued in 1915 to cover the whole work of these courts, in a codification extending to some 300 sections. But much the most significant provision (in Sec. 53) reads: "Decisions of the Mohammedan Law Courts shall be in accordance with the authoritative doctrines of the Hanafia jurists except in matters in which the Grand Kadi otherwise directs in a judicial circular or memorandum, in which case the decisions shall be in accordance with such other doctrines of the Hanafia or other Mohammedan jurists as are set forth in such circular or memorandum." The reference to authoritative Ḥanafite doctrines enshrines the normal practice in the Ottoman Empire; but the reference to circulars and memoranda prescribing other doctrines, which the courts must in certain instances apply instead of the dominant Ḥanafite opinion, opened the door to a series of reforms in the Sudan. Parallels may be found in most of the independent Arab countries, but are virtually unique in the territories here under review.

Of the fifty-four circulars thus far issued under this provision, some refer to comparatively routine matters, but others introduce reforms of a significant and controversial nature. The circulars found ready acceptance in the Sudan because they were issued under the authority of the Grand Qāḍī rather than that of a non-Muslim body or official. The secret of their progressive character is that, until fairly recently, the Grand Qāḍī in the Sudan was always an Egyptian jurist, who was ready to try out in the Sudan ideas that had been under study and discussion in Egypt, sometimes even before their promulgation in their country of origin.

At first these judicial circulars tended to apply the Mālikite doctrine instead of the dominant Ḥanafite opinion, a procedure that was aided by the fact that the overwhelming majority of the Sudanese are, in their private lives, adherents of the Mālikite school. But it was not long before the reforms went well beyond the principle—for which the Ottoman Law of Family Rights of 1917 and the Egyptian Law No. 25 of 1920 provided authority—that the executive or the legislature might instruct the judiciary to apply a "weaker" Ḥanafite dictum, or the dominant view of some other Sunnite school, in order better to serve the public interest. Later circulars were sometimes based on the views of extinct schools, of jurists who lived before the schools had crystallized, or of individuals who did not conform to the accepted views of their schools; at other times they were founded on the views of heterodox schools, although this origin was never acknowledged as such; and occasionally they were derived from a curious combination of part of one view and part of another, in a rule that was really new, although its component parts could each claim some traditional authority.[42]

Space forbids more than a cursory summary of the reforms that have been effected in this way. Ill-used wives have been given the right to claim a judicial dissolution of marriage in a number of specified circumstances; the excessively wide scope previously given to formulas of repudiation uttered by Muslim husbands has been somewhat restricted; after a retrogressive start, a guardian's right to give his daughter in compulsory marriage has been abolished, and child marriage has been made virtually illegal;[43] the law of intestate succession has been reformed; and testators have been given the right to make bequests even to heirs, provided such bequests do not exceed the "bequeathable third," regardless of the attitude of the other heirs. This last point is particularly significant in that it runs counter to what has for centuries been claimed as the consensus of Sunnite Islam.

It is also noteworthy that the Civil Justice Ordinance in the Sudan provides that in matters of

> succession, inheritance, wills, legacies, gifts, marriage, divorce, family relations, or the constitution of wakfs, the rule of decision shall be (*a*) any custom applicable to the parties concerned, which is not contrary to justice, equity or good conscience, and has not been by this or any other enactment altered or abolished and has not been declared void by the decision of a competent Court; (*b*) the Mohammedan Law, in cases where the parties are Mohammedans, except insofar as that law has been modified by such custom as is above referred to.[44]

In addition to the comprehensive scope of legislation in all these countries, it is undeniable that the Islamic law as applied today has also been influenced by English concepts through the decisions of the courts. A few examples must suffice.

In matters of marriage and divorce, a softening of the Islamic doctrine is here and there apparent. As already noted, decrees of restitution of conjugal rights (or "obedience") against recalcitrant wives are not enforced by the police—as they were at one time in the Sudan, for example.[45] In addition, the doctrine that a father may contract an unmarried daughter, even when adult, in compulsory marriage has come to be regarded with reserve and hesitation. In Uganda, indeed, the courts have unequivocally declared that "parents in Uganda have no authority to contract for the marriage of their children, whether Mohammedans or not,"[46] and in the Sudan the compulsory marriage of adult daughters has been abolished by Judicial Circular No. 54 of 1960. Child marriage is becoming increasingly rare, and has been virtually forbidden in the Sudan by the same judicial circular. The Uganda High Court has also taken a lead in declaring that the doctrine of marriage equality (*kafā'a*) is obsolete in that territory.[47]

A similar influence may be seen in questions of guardianship. English courts are inclined to give the greatest weight, whenever and wherever they can, to what they conceive to be the best interests of the minor, even where they regard themselves as administering the Islamic law. Here there is also a tendency for the Islamic law to be replaced by English law.

Much the same may be said in regard to matters of procedure. In this respect the doctrine of the Islamic texts is very rigid, for the testimony of "competent" witnesses is regarded as virtually conclusive,[48] while the testimony of other witnesses is excluded as totally inadmissible. Under the relevant rules the testimony of non-Muslims is precluded in all cases that concern Muslims, the testimony of women is disregarded in a wide variety of cases, and the testimony of "interested" witnesses is wholly rejected. Little imagination is needed to realize how stultifying the strict application of these principles can be in the administration of justice. This difficulty has been seen and emphasized by some of the more progressive Muslim jurists, who have urged that the courts make use of whatever testimony is available in their primary duty of doing justice to the best of their ability, but there can be no doubt that the influence of British courts has tended strongly in the same direction. The influence of English law is also visible in the fact that the courts are inclined to refuse to entertain a case if the plaintiff has allowed an unconscionably long time to elapse before he instituted the proceedings. Such delay without reasonable cause is likely to prejudice the defendant's interests and even to lead to a miscarriage of justice. Periods of limitations are, indeed, sometimes prescribed by legislation, as in Section 51 of the Sudan Mohammedan Law Courts Organization and Procedure Regulations, which provides that "Sharia suits are barred by the lapse of 15 years, provided the plaintiff was competent to plead and that no legal impediment prevented him from doing so, except suits relating to successions and wakfs, which are only barred by the lapse of 33 years subject to the plaintiff being competent to plead and there being no legal impediment."[49]

In all these matters it may fairly be said that the influence of English law has been salutary and progressive. In two respects, however, the rigid application of English concepts has been far less beneficial. First, the English courts have occasionally failed to understand and to apply certain institutions of the Islamic law (notably, the institution of "private" wakfs); second, they have applied with unnecessary strictness the doctrine of *stare decisis* to earlier decisions which were manifestly wrong. Again, cases regarding private wakfs provide an illustration.[50]

The history of judicial misinterpretations of private wakfs began in the nineteenth century in India, where a series of cases culminated in a decision of the Privy Council which invalidated so-called family wakfs if the ultimate dedication to the poor (or to some other charitable purpose, in the English sense of that term) seemed too remote or "illusory."[51] This decision was utterly alien to the Islamic concept, in which the dedication to generation after generation of the descendants of the founder (or, indeed, of anyone else) was itself regarded as an adequate approach to God (*qurba*). It was only Muḥammad ibn al-Ḥasan al-Shaybānī among the Ḥanafites, and certain other jurists, who insisted on an ultimate dedication to a charity which could not fail; the purpose of their insistence was not to introduce a charitable element which would otherwise have been lacking, but to ensure that the wakf would never be left without a named beneficiary.[52] These decisions of the courts so much disturbed Muslim opinion in India that an attempt was made to get back to the doctrines of the *sharī'a* by means of legislation. In the event, however, the Mussalman Wakf Validating Act (1913) left a good deal to be desired in this respect, and even in India and Pakistan the law, as it is now applied by the courts, is contrary to the Islamic doctrine in some respects, and uncertain in others.

None of these decisions were originally applicable in Africa. The judge in an early Kenya case aptly summarized the position by saying that the "pure Mohammedan law" of wakf had been "profoundly modified" in India by judicial decisions; the "Mohammedan law in East Africa has, however, not been subjected to the same modifying influence . . . and remains the same as when the Minhaj [a famous textbook of Shāfi'ite law] was written in the sixth century of the Hijra."[53] Nevertheless, the courts have felt themselves bound by Abul Fata's case, even though it has been recognized by all competent commentators as based on a lamentable (although no doubt understandable) ignorance of Islamic texts. Moreover, this attitude has been authoritatively endorsed by the Judicial Committee itself in Fatuma's case[54] (which seems to me to be one of the most regrettable decisions ever handed down by that august body); their Lordships not only refused to reverse their previous decision, but even to take the easier course of distinguishing it, on any one of two or three perfectly adequate grounds. As a consequence, legislation to rectify the position has had to be introduced not only in India but also in Kenya, Aden, and Zanzibar. In Kenya a not very successful attempt was made to improve on the wording of the India Act and get closer to the pure *sharī'a*. Based on inadequate knowledge and poorly drafted, however, the relevant ordinances, and the rigid and restrictive way in which the courts have interpreted the statutory provisions, have frustrated the hopes of the Muslim communities.[55] The fundamental weakness has always been that the initial misinterpretation of the law is still regarded as binding on the courts, except insofar as the amending legislation explicitly and unequivocally provides to the contrary.

What of the Future?

The "wind of change" is today blowing so widely over Africa, sometimes with almost hurricane force, that any prognosis of further developments is hazardous in the extreme. It seems reasonably clear, however, that the application of Islamic law in all the countries under discussion here will soon be limited to matters of personal status and family law (marriage, divorce, paternity, guardianship, succession, etc.).[56] Moreover, it is highly probable that radical reforms in the Islamic law as applied by the courts even in these matters—such as the reforms already introduced in Egypt, Syria, Morocco, Iraq, Tunisia, and even the Sudan—will before long spread to the countries of East and West Africa. In Ghana a different, and, from some angles, still more radical, tendency has already appeared in the attempt to unify the law of marriage, divorce, and inheritance on a national basis, regardless of religion. Self-evidently, such a development is most attractive to those whose primary objective is national consolidation and progress, but it seems distinctly doubtful whether public opinion (whether Christian, Muslim, or pagan) in most of these countries would be ready to accept such legislation in the foreseeable future—except, of course, on its own terms.[57]

8.

L'EVOLUTION DE LA LEGISLATION DANS LES PAYS AFRICAINS D'EXPRESSION FRANCAISE ET A MADAGASCAR

by Gabriel d'Arboussier

En commençant cet exposé, je pense que le mieux est de donner, par quelques remarques préliminaires, une vue d'ensemble des idées que j'ai rassemblées. J'aimerais attirer l'attention sur quelques-uns des principaux problèmes que nous rencontrons dans les pays d'expression française, peut-être même dans toute l'Afrique, concernant le développement des institutions juridiques de notre temps. J'aimerais aussi ajouter quelques points importants que je n'avais pas inclus dans cet article.

Aujourd'hui, nous nous trouvons en présence de deux problèmes principaux touchant au développement du système juridique en Afrique: (1) le problème de l'adaptation de la loi moderne à la coutume; (2) le choix entre un système d'institutions juridiques multiples ou unifiées. En évoquant le premier problème, j'aimerai commencer en définissant les caractères de la loi coutumière en Afrique qui, je pense, sont totalement différents du caractère de la coutume, au sens européen de terme. Lorsque j'étudiais à la Faculté de Droit, la différence entre loi et coutume, entre règle écrite et tradition, était que la loi écrite était plus rigide et la coutume plus souple, la supériorité de cette dernière étant cette souplesse qui permettait à travers les changements continuels d'adapter la loi à la vie du peuple. J'ai aussi le souvenir d'avoir enseigné que, aux yeux des Anglais, la supériorité de la loi orale était de faciliter l'évolution de la société. Mais quand j'ai etudié et pratiqué la loi en Afrique, j'ai compris que la distinction était exactement le contraire: La loi moderne y est plus souple que la coutume parce que la coutume revêt un caractère qui la rend immuable, sacrée, du fait qu'elle est liée à toutes les croyances, croyances religieuses ou "interdits," toutes choses dont le changement serait considéré comme une offense à Dieu ou aux ancêtres. Ainsi, c'est la première remarque qui–j'en ai le sentiment—est très importante et dont on doit tenir compte pour étudier l'évolution d'un pays. Je pense qu'il ne faut pas utiliser des notions reçues dans un autre pays et un autre contexte.

Ma seconde remarque est que nous nous trouvons maintenant en présence d'un problème, ainsi qu'un grand nombre de jeunes états nouvellement nés qui désirent affirmer leur souveraineté, leur indépendance, et qui veulent avoir leurs propres institutions juridiques sans aucune attache avec l'ancienne puissance dominante, ou avec les nouvelles puissances voisines. C'est pourquoi nous assistons à un développement d'institutions qui, à travers une multiplicité de systèmes juridiques, tend vers l'unité, une unité dont chaque état se proclame aujourd'hui le champion, unité qui nous permettra de fondre les différents systèmes juridiques que nous avons hérités de France, d'Angleterre, ou même de législations locales propres à chaque territoire.

Pour montrer l'importance de cette évolution dans les régions d'expression française, j'aimerais faire quelques remarques sur l'arrière-plan historique, car il est difficile de juger les institutions de ces pays variés selon un même critère. C'est pourquoi je distinguerai trois types d'états: en premier lieu, le Sénégal; ensuite, Madagascar; enfin les autres territoires.

Les raisons de cette triple distinction deviendront évidentes par la suite. Pour des raisons historiques, qu'il est facile de comprendre, je présenterai le Sénégal comme un cas particulier. Le Sénégal a été uni à la France depuis 1636; la ville de Saint-Louis a été construite en 1654; le premier représentant au Parlement français a été élu en 1848; l'exercice du droit de vote a été pratiqué localement au Sénégal depuis la fin du XIXo siècle dans quatre communes dont les citoyens avaient la citoyenneté de Français, citoyenneté de plein exercice. Je pense que cela place le Sénégal dans un situation tout à fait particulière.

L'Ile de Madagascar fut d'abord un protectorat s'étendant sur un royaume et l'annexion proprement dite date seulement de 1895. Jusqu'à cette époque, Madagascar eut ses institutions propres, ce qui est très important puisqu'aucun autre territoire des pays d'expression fançaise n'a possédé le même caractère. (Je ne parle pas des pays d'Afrique du Nord.)

La troisième catégorie comprend tous les autres territoires conquis à la fin du XIXo siècle, territoires qui ne connaissaient ni le droit de vote local, ni la représentation locale, et qui ne furent liés à la France que pendant cinquante, soixante, ou quatre-vingts ans avant l'indépendance; mais ils étaient nombreux et l'effet s'en fit sentir sur leurs institutions.

Si, après avoir fait cette distinction, nous considérons l'évolution et le développement des institutions, nous pouvons distinguer quatre périodes différentes. La première fut celle du "senatus consulte," du 2 mai 1854 de Napoléon III, qui accordait à l'empereur le droit de légiférer pour les colonies. Ce n'était donc pas le Parlement français qui faisait les lois; c'était le président. Et ce système fut imposé à tous les territoires, même au Sénégal, à l'exception des quatre communes de plein exercice. Nous eûmes alors une législation spécifiquement coloniale, émanant directement de l'exécutif, et non du Parlement. Nous avions également deux sources de loi, le président de la République et le gouverneur des territoires, ce dernier pouvant lui aussi édicter des règlements. Ce système a duré jusqu'à la fin de la seconde guerre mondiale, en 1945, lorsque huit députés—dont je fis partie—furent élus au Parlement français, au mois d'octobre de la même année; à cette époque, dans ces nouvelles assemblées constituantes françaises, les problèmes de la législation des territoires coloniaux vint en discussion et nous eûmes alors l'occasion de revendiquer, non le droit d'avoir des institutions propres, mais celui d'avoir un système juridique qui ne serait pas le fait de l'exécutif, et serait conçu par le Parlement où nous étions élus.

Ainsi, dans un sens, nous semblions revendiquer une assimilation avec la France; en fait ce n'était pas cela. Nous désirions être présents pour élaborer, projeter, et rédiger toute la législation concernant nos pays, mais, en même temps, nous affirmions que cette législation devait leur être particulière, et dirigée dans le sens de l'autonomie; car, par tactique, nous ne parlions pas encore d'indépendance.

C'est aussi pour cela qu'au Parlement nous insistions publiquement sur les droits civils, sur le droit d'association, sur le droit de libre expression, et c'est à cette époque que fut votée une loi accordant à tous les habitants de ces territoires la qualité de citoyen français. Mais, au même moment, furent élues les assemblées locales, auprès du gouverneur, et qui étaient, à ce moment-là, simplement des membres de l'exécutif. Cela dura dix ans, de 1946 à 1956. En 1956, évoluant vers l'indépendance, nous avons réclamé l'exécutif local, et la même année une loi nominée "Loi-Cadre" permit l'élection, par une assemblée locale, du premier gouvernement; mais ce gouvernement était encore présidé par un fonctionnaire français, le gouverneur, au côté duquel se trouvait un vice-président qui représentait l'exécutif sur le plan local et qui était responsable devant l'assemblée. Le gouverneur, lui, n'était pas responsable.

Ce système ne dura pas longtemps. Les choses allèrent très vite—un siècle, dix ans, deux ans. En 1958 apparaît la nouvelle constitution qui a reconnu le droit à l'indépendance des pays, aussi bien que le droit pour eux d'être liés à la France, au sein de la Communauté, mais même dans cette Communauté française, le droit de se gouverner réellement soi-même était reconnu non seulement en ce qui concernait le pouvoir exécutif, mais aussi en ce qui concernait le Parlement. Mais certaines compétences relevant de la loi étaient encore au pouvoir du Parlement français pendant deux ans encore: justice, affaires étrangères, enseignement supérieur, armée.

En 1960 tous les territoires eurent leur indépendance et, depuis le pouvoir législatif a été entièrement assumé par le peuple lui-même, sans aucun lien avec le Parlement ou le gouvernement français. Les liens se sont situés au niveau des relations internationales entre deux états par libre agrément, sans que subsistent de liens constitutionels entre les lois de la France et celles de ces territoires.

Ceci est la fresque historique, et je pense qu'il est important d'aborder maintenant le phénomène de l'évolution des institutions à la lumière des deux principales données que j'ai signalées dès le début: l'harmonisation de la loi moderne et de la coutume d'une part, et le choix entre la pluralité ou l'unité des institutions juridiques, d'autre part.

Nous nous plaçons donc en 1960, après que tous ces territoires eurent acquis les pleins pouvoirs de législation ainsi que je l'ai déjà exposé. Il se produit d'abord une sorte de "faim de législation." Puisque les populations aspiraient à faire leurs lois et devaient faire face à l'organisation complète de l'état moderne, nous avons en 1960 organisé toute la vie sur le plan gouvernemental, sur le plan parlementaire, sur le plan social, pour le développement économique. Nous désirions rattraper le temps perdu et en un an nous avons fait passer dix, douze, ou quinze lois dans chaque session de Parlement, parce que nous désirions tout organiser en même temps.

Nous désirions organiser, mais sans pour autant estimer que rien n'avait été fait auparavant. Je crois que cela est très important. Nous n'avions pas à balayer tout le système juridique dont nous avions hérité de l'occupation française, mais à considérer comme essentiel pour le gouvernement l'établissement de la stabilité et la continuité de l'autorité gouvernementale. C'est pourquoi la principale préoccupation à laquelle nous avions à faire face à cette époque, le principal sujet de discussion, fut le problème de la constitution, la recherche d'un nouvel équilibre entre ces pouvoirs que nous venions d'acquérir, celui de la police et de l'armée, ce que nous ne connaissions pas auparavant; le pouvoir judiciaire, l'exécutif, et le législatif.

Nous connaissions, ainsi que je l'ai dit, deux très fortes tendances: d'une part affirmer par la stabilité et la continuité de l'autorité du gouvernement la souveraineté et l'indépendance de notre nouvel état, tout en gardant notre caractère propre, différent des autres territoires; d'autre part nous nous trouvions en présence d'un mouvement tendant à regrouper tous ces territoires, car nous possédons ce grand mythe de l'unité de l'Afrique, chacun de ces états demandant l'unification. Nous considérons que nous ne devons pas, aujourd'hui, rester dans l'immobilisme, mais que nous faisons partie de la grande Afrique, de l'Afrique unique.

C'est ce sentiment trés poussé qui est à l'origine de ces législations dont j'ai parlé qui procèdent à toutes sortes de regroupements en matière monétaire, en matière douanière, de justice, et d'enseignement supérieur. C'est dans ce système juridique que nous avons dû organiser nos états, nos services publics, notre organisation administrative interne, nos institutions religieuses, militaires, notre enseignement supérieur, et tout cela en un ou deux ans. C'est pourquoi certainement nous avons fait beaucoup d'erreurs, mais je crois pouvoir dire que nous pensons en avoir fait le moins possible.

Pour un meilleure démonstration, je prendrai l'exemple de l'état sénégalais pour montrer comment, sur ce problème des lois et de la coutume, nous avons dû faire face au grand problème de l'assimilation. Car le problème, vu sur un plan théorique, est que nous avions une organisation qui, en apparence ou lorsqu'on la considère pour la première fois, semble être une assimilation pure et simple à l'organisation française. Mais, en fait, cette assimilation se situait à un niveau élevé, tandis qu'en dessous la masse continuait à vivre absolument selon la coutume. Ceci parce que la puissance française de l'époque n'a pas réellement assimilé toute la population. Elle n'a cherché à assimiler que ceux qui étaient utiles à l'occupation coloniale. Les lois, en Afrique, servaient les Français dirigeant l'organisation économique, les affaires, les positions commerciales, et quelques-unes de fonctions publiques.

L'assimilation devait préserver le privilège de ces catégories plutôt que de s'étendre à l'ensemble de la population. C'est en réalisant cela que nous avons compris qu'il serait plus facile que nous ne l'avions d'abord pensé d'adapter la loi et la coutume. Nous avions d'abord pensé que la politique d'assimilation avait fait disparaître les fondations de la coutume et qu'il nous serait très difficile d'adapter notre loi aux conditions locales, aux réalités du pays. C'est pourquoi, même sur le plan constitutionnel, nous étions très tentés d'adopter la Constitution française. Mais nous nous sommes très rapidement rendus compte qu'entre les pouvoirs législatifs, exécutifs, et judiciaires nouveaux, nous pouvions créer un nouvel équilibre qui n'était pas exactement celui qui avait fonctionné en France. Je vais apporter quelques précisions sur la réforme des institutions.

D'abord, en France, la distinction entre la juridiction ordinaire et la juridiction administrative est l'un des grands principes de l'organisation. Nous avons pensé et dit que c'est peut-être vrai pour la France, que nous comprenions pourquoi la France faisait cela, mais que la raison pour laquelle les Français devaient le faire en France, n'existait pas en Afrique. Cette raison était que, dans l'ancien régime, la France avait besoin de préserver la très faible autorité de son exécutif contre le Parlement et sa "justice retenue," mais cela n'était pas valable pour nous. D'autre part, cette distinction impose de nouveaux et nombreux cadres pour occuper les nouvelles fonctions. Ce qui coute très cher. Alors pourquoi imiter? Et nous avons décidé—je pense qu'en France cela a fait une sorte de révolution quand nous l'avons exposé—que nous ne reconnaissions pas que le Conseil d'Etat et la Cour Suprême devraient former deux corps, mais un seul corps qui serait juge aux affaires civiles aussi bien qu'aux affaires administratives. En instituant cette nouvelle organisation, nous innovions mais de façon conforme à la situation de notre pays. En ce qui concerne l'équilibre entre les pouvoirs, nous nous tournons beaucoup vers la Constitution américaine et sa justice; quant à la Cour Suprême, nous ne pourrions lui donner, au début, la même puissance. La justice était un nouveau pouvoir. L'Assemblée et le gouvernement étaient très jaloux de leur autorité récente, mais pourtant plus ancienne que celle de la justice, et il apparaissait difficile de leur imposer une seconde cour. Tout d'abord, dans un premier temps nous avons limité la compétence de la seconde cour au domaine de la juridiction et de l'organisation, mais non au domaine politique et constitutionnel.

Nous devions aussi fixer le statut de l'institution la plus ancienne que nous ayons eue, celle de parti. Le parti a été le premier corps constitué que nous ayons eu; il fonctionne depuis quinze ans dans tous ces territoires. Il a participé aux actions de gouvernement, de Parlement, et de toute la vie publique depuis quinze ans. Nous ne pouvions pas balayer cela, et nous avons essayé d'organiser ce parti, non comme arbitre des institutions, parce nous étions décidés à refuser un "parti unique" dont nous n'acceptions pas le principe. Nous avons pensé que le parti était une sorte de "courroie de transmission" entre les différents organes du pouvoir, et entre ceux-ci et la population. Et c'est le rôle que nous lui avons attribué. C'est ce que nous appelons la "quatrième force." Nous avons essayé d'organiser alors cette quatrième force dans une sorte de nouvel équilibre qui, pensions-nous, préserverait les libertés humaines et civiles, et c'était réellement l'idéal que nous poursuivions.

Puis, dans un second temps, juste après la crise que nous avons connue en décembre 1962 au Sénégal, nous avons fait un nouveau pas très important dans la transformation de notre système juridique. Cette crise a montré que, malgré toutes les précautions que nous avions prises pour ne pas nous orienter vers un parti unique ou pour ne pas permettre que l'Assemblée soit dominée par l'exécutif, le gouvernement tenait en réalité tout le pouvoir entre ses mains et utilisait le parti comme un parti unique. C'est pourquoi cette crise a été, pour nous, pleine d'enseignement. Nous avons dû prendre deux nouvelles dispositions: le première pour l'équilibre entre les trois pouvoirs, renforçant davantage la puissance de la Cour Suprême qui devient un arbitre entre l'exécutif et l'Assemblée. Nous devions aussi préciser la position du parti par rapport à la Constitution, parce que, lors de la crise, nous avions vu que les militants du parti unique voulaient mettre ce dernier au sommet des institutions. Nous avons alors affirmé que le parti ne représentait qu'une fraction de la population, et non la population tout entière. C'est le Parlement qui, seul, représente celle-ci; c'est le gouvernement qui en exprime la volonté pendant que la Cour Suprême reste juge des conflits entre les différentes fractions de la société. Le parti, par contre, ne peut pas être au sommet de ces institutions; le rôle du parti est d'être soumis à la loi et non pas de fixer la loi. Cela a été notre grande réforme, qui est une très riche promesse pour l'avenir, car le grand problème pour les territoires et états africain est le suivant: Sommes-nous sur le chemin d'un système démocratique, ou allons-nous vers l'autocratie?

Le but de mon exposé est de montrer que nous avons élaboré un système juridique nouveau, sur les bases de la loi française et des coutumes. Les institutions doivent être adaptées au courant qui tend à l'unité de l'Afrique. Nous ne pouvons avoir et nous n'aurons pas plusieurs systèmes juridiques, mais une sorte de "loi commune" qui adaptera sans doute la loi moderne et la coutume. Le courant pour l'unité sera le même pour tous les territoires. En ce qui concerne l'organisation constitutionnelle, je pense que la plupart des territoires auront une sorte de régime présidentiel, mais ce régime présidentiel pourra tendre vers un régime personnel si la Cour Suprême dans le pays n'est pas assez forte pour servir d'arbitre entre l'exécutif et le législatif, et si l'Assemblée n'a pas de pouvoirs complets, comme cela se passe dans certains pays.

Enfin, l'importance du développement économique actuel a donné un nouvel essor au développement de nos institutions, ainsi que je l'ai indiqué dans le journal *Socialisme africain*, et cela aura une grande influence sur le développement des institutions de cette partie de l'Afrique qui, je le sais, est très différent du développement des territoires d'expression anglaise. Je pense que les grands moyens dont nous disposons, que les grandes similitudes de culture qui existent entre tous les pays d'expression française et d'expression anglaise, et aussi l'idéal commun que nous avons, à savoir que l'homme est à la base de toute constitution et toute organisation sociale, pourrait nous conduire vers un système juridique qui servira à l'Afrique.

Les états africains, issus de l'ancienne Union française, ont subi de profondes transformations depuis qu'ils ont acquis leur indépendance. Ces mutations apparentes particulièrement dans les domaines économiques et politiques se manifestent clairement à travers l'évolution législative de chacun de ces jeunes états. L'abondance même de cette législation est significative; bien qu'ils aient affirmé et prouvé qu'ils ne voulaient en aucun cas faire systématiquement table rase des structures héritées du régime précédent, ces pays se sont trouvés dans l'obligation d'adapter les lois aux conditions nouvelles issues de l'indépendance et souvent même de créer des institutions originales.

L'activité de ces états pendant ces trois dernières années apparaît ainsi particulièrement riche et constructive. A partir du régime existant au moment de la proclamation de l'indépendance, des systèmes juridiques nouveaux ont pris corps, systèmes souvent complexes mais destinés à assurer l'évolution harmonieuse des institutions, de l'économie, et de la société vers un nouvel équilibre.

L'histoire constitutionnelle des pays africains francophones est fort intéressante. Il n'est pas exagéré dès maintenant de parler d'histoire; ces états ont eu en effet, dans ce domaine, une vie mouvementée, tous ont connu au moins deux constitutions successives. Si plusieurs de ce constitutions ne sont pas sans rappeler la Constitution française du 4 octobre 1958, il est bon de souligner qu'il s'agit d'un phénomène courant en matière constitutionnelle où l'imitation est la règle.

L'idée directrice qui a présidé à ces travaux est partagée par l'ensemble des hommes politiques africains: il s'agissait avant tout d'assurer la stabilité et la continuité du pouvoir gouvernemental. Les techniques parlementaires héritées de la IVe République française n'ont permis d'obtenir ni cette stabilité ni cette continuité. D'où le recours général dans l'ensemble des états africains francophones au régime présidentiel.

Cette recherche de cohésion ne s'est pas manifestée seulement à l'intérieur des états. On a assisté à un effort continu vers un regroupement des états francophones. C'est ainsi que les douze états d'expression française—Cameroun, République centrafricaine, Congo-Brazzaville, Côte d'Ivoire, Dahomey, Gabon, Haute-Volta, Madagascar, Mauritanie, Niger, Sénégal, Tchad, signataires le 28 mars 1961 du traité instituant l'Organisation Africaine et Malgache de Coopération Economique (OAMCE)—ont ensuite fondé le 7 septembre 1961 l'Union Africaine et Malgache (UAM). Ils ont poursuivi la ratification des divers accords conclus à l'occasion de la création de ces organismes: charte constitutive, conventions diverses, et pacte de défense économique.

Tandis que s'affirmait cet effort vers l'unité africaine, l'activité diplomatique africaine et malgache se développait d'une façon considérable aussi bien en ce qui concerne, pour chaque état, la conclusion d'accords bilatéraux avec des pays du monde entier et notamment la France, l'adhésion aux conventions et organismes internationaux, qu'en ce qui concerne la coopération interafricaine qui se caractérise par une action concertée pour la réalisation d'objectifs communs sans que la personnalité politique des états en soit affectée.

La situation des pays africains est réellement celle des pays neufs. Il faut tout construire en même temps. C'est ainsi que parallèlement à l'effort de construction politique, dont nous venons de voir les manifestations, s'est poursuivi la recherche des mesures les plus aptes à assurer le développement économique, condition essentielle pour l'acquisition d'une véritable indépendance. A travers la diversité des textes publiés, il faut souligner dans ce domaine la tendance générale à l'organisation concrète des instruments du développement et l'intéret porté par le législateur à certaines branches particulières comme le statut de la recherche et de l'exploitation minière, du problème des échanges commerciaux et de la commercialisation des produits locaux—café, cacao, arachide, coton, et ainsi de suite—ainsi qu'à leur conditionnement.

La réglementation monétaire confirme à la fois la tendance vers la consolidation de l'indépendance de chacun des pays et vers le regroupement africain et la coopération inter-ètats. Le Togo a décidé en 1962 la création du franc togolais et d'une banque centrale. Madagascar a installé son Institut d'Emission tandis que le régime de l'émission était réorganisé. Le Mali a procédé à une réforme monétaire plus avancée de la monnaie malienne. Le franc CFA enfin a été introduit au Cameroun oriental. La confirmation du regroupement africain s'est, elle, manifestée par la création de l'Union Monétaire Ouest Africaine, création qui a été assortie d'un accord de coopération avec la République française portant notamment sur la transformation des institutions monétaires existantes.

La législation douanière et fiscale est particulièrement représentative des préoccupations économiques des gouvernements africains; elle témoigne du souci des états de favoriser l'apport des capitaux étrangers nécessaires aux investissements par la création de codes d'investissements et de régimes fiscaux de longue durée. Mais cette législation illustre aussi la prise de conscience de plus en plus vive de la solidarité africaine. En Afrique équatoriale, en effet, l'activité législative en matière douanière a été marquée principalement par les décisions de l'Union Douanière Equatoriale (UDE). Celle-ci fondée sur une convention du 7 décembre 1959, groupe le Congo et le Tchad, ainsi que le Gabon qui tient au sein de l'UDE une position à part, quelque peu en retrait, puisqu'il ne fait pas partie du bureau commun des douanes. Or, on a assisté à une extension du cadre de l'UDE qui s'est associé le Cameroun à compter du 1er janvier 1962. En application de ce principe d'association a été institué un tarif douanier extérieur commun aux états membres et à la République fédérale du Cameroun.

La même tendance se fait jour en matière d'assurances. Plusieurs états ont défini leur réglementation propre, tandis qu'une convention de coopération en matière de contrôle des entreprises et opérations d'assurance a été signée le 27 juillet 1962 par douze états africains: Cameroun, République centrafricaine, Congo, Côte d'Ivoire, Dahomey, Gabon, Haute-Volta, Mauritanie, Niger, Sénégal, Tchad, ainsi que par la France et par Madagascar.

Parallèlment à cet effort de construction politique et économique, les gouvernements africains se sont attaqués au problème de la structure même des états.

L'organisation de la fonction publique a été l'un des soucis dominants. Presque tous les états ont mis sur pied des statuts de la fonction publique tandis que la formation des cadres était assurée par la création simultanée d'écoles nationales d'administration.

De profondes modifications ont également marqué l'évolution de l'organisation administrative intérieure. Certains états optaient pour la division du territoire en préfectures et sous-préfectures, d'autres adoptaient le système provincial ou bien encore un quadrillage en régions permettant ainsi la présence administrative nécessaire au développement économique.

L'organisation judiciaire elle aussi s'est progressivement transformée. Les états ont poursuivi la réforme de leurs juridictions créant, pour la plupart d'entre eux, des cours suprêmes qui groupent, en leur sein, les attributions de la cour de cassation, du conseil d'état, de la cour des comtes, voire même du conseil constitutionnel. Dans ce domaine, plus que dans tous les autres, ont prévalu la simplification et l'efficacité. C'est ainsi qu'au Sénégal un seul ordre de juridiction est compétent pour juger tous les citoyens sans distinction de statut et tous les procès. En effet, les principes sur lesquels se sont appuyés les rédacteurs de cette réforme judicaire sont la suppression des juridictions de droit local de façon à donner à un ordre de juridiction unique compétence à l'ègard de tous les citoyens et de favoriser l'interpénétration judicaire du droit moderne et du droit coutumier. Ce même principe a conduit à la suppression de la juridiction administrative. L'autre principe important qui présidait à la réalisation de la réforme judiciaire est celui de rapprocher notamment en matière pénale le juge du justiciable; c'est pourquoi des justices de paix ont été instituées au chef lieu de chaque cercle.

Cette réorganisation judiciaire a été dominée par le souci de créer des institutions simples, efficaces, et favorisant la sécurité des transactions. Elle assure aux plaideurs un débat aussi large que possible devant des juges dont la compétence et attestée par la formation professionnelle exigée d'eux, et dont l'impartialité est protégée par des garanties statutaires précises. La plupart des états africains ont suivi le même voie.

Enfin un secteur particulièrement important, puisqu'il met directement en cause l'avenir même de l'état, l'éducation nationale, a fait l'objet d'une réglementation très abondante; if s'est agi d'abord d'augmenter le plus possible le taux de scolarisation et d'organiser l'enseignement supérieur. C'est ainsi qu'au Cameroun, l'Institut National d'Etudes Universitaires préfigure l'université, qui déjà existe au Sénégal, à Madagascar, et en Côte d'Ivoire.

Mais dans ce secteur également on retrouve cette tendance profonde et particulièrement réconfortante à l'harmonisation des programmes dans l'ensemble des états africains; 1962 a vu se réaliser l'accord des quatre états d'Afrique équatoriale—République centrafricaine, Congo, Gabon, et Tchad—sur un programme commun en matière d'enseignement supérieur. La conférence des chefs d'état de ces pays a, en effet, adopté le principe de création d'une université d'Afrique centrale. La convention signée par ces derniers le II décembre 1961, et portant organisation de l'enseignement supérieur en Afrique centrale, prévoit dans ce but l'institution d'un organisme commun, la fondation de l'enseignement supérieur en Afrique centrale, chargée de dispenser cet ordre d'enseignement pour l'ensemble de leurs territoires. L'accord de coopération signé le 12 décembre 1961 par les quatre états ainsi que la République française dispose, en particulier, que celle-ci fait apport du centre d'enseignement supérieur de Brazzaville à cette fondation. Quel meilleur moyen peut-on espérer trouver pour assurer l'avenir de la coopération entre états africains que de favoriser d'abord le rapproachment entre les futures élites par un enseignement commun?

Cette étude de l'évolution législative dans les états issus de l'ancienne Union française met donc bien en relief les préoccupations majeures des hommes politiques africains qui sont d'ailleurs celles de tous les pays neufs: asseoir solidement l'indépendance par la consolidation de l'autonomie politique et autant que possible économique, mais aussi coopérer avec les autres états qui ont des problèmes similaires à résoudre. Il est donc nécesaire de considérer ces législations en fonction d'abord de l'histoire de ces pays, mais aussi et surtout en regardant vers l'avenir qui se construit aujourd'hui.

Pour mieux comprendre cette situation générale, j'ai cru bon d'examiner plus en détail la situation particulière de l'état sénégalais. Quatre ans déjà ont passé depuis les profondes mutations, à mon sens inévitables et irréversibles, qui ont transformé l'ensemble des territoires qui constituaient l'Union française. Les passions se sont apaisées, et cependant des esprits que leur rigeur morale place au dessus de toute suspicion s'interrogent sur l'efficacité de cette évolution et sur ses chances futures du point de vue économique, tandis que d'autres se prennent à regretter qu'une orientation différente n'ait pas été suivie.

Dans le cadre du séminaire sur "l'Adaptation et le Développement des Systèmes légaux," il me paraît donc utile de relever ce que cette évolution a apporté immédiatement aux Sénégalais sur le plan de la liberté de l'homme et du respect de la personne humaine. Je laisserai naturellement de coté tout ce qui a traît au développement économique et à l'amélioration des niveaux de vie, comme n'entrant pas dans l'objet de ce colloque.

Avant tout il convient de rappeler que l'élaboration des institutions de l'état nouveau est tout entière dominée par volonté délibérée de ne pas faire systématiquement table rase des institutions existantes, mais de les remplacer ou, selon les cas, de les modifier de façon plus ou moins profonde lorsqu'il ne s'agissait pas de créer des institutions entièrement nouvelles. Cette conception a été celle de la première Assemblé Constituante Sénégalaise lorsqu'elle a élaboré la Constitution du 24 janvier 1959, dans le cadre de la Fédération du Mali, ainsi que de la seconde Assemblée qui, après l'éclatment de cette fédération, a adopté la Constitution de 26 août 1960. C'est aussi le principe qui a inspiré l'action de tous les gouvernements qui se sont succédés à la tête de l'état.

Cette méthode, qui était seule de nature à éviter l'anarchie, mérite d'être signalée, car elle ne s'imposait pas à priori. Il suffit pour s'en convaincre de rappeler qu'après l'effondrement du régime politique de l'état français, le gouvernement qui lui a succédé a adopté le principe contraire, et par l'ordonnance du 9 août 1944 relative au rétablissement de la légalité républicaine, a déclaré nuls toutes les lois, ordonnances, et décrets promulgués par le gouvernement de Vichy, sous réserve de ceux expressément ou tacitement validés par le gouvernement provisoire de la République française.

Il est certain que si cette dernière méthode eut pu présenter au Sénégal l'avantage d'obliger à un examen systématique d'un passé dont les principes et les méthodes sont condamnés, elle aurait eu l'inconvénient de contraindre à un immense effort de compréhension et de révision par un personnel peu nombreux et déjà surchargé, alors qu'à défaut de publications juridiques spéciales au Sénégal, les textes en vigueur étaient, en certaines domaines, difficiles à connaître. Au surplus, les hommes qui depuis dix ans menaient la lutte pour l'indépendance de leur pays savaient parfaitement quelles institutions devaient être immédiatement abolies, ou profondément transformées.

En définitive, pour être en un sens plus empirique, la méthode s'est révélée, dans son application, immédiatement efficace. Elle a été ultérieurement complétée par des études conduites systématiquement par les différents ministères, souvent animées par la commission de codification créée au Secrétariat Général du gouvernement, études dont le but tendait à codifier les dispositions éparses dans des décrets, des arrêtés du gouverneur générale et du gouverneur du Sénégal, et à les mettre en harmonie avec l'organisation constitutionnelle, gouvernementale, judiciaire, et administrative de la République.

Cette objectif a été réalisé principalement au cours des années 1960, 1961, et 1962. Les textes constitutionnels et législatifs, ainsi que les principaux textes réglementaires, sont rapportés dans les dix volumes du *Recueil de Législation et de Jurisprudence*, édités par la Cour d'Appel de Dakar. En raison de l'importance même de l'œuvre réalisée, il ne saurait être question de procéder à son étude exhaustive dans le cadre limité de cette étude. Je me bornerai donc à l'étude des règles juridiques qui se rattachent au principe de légalité reconnu par les Congrès de Delhi et de Lagos comme la condition nécessaire du libre épanouissement de la personne humaine.

Le principe de la séparation des pouvoirs législatif, exécutif, et judiciaire a reçu dès la première Constitution une consécration d'autant plus éclatante qu'il était moins appliqué avant l'indépendance. En effet, la séparation de l'exécutif et du législatif ne s'appliquait qu'à un domaine très restreint; si dans la Constitution de 1875, le principe de la délimitation par le Parlement des domaines lesquels l'exécutif pouvait édicter des règles légales par décret était le même aux colonies que dans la métropole. En fait, d'une part, les matières dans lesquelles le Parlement avait lui-même légiféré pour les colonies étaient peu nombreuses, et, d'autre part, le sénatus-consulte du 2 mai 1854, maintenu en vigeur, conférait au président de la République le droit de légiférer le plus étendu.

La Constitution française du 27 octobre 1946 marque une première, mais modeste, étape en réservant à la compétence exclusive du Parlement métropolitain où siégeaient des députés des territoires d'outre-mer, la législation criminelle, le régime des libertés publiques, et l'organisation politique et administrative. Il convient d'ajouter toutefois que dans chaque territoire ou groupe de territoires des assemblées élues avaient reçu compétence pour légiférer certaines matières déterminées.

S'il eut été vain et dangereux pour les juristes sénégalais, nourris aux sources du droit français, de vouloir adopter l'orgueilleuse épigraphe de Montesquieu pour "l'Esprit des Lois"—*prolem sine matre creatam*, "un enfant né sans mère"—nous avons déjà eu l'occasion de souligner* les caractères originaux qu'ils ont imprimé à leur charte fondamentale, d'une part en inscrivant dans les quinze articles de son livre II le respect et la garantie intangibles des libertés politiques, des libertés syndicales, des droits et libertés de la personne humaine, de la famille, et des collectivités locales, des libertés philosophiques et religieuses, du droit de propriété individuelle et collective, des droits économiques et sociaux.

En érigeant en règles de droit positif, se qui n'était jusque-là que pétition de principe, les constituants sénégalais, sans doute sensibilisés par leur histoire récente au respect de la personne humaine, ont proclamé, dès le premier jour, leur volonté d'apporter leur contribution à la civilisation de l'universel. D'autre part, dès sa mise en œuvre, la Constitution du 26 août 1960 a fait l'objet d'une application originale en ce qui con-

*Discours prononcé au Congrès Africain sur la Primauté du Droit, tenu à Lagos en janvier 1961, reproduit dans *La Justice au Sénégal* (Rufisque: Imprimerie Officielle).

cerne la distinction entre le pouvoir de légiférer de droit commun, dévolu au gouvernement, et le pouvoir législatif d'attribution réservé à l'Assemblée Nationale pour les seules matières comprises dans une énumération limitative.

L'esprit des constituants, qui recherchèrent beaucoup plus la collaboration entre les fonctions que leur controle respectif, a permis au gouvernement de soumettre à l'examen et au vote de l'Assemblée des textes qu'il pouvait légalement promulguer sans son accord. Cette interprétation, plus conforme à l'esprit de la Constitution qu'à sa lettre, a été contestée par certains juristes. Selons cette opinion, même si le gouvernement l'y invitait, l'Assemblée Nationale ne pouvait franchir les limites de son domaine, limites d'ailleurs souvent imprécises et difficiles à définir. Pour mettre un terme à ces discussions stériles, la lettre de la Constitution a été mise en harmonie avec cette volonté commune du gouvernement et de l'Assemblée.

Soulignons que le caractère insolite en régime démocratique de ce pouvoir législatif général, conféré à l'exécutif, ne se justifie que par le caractère très technique de certaines dispositions générales, la rapidité nécessaire à la promulgation d'une grande masse de textes, mais en tout cas sous la garantie d'un controle juridictionnel accru exercé par une autorité judiciaire dont l'indépendance est assurée.

En permettant, par la loi constitutionnelle n° 61-63 du 12 novembre 1961, à l'Assemblée Nationale de se prononcer sur des projets relatifs à des matières ne rentrant pas dans son domaine d'attribution, mais que le gouvernement estime devoir lui soumettre en raison de leur importance sociale, économique, ou financière, les constituants ont opéré un retour vers la source de tout pouvoir politique dans un régime démocratique. En effet, dans un tel régime, les décisions des élus du peuple au suffrage direct, en l'espèce l'Assemblée, doivent prévaloir sur les décisions de ceux qui n'en sont que l'émanation indirecte, en l'espèce le gouvernement. Ajoutons encore que le schéma constitutionnel s'est trouvé considérablement influencé dans les faits par l'existence d'un parti dominant, jouissant à l'Assemblée Nationale de 79 sièges sur 80, et par la circonstance que le président de la République et le président du Conseil des Ministres cumulaient ces fonctions avec celles de chef du parti en sorte que ce qui avait été décidé par le parti n'était pas sérieusement discuté par l'Assemblée.

Cette situation aurait pu présenter le grave danger d'abandonner aux organes constitutionnellement irresponsables du parti des décisions incombant aux élus de l'ensemble de la nation. Mais la vivacité de la réaction de l'Assemblée Nationale lors des évènements du 17 decembre 1962 a montré que celle-ci savait user de toutes ses prérogatives et prendre ses responsabilités lorsque le fonctionnement régulier de la constitution était mis en cause.

Les empiètements du législatif sur le judiciaire sont difficilement concevables à l'époque moderne, et sans doute aussi seraient-ils difficilement réalisables. Quant au risque d'empiètements éventuels des cours et tribunaux dans le domaine législatif ou réglementaire, par la voie d'arrêts de règlements hors des domaines où, comme en matière de conflits collectifs du travail la loi l'a expressément organisé, il a été définitivement éliminé tant par les sanctions pénales édictées par le législateur de la période révolutionnaire française toujours en vigueur, que les traditions que depuis un siècle et demi s'est forgée la magistrature française, traditions dont la magistrature sénégalaise a hérité.

C'est donc seulement sous l'angle de la séparation des pouvoirs judiciare et exécutif qu'il convient d'examiner le second aspect du principe de la séparation des pouvoirs.

Jusqu'en 1946, l'indépendance des juges était fort mal assurée, et l'on peut dire que pour la grande masse des justiciables la justice n'offrait que de très faibles garanties d'impartialité. En effet, d'une part, les tribunaux indigènes baptisés ultérieurement tribunaux de droit local, qui statuaient tant au civil qu'a pénal, étaient présidés par le chef de la juridiction administrative assisté d'assesseurs désignés sur sa proposition, et, il faut bien le dire, choisis souvent beacoup plus en fonction de leur plus ou moins grande docilité, que de leur compétence en matière coutumière, compétence d'ailleurs difficile à apprécier. Mais un décret du 30 avril 1946 est venu supprimer la compétence des tribunaux indigènes en matière pénale. Dès ce moment la majorité des justiciables a rejoint la minorité des citoyens qui jusque-là relevait seule de la compétence des tribunaux de droit français.

D'autre part, les magistrats du siège composant ces tribunaux qui, à la différence de leurs collègues servant dans la métropole, n'étaient auparavant pas inamovibles, se sont trouvés régis par les dispositions de la Constitution du 27 octobre 1946, garantissant leur indépendance par l'organe du Conseil Supérieur de la magistrature. Ainsi la même année la grosse masse des habitants a échappé en matière pénale aux tribunaux indigènes pour relever désormais des tribunaux du droit français, dont l'indépendance était pour la première fois garantie.

Dans la première Constitution du Sénégal, l'organisation et le fonctionnement des tribunaux judiciares relevait de la compétence de la Fédération du Mali. La Constitution fédérale se bornait à poser le principe de l'indépendance de l'autorité judiciaire à l'égard de l'exécutif et du législatif. La fédération a été dissoute avant d'avoir pu organiser cette indépendance. Avec la Constitution sénégalaise du 26 août 1960, le président de la République, arbitre entre les autres pouvoirs de l'état, devient le garant de l'indépendance de l'autorité judiciaire. A ce titre, c'est lui qui nomme les magistrats, tant ceux du ministère public que ceux du siège avec, pour ces derniers, le concours du Conseil Supérieur de la magistrature.

Corrélativement a été décrétée la suppression des juridictions de droit local (tribunaux coutumiers, tribunaux du 1er et du 2ème degré, et tribunal supérieur de droit local), qui énchappent aux garanties exposées ci-avant, pour donner compétence aux juridictions ordinaires. La substitution progressive des unes par les autres devra être achevée au cours de l'exécution du premier Plan Quadriennal de développement.

Mais la réforme fondamentale pour le respect des droits de citoyens consiste dans la suppression de juridictions administratives, jusque-là compétentes pour juger le contentieux administratif. En effet, l'organisation française comprenait le Conseil du Contentieux Administratif, compétent en premier ressort à charge d'appel devant le Conseil d'Etat, pour juger le contentieux relatif aux actes des autorités locales et fédérales ou mettant en cause les deniers des budgets locaux ou fédéraux. En outre, le Conseil d'Etat siégeant à Paris, était juge de droit commun de l'excès de pouvoir, hormis pour les décisions des autorités locales et fédérales concernant les fonctionnaires soumis à leur autorité.

Ce système, onéreux pour le budget, complexe, déroutant pour le plaideur, d'une ordre de juridiction spécialement organisé pour juger l'administration et les actes juridiques du gouvernement, composé de fonctionnaires qui sont tantôt les conseillers du governement et tantôt ses censeurs et enfin nécessairement coiffé d'un tribunal des conflits, pour trancher les inévitables conflits de compétence avec les tribunaux judiciaires, n'a pas trouvé de défenseurs au Sénégal. En conséquence, au Sénégal, l'état et les collectivités publiques ont cessé d'être des plaideurs privilégiés; en application de l'ordonnance no 60-65 du 14 novembre 1960, tous sont justiciables du tribunal civil, de la Cour d'Appel, et de la Cour Suprême, comme des plaideurs ordinaires. L'administration devra la première se soumettre aux règlements, qu'elle édicte pour le bien commun de la nation et de ses citoyens.

Ce contrôle juridictionnel, exercé par la voie du recours en annulation contre les actes réglementaires, est de la compétence exclusive de la Cour Suprême, dont les membres sont nommés à vie et dont les fonctions sont incompatibles avec la qualité de membres du gouvernement, de l'Assemblée Nationale, ou d'un cabinet ministériel, avec l'exercice des professions d'avocat, d'officier ministériel, d'auxiliaire de la justice, et toute activité professionnelle privée.

Nous en aurons terminé avec le développement qu'a subi, depuis l'indépendance, le principe de la séparation des pouvoirs en indiquant que le contrôle a priori de la constitutionalité des lois incombe à la Cour Suprême, qui peut être saisie par le président de la République, gardien de la Constitution, que celle-ci est obligatoirement consultée avant la promulgation des lois qualifiées d'organiques par la Constitution, et qu'enfin c'est à elle qu'il incombe de dire si une matière régie par un texte de forme législative promulgué antérieurement au 26 août 1960 peut être modifié par le gouvernement en raison de la nouvelle répartition des compétences.

Si nous passons maintenant du plan des institutions à celui de leur mise en œuvre, nous trouvons en premier lieu l'organisation d'un barreau. Avant l'indépendance il existait certes un corps d'avocats-défenseurs, nommés par le gouverneur général, administré par lui, et soumis à l'autorité du procureur général. Le barreau organisé par un décret no 60-309 du 3 septembre 1960 est ouvert à tous ceux qui désirent s'y inscrire, sous la seule condition de justifier des capacités techniques et d'être de bonnes vies et mœurs. Les avocats ont libre accès devant toutes les juridictions, même devant les juridictions coutumières provisoirement maintenues, dont l'accès était interdit aux avocats-défenseurs.

Ainsi donc, les traits dominants des nouvelles institutions sénégalaises sont (1) un pouvoir exécutif muni de pouvoirs très grands lui permettant d'agir instantanément et efficacement pour la solution des problèmes quotidiens aigus suscités par la construction d'un état nouveau; (2) des possibilitiés de large et efficace collaboration entre les diverses fonctions constitutionnelles, collaboration qui s'est traduite par un volume considérable de textes législatifs et réglementaires promulgués en trois ans, ainsi que par l'adoption d'un plan quadriennal de développement coordonné, s'appliquant à tous les domaines des activités humaines; and (3) la sauvegarde des droits des individus par des organes juridictionnels présentant des garanties réelles d'indépendance, condition indispensable de leur impartialité.

A la suite des évènements de décembre 1962, la réforme constitutionnelle, intervenue sur la base de ces principes, mérite cependant d'être exposée. Les trois organes essentiels de la République du Sénégal sont désormais le président de la République, en même temps chef de gouvernement, l'Assemblée Nationale, et la Cour Suprême.

Ces organes étaient d'ailleurs les mêmes dans l'ancienne Constitution sénégalaise, représentant ainsi l'exécutif, le législatif, et le judiciarie, que le Sénégal a toujours tenu à ériger en organes indépendants. Mais dans la Constitution ancienne, l'exécutif comportait et le président de la République et le président du Conseil d'Etat, le président de la République étant en même temps le gardien de la Constitution et l'arbitre entre l'exécutif et le parlementaire, en s'appuyant sur l'autorité judicaire. En fait, les empiètements incessants du chef du gouvernement sur les prérogatives du président de la République l'avaient empêché d'exercer sa fonction arbitrale, ce qui fut l'une des causes essentielles de la crise. C'est pourquoi, sans contrevenir aux principes fondamentaux qui régissaient l'ancienne Constitution et qui organisaient également la séparation et la collaboration des pouvoirs, la nouvelle Constitution a essayé d'éviter tout ce qui pouvait nuire à l'équilibre des pouvoirs.

Dans l'ancienne Constitution, amendée d'ailleurs par des dispositions ultérieures, l'équilibre entre l'exécutif et le parlementaire était fondé sur le pouvoir de dissolution du gouvernement à l'égard de l'Assemblée et sur la possibilité de censure du gouvernement par l'Assembée. C'est parce que ces dispositions ont été remises en cause par l'ancien chef du gouvernement que des dispositions nouvelles ont été adoptées. En cette matière, elles sont exactement l'inverse des dispositions anciennes, établissant l'équilibre non plus sur le pouvoir de dissolution et la motion de censure, mais, au contraire, sur l'absence de pouvoir de dissolution et l'absence de motion de censure.

Désormais le président de la République, chef du gouvernement, ne peut pas dissoudre l'Assemblée Nationale et l'Assemblée ne peut, non plus, renverser le gouvernement. Le conflit entre l'exécutif et le parlementaire doit donc être tranché par un autre organisme, précisément la Cour Suprême qui déjà exerçait, dans l'ancienne Constitution, un pouvoir de contrôle, mais d'une façon moins nette.

Ainsi donc, nous n'avons plus de responsabilité du gouvernement devant l'Assemblée Nationale, mais la reponsabilité des ministres devant le président de la République qui nomme les ministres et secrétaires d'état, fixe leurs attributions, et met fin à leurs fonctions. La nature même de la fonction ministérielle est ainsi profondément modifiée. Le ministre n'est plus qu'un auxiliare du président de la République; il n'y a plus de conseil de cabinet au sens technique du terme, c'est-à-dire, il n'y a plus d'organe collectif ayant pouvoir de décision. Cette soumission des ministres au président et la séparation des pouvoirs entre l'exécutif et le législatif rend incompatible la qualité de ministre ou secrétaire d'état avec l'exercice d'un mandat parlementaire. C'est là une innovation importante de la nouvelle Constitution.

L'Assemblée Nationale constitue un second organe fondamental de la République. Ici, il y a peu de changements par rapport au système précédent; la composition de l'Assemblée et le statut de ses membres sont indépendants du caractère présidentiel, et non du régime.

Enfin, le troisième organe essentiel, la Cour Suprême, a subi peu de modifications, mais l'inamovibilité des magistrats donne à ses décisions une autorité particulière; l'article 82 de la Constitution dispose qu'elle connaît des conflits de compétence entre l'exécutif et le législatif. La loi organique organisant la Cour Suprême doit précisément être modifiée pour tenir compte de cette nouvelle disposition constitutionnelle fondamentale.

Dans la première partie de notre exposé nous avons essayé de voir quelle était l'évolution de la législation dans l'ensemble des pays africains et malgache d'expression française, évolution marquée, d'une part, par le fond juridique comme hérité du droit français et, d'autre part, par la tendance à l'unité africaine qui crée, de son côté, une certaine communauté de législation.

Dans la deuxième partie, l'example sénégalais qui, à notre sens, apparaît comme le plus élaboré est significtaif car, ayant conçu un système parlementaire s'apparentant assez étroitement au système parlementaire occidental et français; en particulier, il a évolué vers un régime présidentiel qui le rapproche de la structure constitutionnelle de l'ensemble des autres états d'expression française. Cette tendance n'en n'a pas moins laissé à la Constitution sénégalaise son caractère très original pour deux raisons essentielles. La première raison est que cette Constitution s'inspire de la primauté du droit en ce qui concerne, en particulier, les rapports du parti et du gouvernement en admettant que les partis politiques fonctionnent conformément à la loi et qu'aucun d'entre eux, aussi prédominant soit il, du point de vue électoral, n'est au dessus de la Constitution. La seconde raison est l'importance donnée au pouvoir judiciaire qui, de ce fait, apparente, dans une certaine mesure, la Constitution sénégalaise à la Constitution américaine sans, toutefois, donner à la Cour Suprême sénégalaise les mêmes pouvoirs que ceux de la Cour Suprême des Etats Unis d'Amérique. Il y a là, me semble t-il, une position de principe extrêmement intéressante qui tend à éviter à la fois l'évolution des systèmes politiques africains vers le totalitarisme et vers le pouvoir personnel.

Enfin, dans toute l'évolution législative actuelle des pays africains de langue française, il importe de souligner l'importance donnée au problème du développement économique qui donne naissance, ainsi, à une législation économique fort importante et au développement d'une idéologie que l'on qualifie tantôt de socialisme africain, tantôt de voie africaine vers le socialisme.

Ainsi donc, on voit que l'évolution des systèmes législatifs en Afrique d'expression française, ayant abordé d'abord la phase initiale d'une telle décolonisation par l'adaptation de la législation antérieure coloniale aux impératifs de l'indépendance, abordent maintenant la phase de la construction de l'Afrique, tant sur le plan intérieur des états existants, que sur le plan de la coopération entre ces états en vue de l'unité africaine.

Telles m'apparaissent les grandes lignes de l'évolution actuellement suivie par le système législatif dans ces pays.

9.

THE EVOLUTION OF LAW AND GOVERNMENT IN MODERN AFRICA

by T. O. Elias

As the various European powers established their rule over African territories, whether by annexation or by conquest or by cession, they sooner or later introduced their particular systems of law, albeit into only a limited part of the territory that came under their sway. There were obvious differences as regards both the manner of introduction and the subject matter of the law thus introduced. The British policy was to say, in the beginning, that Englishmen took the principles and the practices of the English common law with them into foreign lands to which they migrated. It was, therefore, inevitable that English law was limited to the colony area of the new dominion, and that its subsequent application to the rest of the country was often limited or qualified. It was always a cardinal principle of British colonial policy to give explicit recognition to the claims of such immemorial customs and usages as bore the characteristics of rules of law, as understood and applied in the indigenous communities.

The French colonial policy of assimilation was to some extent similar in that French law was also introduced into French overseas territories, ostensibly to govern the area of strictly French settlement; in practice, however, the French system of Direct Rule tended to leave little room for the flowering of customary law. The British system of Indirect Rule, on the other hand, encouraged the practice as well as the development of customary law through the use of the institutions of chieftaincy, local councils, and traditional tribunals as the organs of local government.

The Portuguese and the Spanish colonial theory, that their overseas dependencies are integral portions of metropolitan Portugal and Spain, gives no conscious recognition to the existence of the customs and usages of the people over whom they rule. Portuguese and Spanish laws were introduced holus-bolus into the African territories of Portugal and Spain as if those lands were inhabited entirely by Iberian communities. It must, of course, be said that some latitude is allowed in practice when both these systems of law are being applied at the lowest level, as the legal regime recognizes certain degrees of assimilation to Portuguese or Spanish citizenship.

It is therefore clear that, insofar as French, Portuguese, and Spanish African territories are concerned, problems of conflict of laws are confined to status-bearing groups on the one hand, and to the ordinary unsophisticated Africans on the other. All those who qualify as *évolués* or *assimilados*, whether they are Africans or Europeans, come under the imported European legal order, while all others live under a watered-down version of that system with some admixture of acceptable local usages.

The British system offers the most definitive field of study in acculturation owing to the interaction between imported European laws and the various bodies of customary law in Africa. English law is operative, as we have seen, in its overseas dependencies according as these fall into the category of colonies, protectorates, or mandated (or trust) territories. The theory is that English law operates to the fullest extent possible, having regard to local circumstances, in the colonies, whether they have been settled or ceded or annexed. Into the often subtle differences in the application of English law in these three categories of colonies we need not enter here. The inhabitants of protectorates are not regarded as British subjects, but only as British-protected persons; only the inhabitants of a colony are British subjects. The practical result of this distinction may be seen in the Privy Council decision in *King v. Crewe*[1] that the inhabitants of a protectorate are not entitled as of right to the issue of the prerogative writ of habeas corpus, and that only British subjects in the United Kingdom and in the colonies are so entitled. The inhabitants of a mandated or trust territory are neither British subjects nor British-protected persons in the strict legal sense; nevertheless, they are entitled to the protection of the administering power insofar as external relations are concerned. The inhabitants of protectorates and of mandated or trust territories, however, do enjoy the same diplomatic privileges—for example, the carrying of British passports—as British subjects in the colonies. Whether a person belongs to a colony, a protectorate, or a mandated (or trust) territory, he is accorded the same treatment in the administration of justice according to law, even though different methods may sometimes be employed to achieve the required result.

When English law is introduced into a British dependency, the prac-

[1] For notes to chapter 9, see page 252.

tice has been to make it applicable to all the inhabitants of a colony with effect from a given date and subject to such variations as local circumstances might warrant; local legislatures pass the necessary amending enactments to provide for the variations. Two important qualifications to this general statement of principle relate to (1) the class of persons, and (2) the extent of the subject matter.

Although English law applies to all persons within a colonial territory, with or without local modifications, individuals are free in certain instances to decide that their relationships shall be governed by customary law, with jurisdiction exercised by the customary courts. The decision in *Re Bethell*[2] suggests that only Africans may so choose a system of customary law to govern their relationships. In the case itself, it was held that an Englishman was incapable of contracting a customary-law marriage with an African woman of the Baralong tribe in Southern Rhodesia, for the reason that marriage under the law of that community was potentially polygamous. The basis of this decision would seem to be bad both in law and in logic. It is bad in law because the customary law in question did not discriminate against the Englishman on the ground of nationality; indeed, the local elders gave the marriage the traditional blessing. The reason is bad in logic because it was not proved that the woman belonged to a polyandrous community, and there was no likelihood that she would marry another man contemporaneously with her present husband. As for the husband taking another woman to wife, only considerations of policy, not of law, could hold his instant marriage as null and void on that score.

The second qualification in regard to the introduction of English law into a colony may be found in almost all the relevant legislative enactments. These generally provide that the courts shall apply English law in all matters in dispute brought before them for adjudication, except in cases relating to marriage and the family, land tenure, succession and inheritance, and, by implication or sometimes by law, chieftaincy and traditional matters. These matters of customary law and tradition are thus excluded from the purview of English law and of British-established courts, at least as a matter of first instance, and only the various customary courts have jurisdiction over them.[3] We shall see presently how this dualism of legal competences operates in practice.

It is not possible to examine here all the possible cases of conflict between English law and the various bodies of customary law, between English law and the varieties of Islamic law, between two or more bodies of customary law or of Islamic law, or between one body of customary law and another variety of Islamic law. The conflict between the imported and the local law may arise from general principles of law, such as the opposition of English common law and equity to principles of the local law, or it may arise from more specific disagreement, such as that between an imported statute law and a local rule of traditional law. Sometimes a statute that sets up a system of choice of law for parties to a dispute is employed to resolve the conflict; at other times the matter is left to judicial interpretation.[4] In certain territories or areas such as Northern Nigeria, where two or more African communities or ethnic groups live in close proximity, a mixed court, composed of leading representatives of the groups concerned, is established to apply a kind of *jus gentium* in the adjudication of disputes between two or more members of different communities. The practice and the procedure followed in such a court are in many ways similar to those of the higher grades of customary courts (or local courts) and are no less flexible, so long as substantial justice is done. But the vast majority of the cases of conflict, whether between two or more Africans belonging to different ethnic groups or between an African and a non-African, are dealt with by the ordinary courts within the national legal system. The rules for handling such cases, already well established in some territories, are in the process of being set up in others. The aim is the progressive development of a common law applicable to all alike within each territory.

The recognition of customary law in Africa was first given express definition in connection with Sir Frederick (later, Lord) Lugard's famous theory and practice of Indirect Rule. The doctrine of Indirect Rule implies the use of the traditional chief, his council, and his court as the pivot around which local administration revolves. Lugard found these institutions most fully developed in Northern Nigeria, where he began his experiment at the close of the last century. As the traditional courts were well organized into different grades, he simply adopted and classified them as A, B, C, and D, in a descending order of magnitude, that is, from the powerful emir's court down to simple village tribunals. Subject to the supervision of British residents in charge of the principal administrative units into which Northern Nigeria was divided, the emirs' courts were permitted to exercise unlimited jurisdiction, including the power of life and death. They usually applied the Islamic law of the Mālikite school, although the pristine customary law prevailed in the sphere of land tenure and succession.

The system of Indirect Rule was subsequently applied to southern Nigeria, and later, in the early 1930's, to Tanganyika. Still later, it was applied to the Gold Coast (now Ghana) and to all British dependencies in Africa. The traditional courts were not always and everywhere classified into the four grades used in Northern Nigeria, for the degree of social and political organization, varying from territory to territory, largely dictated the particular pattern of the hierarchy of courts. But whether courts were classified into two, three, or four grades, the important aspects were the express delimitation of their respective jurisdictions and the attempt to systematize their procedures. The procedures, however, did not have to be identical with or conform to English rules of evidence and procedure.

Development in the practice of this aspect of Indirect Rule nevertheless followed two divergent lines. Nigeria may be said to typify one approach, while Tanganyika typifies another. In Nigeria and in practically all British West African territories, the system of customary or native courts was integrated with the system of British-established courts, consisting of two or three grades of magistrates' courts and a high or supreme court. Ultimate appeal from the latter formerly lay to the West African Court of Appeal, and thereafter to Her Majesty's Judicial Committee of the Privy Council in the United Kingdom. The four grades of customary courts had their own system of appeals and of transference of cases from one court to another, with appeals to the magistrates' courts or to the high court according to well-defined principles, based on the particular grade of customary courts. In some places area customary courts of appeal were established as intermediaries between customary courts and British-established courts. Through this system of vertical or integral structure of all courts of a particular territory in West Africa, legal dualism was brought under effective control. The beginnings of the evolution of a common law were discernible.

The Tanganyikan pattern, which prevails in most East and Central African territories, tended toward parallelism between the customary (or local) courts and the British-established magistrates' and high courts. Until comparatively recently, a system of reviews and remissions by judicial assessors was all that obtained to ensure as impartial an administration of justice as was practicable; there were few, if any, direct appeals from the reformed traditional courts to British-established courts. This subject has received constant and careful study by all those concerned with the administration of justice in Africa, and efforts have been and are being made to bring about integration between the two systems.[5]

Constitutional changes in the past decade or two have brought about important alterations in the traditional roles of the chief, his council, and his court, almost everywhere in Africa. First, the sole native authorities, with the hallmark of personal rule, have been converted into chiefs-in-council in order to emphasize the democratic idea that the chief must exercise his powers only as *primus inter pares*. Second, the old councils have been reorganized to differentiate administrative from judicial functions within the local or native authority bodies. With the differentiation of functions has also come differentiation of those engaged in pure administration from those who adjudicate disputes. Third, the membership of the traditional local authority councils has been broadened to take in a reasonable proportion, varying in some places from one-third to one-half of the members, of ordinary individuals who were formerly regarded as outside the pale. Similarly, traditional tribunals, membership in which has never been based upon systematic training in the applicable customary law, have been modernized to take in only those who, either through long experience of local customs and usages or through practical administration as registrars in British-established courts, have acquired the necessary competence to administer not only the customary law but also a limited number of simple legislative enactments, dealing with traffic offenses and the like.[6] Finally, the advent of independence has blurred for all practical purposes the erstwhile distinction between British subjects in the colonies and British-protected persons in the protectorates. There is now only one territory and only one citizenship in each of the newly independent, sovereign states of Africa. This merging together of the various ethnic communities within the territory of a single state into one common citizenship is a significant event in the evolution of political societies in Africa. As Fortes and Evans-Pritchard have pointed out,[7] African societies may be roughly classified into two main categories: (1) those with well-organized political and administrative machinery and judicial institutions, under a paramount chief or king; and (2) those with rudimentary political and administrative arrangements and insufficiently institutionalized judicial organs, usually lacking a well-defined chiefly system. Societies of the first type are often more heterogeneous, cosmopolitan, and sophisticated than the latter, which are characterized by homogeneity, close kinship ties, and a republican arrangement of communities into mutually balancing segments. The effect of the recent constitutional changes is therefore more profound on chiefless than on chiefly societies.

The examination of the effects of recent constitutional changes and political developments upon the traditional institutions of African societies leads to a consideration of the position of chiefs within the existing framework. As we have seen, the chief-in-council has replaced the chief who was a sole native authority. A further development has been the separation of the chief from the newly reformed local government councils; the chief has in most instances become merely the president, that is, the ceremonial head of a local council who formally opens each session and delivers an address once or twice a year. The day-to-day business of the council is entrusted to an elected chairman chosen from among the councilors on personal merit, insofar as possible.[8]

By far the most important problem relating to chiefs, however, has been to decide what use can be made of them under modern constitutional arrangements. In some countries, what many regard as a proper place for the chief has been found by the creation of bicameral legislatures with an elected lower house and an upper house made up of chiefs. This plan has been implemented in each of the regions of Nigeria, for example, even in the Eastern Region, where the institution of chieftaincy has not always been a marked feature of the republican polity. At the federal level, some lesser chiefs have been elected as members of the House of Representatives, and chiefs from all parts of the country, selected by electoral colleges set up by the regional legislatures, constitute nearly a third of the Senate. By and large, this system has proven satisfactory in Nigeria.

In other countries, such as Ghana and Tanganyika, the adoption of a unicameral legislature has relegated the chief to at least a secondary position. Ghana's regional assemblies, composed predominantly of chiefs, perform purely advisory functions related to chieftaincy and other traditional matters. This arrangement was intended to preclude the possibility of divided loyalties on the part of the people toward chiefs, as traditional rulers, and toward the new charismatic leader, as head of state or government. It has been argued, however, that some of Ghana's present-day political and governmental problems can be traced to the manner of handling chiefs under the new constitutions. In Tanganyika, the chief seems to have fared even less well than in Ghana; there is neither an institutional assembly of chiefs, nor specific constitutional machinery for consulting with them. They are apparently expected to take their place in the queue of ordinary men and women as electors or candidates for election. This solution looks democratic enough, and should work well in the absence of paramount or other strongly established chiefs in the local polity. Time alone will test the wisdom of the arrangement in Tanganyika. If it succeeds, it may well set the course of advance in chiefless societies in other parts of Africa.

No proper appraisal of the political problems of Uganda should underrate the importance of the chief. The existing constitution is a compromise solution to the thorny problem of the relationship between

Buganda on the one hand, and the kingdoms of Toro, Ankole, and Bunyoro, as well as Busoga, on the other. The current dispute between Buganda and Bunyoro over the so-called lost counties is an illustration of the problem. Any parliamentary arrangement that fails to find a proper place for the Kabaka of Buganda, in particular, and the other paramount chieftains in the rest of the country would be doomed to failure from the outset.

During our work in the Congo in the summer of 1963 as the United Nations Commission of Constitutional Experts charged with the task of drafting a federal constitution for the Congo, several informants from Katanga assured us that the success of Moise Tshombe's intransigence should be partly attributed to his reliance on an unofficial body of local chiefs for advice on all important issues between him and the rest of the Republic. The central government agreed with us that the federal constitution must provide for the participation of chiefs, not only in the provincial assemblies, but also in the central legislature, along the lines followed in Nigeria. This constitution also reorganizes the legal system of the country so as to ensure the integration of traditional tribunals, and of the various bodies of customary law which they administer, with the national system of administration of justice.

In the ex-French territories, as we have seen, the application of Direct Rule has so emasculated the chief, with his trappings of traditional authority and influence, that he no longer constitutes a real problem for the "new" men now in authority. It has thus been possible for most of these territories to adopt presidential systems of government, usually on the de Gaulle model. The question remains, however, as to whether the peculiar circumstances that justified the emergence, as well as the maintenance, of the de Gaulle hegemony over France could be said to exist in these territories, or whether the new African presidents necessarily stand in relation to their respective peoples as de Gaulle seems to stand in relation to the French people.

Almost all the postindependence agreements which these territories, as members of the French Community, concluded with France have retained some form of judicial association with the Conseil d'Etat and the Cour de Cassation of France, thus establishing a system of references and appeals from their highest local tribunals to those of France. There is some similarity between this system and the system of limited appeals from the highest courts in some ex-British territories to the Judicial Committee of the Privy Council. But the comparison would be superficial if it did not differentiate between the judicial appeals of the British system, restricted to well-defined categories of cases and circumstances, and judicial appeals of the French system, extended to administrative as well as legal relationships between African institutions and the French. Moreover, the French system permits the continued association of the African republics with French administrative and judicial institutions in Paris, whereas the British system recognizes the legal fact that a republican member of the Commonwealth maintains no system of appeal to the Judicial Committee of the Privy Council.

Another interesting aspect of the comparison between ex-French and ex-British territories in Africa is the difference in attitude toward the former metropolitan legal systems and institutions. Whereas ex-British territories tend to be selective, even eclectic, in their adoption of English and other systems of law in their postindependence judicial and legal experiments, ex-French territories, almost without exception, have adopted not only the text but also the machinery and the procedures of the Code Napoléon and other French laws. In these territories the study of indigenous customary law and of comparative law in general forms little or no part of the legal curriculum in local universities. In contrast, many ex-British territories, while continuing to base their legal systems upon the British common law, have shown a desire to improve their own systems by borrowing freely from other legal systems and by encouraging the study of comparative law, as well as the progressive development of various bodies of customary law, in their universities. This is not to say that French jurists have not made scholarly contributions to the study of the customary laws of French dependencies. The point is that such efforts have yet to provoke complementary contributions from French African jurists.

What has been the effect of the interaction between imported ideas of law and government and those of customary law and politics on the ordinary people in African countries? For all the recent judicial and constitutional developments, the task of nation building is yet to be accomplished in Africa. On the whole, the recent changes have tended toward the securing of common legal principles in the sphere of nationality and citizenship; nevertheless, ethnic particularisms too often tend to assert themselves amid the general clamor for self-determination and national sovereignty. Whenever the stage has been reached that the metropolitan power is about to withdraw from a dependent territory, new demands on the part of elements in the local community have come to the fore. These may be summarized into three main groups.

The first demand has arisen out of the fears and anxieties of certain ethnic minorities that the group that would assume power at political independence might oppress them in one way or another. They accordingly demand that, for the existing unitary system of government, a federal one that would allow, insofar as possible, for a measure of regional or ethnic autonomy within the federal constitutional framework should be substituted. Nigeria affords a unique example of this process, although Uganda and Kenya seem to be following suit. When a similar demand was made by the opposition parties in Ghana in 1956, Nkrumah's Convention People's Party successfully resisted the suggested adoption of a federal system, mainly on the ground that it would promote the fissiparous tendencies engendered by tribal loyalties and assertiveness. The most that was conceded was the advisory regional assemblies, to which I have referred earlier.[9] The relatively smaller size of Ghana, in terms of both population and territory, might be regarded as justifying such a stand, but a country with the size and population of Nigeria could not have ignored the demand.

In the ex-French African territories, the reverse process has in fact taken place. The quasi-federal government of former French West Africa, consisting of eight territories, and of former French Equatorial Africa, made up of four territories, broke up, at independence, into twelve separate sovereign states, all but one of them remaining in the French Community. In only one instance did two of these territories—Senegal and the French Sudan—attempt a federal union after independence, under the name of the Federation of Mali, but the experiment was short-lived. It is possible that some of the ex-French territories would be better served by some form of wider political aggregation.

In addition to demanding a federal system of government, ethnic and other minority elements have insisted on the incorporation of a set of fundamental rights and freedoms into the independence constitutions. Here, again, Nigeria is the exemplar. It was not that the existing legal system or the administration of justice had not recognized the personal liberty of the subject or the inviolability of property rights, but that many minority groups felt that the spelling out of these fundamental rights and freedoms in considerable detail would serve as an effective bulwark against possible tyranny. Many African territories have since followed the Nigerian experiment, including a country like Sierra Leone, which has no federal constitution but does have ethnic problems. It is significant that Ghana has not included in her constitution the bill of rights demanded by the opposition parties on the eve of independence; the Ghana government felt that litigation in court in connection with such entrenched rights could give rise to intertribal or even personal conflicts within the new state. Possibly, also, it feared that a system that permits the interpretation of a written constitution by the courts would give the judiciary too much power. Tanganyika, following Ghana's example, has given the latter reason, among others, for excluding a bill of rights from its independence constitution.

Ethnic considerations have led to the entrenchment of fundamental rights in the recent constitutions of Uganda, Kenya, and almost all the ex-French African territories. In order to allay the anxieties and the mutual suspicions of rival ethnic and provincial groups in the Congo, we have recently incorporated in its federal constitution fundamental rights provisions which are at least as detailed as those in the Nigerian Constitution. The strength of ethnic self-assertiveness may be judged from the sudden breakup of the former six provinces into seventeen to twenty new provinces which are apparently based on ethnic considerations alone. Such a development could create more problems than it is intended to solve, and it seems a mere concession to expediency. In addition to guaranteeing the usual freedoms of speech and expression, of assembly and association, of conscience and of political and religious beliefs, all these recent bills of rights contain provisions forbidding all forms of slavery and slave dealing, inhuman treatment, and discrimination on the ground of tribe, religion, or other group affiliation.

A third feature of recent independence constitutions has been the demand of whole communities or groups, or even administrative units, for the allocation of the total revenue of the state on the basis of the production or the consumption of the various sources from which particular revenues are derived. It has often been claimed that, under the former centralized system of government, certain areas of the country benefited more than others in the use of the national revenue for social and economic development. To redress the balance, an often complicated formula for the division of revenue has been embodied in some of these constitutions, the Nigerian one being probably the most detailed. The revenue allocation system under the federal constitution of the Congo has been modeled on the Nigerian system, though in a more simplified form.

In addition to these three major characteristics of the recent constitutions, there are other less spectacular, but equally important, devices for allaying the fears of individuals as well as of ethnic minorities. (1) The Public Service Commission is designed to ensure absolute impartiality in appointment, discipline, and termination of service of public servants. (2) The Judicial Service Commission,[10] presided over by the chief justice of the country and composed of other judges, is responsible for all judicial appointments. (3) The electoral commissions are responsible for the delimitation of constituencies as well as the organization and supervision of all elections. The independence and impartiality of the judiciary is further guaranteed by the constitutional provision that the salaries of all judges are first charges upon the Consolidated Revenue Fund of the country; in other words, the emoluments of judges are not subject to the annual parliamentary debates on the budget. There is also a provision that judges' salaries and other conditions of service may not be altered to their detriment during their tenure of office. Nor may judges be removed from office except by a complicated procedure involving the setting up of a special judicial tribunal which must recommend such removal, and the subsequent approval of that recommendation by the Judicial Committee of the Privy Council. This last provision does not apply to Ghana, which, as a republic owing no allegiance to the Crown, no longer uses the machinery of the Privy Council. But even in territories like Nigeria, there is already a feeling that the removal of judges should be made subject to some other purely internal procedure compatible with democratic principles.[11]

The survey attempted here has touched upon so many issues of contemporary government and politics in Africa that full justice can hardly be said to have been done to any one subject. The nature of the interaction between African institutions and laws and those imported from Europe is such that, in an interdisciplinary seminar, it would be unwise to specialize. I hope, however, that I have pointed up a number of vital questions for students of sociology, law, government, politics, and economics.

10.

THE ADAPTATION OF CUSTOMARY FAMILY LAW IN SOUTH AFRICA

by Leslie Rubin

More than three centuries of rule by the white man have wrought profound changes in the structure of traditional African society in South Africa. In three important fields—land rights, chieftaincy, and customary law—conquest of the African tribes and the consequent imposition of European government and administration have undermined concepts and institutions that contributed to the stability of African life. Today ownership of land by Africans (11 million in a total population of 16 million) is limited to areas known as the reserves which constitute about 12.9 percent of the total area of South Africa; within those areas the traditional system of allocation of land by the chief as custodian of tribal lands has been replaced by several types of land tenure subject to a variety of legal and administrative restrictions on use and disposition. In traditional African society the chief was the center of an efficient system for maintaining social order. As he was vested with extensive political power and authority, his actions and decisions were, as a rule, required to express the wishes of his people, ascertained by constant consultation with elders and periodic consultation with larger groups. Today the chief is an administrative official performing functions whose nature, scope, and extent are determined, not by the traditions of his people, but by the government of South Africa which appoints him and may dismiss him at will.

These two questions—the effect of European conquest on traditional African land rights and its impact on political institutions—have received much attention. The purpose of this paper is to discuss the third issue, namely, the effect of European conquest and rule on traditional African law.

In South Africa today much of the law that regulates the life of the

African population is uncertain and confused. This state of affairs arises from the coexistence within the South African polity of two distinct bodies of law: the common law (Roman-Dutch law, or more accurately, South African law[1]) and customary law.[2] Before we discuss the interaction of South African law and customary law, it is appropriate to note that South African law is itself the result of interaction between Roman-Dutch law and English law.

Origins and Development of South African Law

At the date of the first British occupation of the Cape of Good Hope in 1795, Roman-Dutch law had been in force in the settlement for more than a century.[3] Although there was no express declaration to that effect, the first governor recognized the existing system, and Roman-Dutch law was applied even to British-born subjects.[4] In 1858, despite an official recommendation, made thirty years earlier, that the English law should gradually be substituted, the Commission of Enquiry reporting on the state of law at the Cape said that "Roman-Dutch law, which consists of the civil or Roman laws as modified by the legislature of Holland, and by the customs of that country, forms the great bulk of the law of the colony."[5]

The retention of Roman-Dutch law was in accord with settled English policy that inhabitants of conquered territories should continue to live under their own laws.[6] It was inevitable, however, that English law would play an important part in the development of a system of law for the colony. In the first place, there were penal provisions of the Roman-Dutch law whose harshness and cruelties were repugnant to the spirit of English law. These were abolished at an early date by legislation, and before long criminal procedure was brought into line with the recently revised criminal procedure applicable in England, and the English law of evidence, subject to certain modifications, was introduced.[7] Then, economic development in the colony served to show that Roman-Dutch principles were inadequate to satisfy the requirements of a changing society, and the laws relating to such matters as shipping, insurance, insolvency, and companies, in force in England, were introduced (in some instances without modification) in the Cape.[8] Finally, English doctrines and principles were introduced, apart from legislation, through the application of the law in the courts. This development followed naturally from the fact that the law was being interpreted by judges trained in England, who were likely to refer to deci-

[1] For notes to chapter 10, see page 253.

sions of the English courts and to English textbooks rather than to the works of Roman-Dutch writers.[9] The Cape pattern of a basis of Roman-Dutch law modified by, and with substantial additions from, English law extended to the republics of the Transvaal and the Orange Free State, and to Natal.[10]

The conclusion of the Boer War, followed by the annexation of the two republics, revived in some quarters the proposal that English law be substituted for Roman-Dutch law, but the suggestion met with no success.[11] By 1910, when the Union of South Africa came into existence, Roman-Dutch law (modified in the manner and to the extent described above) was firmly established as the common law in the four colonies then under British rule. In the law of persons and family relations, the law of property, and the law of delict, the principles of the original Roman-Dutch law in force in the Cape at the date of British occupation were applied with little change. In the law of contract, on the other hand, the influence of English law has been considerable.

British rule had thus kept faith with the principle that the customary law of the conquered people in her colonies should be recognized. Where that law was modified, the modification was a response to the requirements of a changing society, not the result of arbitrary imposition of the will of the ruling power. The establishment of union, bringing with it a centralized legislature and the Supreme Court of South Africa, headed by the Appellate Division, accelerated the process of creating an integrated system of law for the country as a whole. Although there has been a tendency to emphasize Roman-Dutch foundations, and to resist excessive reception of English ideas,[12] South African law today has taken shape as a coherent system constituting an amalgam of Roman-Dutch and English law.[13]

Recognition of African Customary Law before Union

With the advance of British rule in the Cape during the nineteenth century, African tribes became part of the settled population subject to British administration. The task of governing them compelled the colonial administrators, before long, to recognize that these new subjects regulated their lives according to their own systems of law. The control of Fingo chiefs by British superintendents in 1847 gave rise to the first manifestation of conflict between European law and African customary law.[14] Customary law was the body of oral law which, despite variations from tribe to tribe, presented in its main institutions features common to the Bantu-speaking tribes of southern Africa.[15] It resembled closely the laws of the Anglo-Saxon, Germanic, and Frankish peoples before the feudal era, but in some respects, such as abandonment of the judicial duel and recognition of a distinction between crime and wrong, had reached a stage of development found in Europe in the early Middle Ages.[16]

Customary law was well developed in the sphere of family relationships, and underdeveloped in the sphere of contract. Marriage was polygamous, and the head of the family was the senior common ancestor in the male line. Marriage, following upon arrangements concluded between the respective families of the spouses, did not require the seal of tribal authority for its validity. A marriage was concluded with the transfer of the bride to the bridegroom's family and the payment of valuable consideration, usually cattle (*lobolo*) to the bride's family. Divorce took place at the instance of either spouse without reference to the courts, provided agreement was reached on whether (and if so, how much of) the lobolo paid had to be restored to the husband. Women were not permitted to perform valid legal acts without the consent of a male guardian, had very limited rights to property, and could never be guardians of their children. The levirate required a widow to remain with her husband's family and, by entering into a union with one of his relations, to bear children in her husband's name. Testamentary succession was unknown; as a rule the eldest son succeeded to the family property on the death of the head of the family. There was a rudimentary distinction between crime and delict in that homicide was treated as an injury to the chief, whereas theft was regarded as a private wrong entitling the victim to compensation and damages. Among the private wrongs justifying damages were adultery and seduction, the former giving rise to an action by the husband, and the latter, to an action by the girl's father.

Different approaches to the conflict between the law of the land and customary law developed in the four colonies. Within the Cape Colony there were differences between one area and another. Everywhere, as the African came increasingly under European influence and was drawn more closely within the white economy, the question whether customary law should be recognized or not had to be faced as a practical aspect of government and administration. Whenever recognition was accorded, the decision to do so brought in its train two difficulties. First, recognition presupposes ascertainment of the law to be recognized. The rules of conduct recognized as binding in tribal society were unwritten, expounded unsystematically by chiefs and elders from time to time, and handed down in this form from generation to generation. It follows that these rules require, not only to be recorded, but also to be expounded as a coherent body of legal principles. Although the work of anthropologists has combined with an extensive body of case law to make a valuable contribution to this end, some of the law of all tribes in South Africa, as well as the larger part of the law of some tribes, still awaits adequate study and definitive recording. Second, the customary law to be recognized has itself undergone modification in some respects:

> The customs recognized as Native law are ancient ones. But in actual fact many of these customs, or certain features of them, are changing as the social and economic conditions of Native life change. Nowhere in the world has social change been as swift and as far-reaching as it has in Africa in the last two or three decades. Where customs of marriage or family life have undergone significant change, which form of the custom shall the courts recognize as Native law? Shall they countenance only the practice of the oldest generation? Or shall they seek to find current or temporary custom in the practice of younger people?[17]

Under the influence of the liberal doctrine later expressed in the maxim, "Equal rights for all civilized men," the law of the Cape Colony applied to all. There was no formal recognition of customary law, although the practice grew of giving effect to transactions based on customary law when it did not conflict with the law of the colony, and was not repugnant to morality or public policy. Marriage according to customary law was an illicit union in the eyes of the law of the colony, and it could not therefore give rise to rights enforceable in the courts. From time to time, however, the courts did grant relief to Africans who had regulated their affairs according to customary law without recognizing the legality of the customary institutions concerned. But the decisions were not consistent.[18] In 1864, with the enactment of the Native Succession Act, the colony accorded a limited recognition to customary law. Under this law the estates of Africans residing permanently in the colony were administered according to customary law. British Kaffraria, which was incorporated in 1865, became subject to the same system; that is, the law of the colony was applied except in the sphere of succession. In fact, the practice that had developed in British Kaffraria of permitting magistrates to apply "their own ideas of equity, Cape and native law" continued. In deciding what "native law" was, the magistrates looked to the *Compendium of Kaffir Laws and Customs*, compiled in 1858 by Colonel Maclean, the chief commissioner of British Kaffraria.[19] In the Transkei—the large area comprising a number of territories annexed between 1877 and 1894—customary law was recognized from the date of its incorporation in the Cape Colony. Magistrates' courts established in districts throughout the territory were required to apply the law of the colony, but were vested with a discretion to apply customary law in suits in which all the parties were Africans. The Supreme Court had no such discretion. In the exercise of its appellate jurisdiction, however, it could apply customary law in determining whether the magistrate's court had made a proper exercise of its statutory discretion to recognize customary law.[20] The Supreme Court was deprived of its right to hear civil appeals by Africans in 1894, when the Native Appeal Court with exclusive jurisdiction in such appeals was created. From 1898 an appeal lay against a decision of the Native Appeal Court to the Supreme Court.[21] Within the Cape Colony, therefore, two systems were in operation. In the Transkei, both the law of the colony and customary law, subject to judicial discretion, applied. In the remainder of the colony (save for the practice that had grown up in British Kaffraria) the law of the colony alone, subject to the provisions of the Native Succession Act, applied.

In Natal, customary law was recognized shortly after annexation of the colony in 1843. It was provided that customary law was to be preserved except where it was "repugnant to the general principles of humanity recognized throughout the whole civilized world." [22] For the next thirty years a policy developed which was in marked contrast with the Cape policy of assimilation. Directed by Theophilus Shepstone, the policy aimed at preserving the tribal system where it existed, and restoring it where it had broken down. In accordance with this policy, chiefs continued to exercise their customary judicial functions, subject to the supervision of colonial officials. In 1875 the Native Administration Act transferred most of the civil jurisdiction formerly exercised by the chiefs to courts of administrators of native law. An appeal lay from these courts to a native high court, with a further appeal to the Supreme Court.[23] At the date of union, magistrates, taking the place of the administrators of native law, were vested with minor civil and criminal jurisdiction over Africans. Specified civil matters and criminal offenses were to be dealt with by the Supreme Court, but all other civil disputes and criminal prosecutions came before the Native High Court.[24] Civil actions were to be tried "according to Native laws, customs and usages save so far as may be otherwise specially provided by law, or as may be of a nature to work some manifest injustice or to be repugnant to the settled principles and policy of natural equity."[25]

In 1878 the Code of Native Law was introduced, comprising rules of substantive law and administrative provisions. It was not exhaustive. In those branches of law not covered by the code, the unwritten law, applied in accordance with the principle of repugnancy, remained in force. But where the provisions of the code "embody the rules of law in distinct terms, then those rules must be operative in all cases not expressly or impliedly excluded."[26] While some of these provisions merely gave legislative force to the existing customary law, others altered the law. The original code has been amended, but a substantial part of the customary law applicable in Natal today comprises rules that were formulated in 1878.[27]

The system of exemption from the operation of customary law, "one of Natal's major contributions to colonial policy,"[28] was introduced in 1865. The intention was to offer an enhanced status to Africans who were not "either so ignorant or so unfitted by habit or otherwise as to render them incapable of exercising and understanding the ordinary duties of civilised life." [29] A successful applicant for letters of exemption, while ceasing to be subject to customary law, did not acquire the legal status of a white and continued to be subject to the law of the land insofar as it discriminated against Africans.[30]

Early republican policy in the Transvaal made no provision for the recognition of customary law. Law 3 of 1876 provided that, in the interests of morality, polygamy and lobolo should not be recognized. But the first marriage law enacted permitted whites only to enter into a valid marriage.[31] An undertaking embodied in that law, to introduce separate legislation regulating marriages between nonwhites, was not honored until twenty-six years had elapsed.[32] When a bill was finally introduced in the Volksraad in 1895, it gave rise to petitions calling for its rejection, and met with vigorous opposition during the debates; it was passed two years later by a majority of thirteen votes to twelve. Objection to the proposed law rested fundamentally on the contention that it would encourage equality between black and white.[33]

Law 4 of 1885, which was based on a law introduced in the short period of British rule between 1877 and 1881 and reflected the Natal policy of Shepstone, provided for the recognition of customary law so long as it was not "inconsistent with the general principles of civilisation recognized in the civilised world." Jurisdiction in civil suits between Africans vested in native commissioners, subcommissioners, and chiefs appointed by the government for specified districts or tribes, with a final appeal to the superintendent of natives. But all judgments were subject to the overriding control of the government. No judgment could take effect until it had been considered by the government, which had the power to set it aside or amend it. Later, again under British rule, Law 4 was amended by removing the powers vested in the superintendent of natives and the government and providing for an appeal to the Supreme Court against decisions of a chief or a native commissioner, but the limitation on the recognition of customary law remained (Proclamation No. 28 of 1902). In a number of decisions on appeals from the courts of native commissioners, the Supreme Court declined to accord recognition to customary marriages on the ground that it was "inconsistent with the general principles of civilisation recognized in the civilised world."[34] At the opening of the first session of the Native Appeal Court for the Transvaal and Natal in 1929, the president, dealing with the effect of these decisions on the African people, described the act as having "bastardised almost the entire Native population of the Transvaal, . . . deprived practically every Native father of guardianship or other rights to his children, . . . destroyed any equitable claim in property, the passing of which, to the Native mind, alone differentiates marriage and prostitution and finally so undermined the fundamental native customs that there was very little left as regards status." [35] Statutory provision had been made for the recognition of the customary law of succession in 1902.[36]

In the Orange Free State, where no settlement of Africans occurred in large numbers, the question of recognizing customary law was not so pressing as it had been in the other colonies. Here, too, however, provision was made for rights of succession by children of a customary marriage, and for the legal guardianship of such children by their parents in certain circumstances.[37]

Recognition of Customary Law in South Africa

The diversity in policy, law, and procedure continued after the four colonies had combined to form the Union of South Africa in 1910. In 1927 the Native Administration Act was passed with the object of establishing uniform recognition of customary law throughout the country. The act provided for the creation of a system of courts to deal with disputes in accordance with customary law. Accepting legal pluralism, it allowed the courts to determine whether South African law or customary law should apply, but attached certain conditions to the recognition of customary law. The act did, however, make certain changes in the law relating to marriage and succession.[38] It also empowered the government to amend the Natal Code of Native Law, and to extend its operation to Zululand. An amended Natal Code was promulgated pursuant to these powers.[39]

How far implementation of the provisions of the Native Administration Act has served to resolve the problems caused by the conflict between South African law and customary law will appear from the description of the tribunals applying customary law, and from the discussion of the principles applied in choosing between the two systems.

Customary Law in the Courts

Four courts have jurisdiction over Africans only: chiefs' courts, native commissioners' courts, native appeal courts, and native divorce courts.[40] A chief's court has unlimited civil jurisdiction in disputes arising from customary law between Africans resident within the chief's area, but it may not determine questions of nullity, separation, or divorce relating to a civil marriage. Criminal jurisdiction includes all offenses known to customary law and, since 1952, all but the most serious offenses under the law of the land. Only a chief or a headman authorized to do so in terms of the act may exercise civil or criminal jurisdiction. An appeal lies to the native commissioner who, because evidence in the chief's court is not recorded, hears the evidence afresh and records it.[41]

A native commissioner's court has jurisdiction only in "civil causes between Native and Native," regardless of the amount of the claim, but subject to specified limitations as to causes of action.[42] The court is vested with a discretion to apply customary law, and its judgment may be taken on appeal to the appropriate native appeal court. The decision of the native appeal court is final, but the court may itself grant leave for a further appeal to the Appellate Division of the Supreme Court.[43] If the minister of native affairs doubts the correctness of a decision of the court, he may state a case for determination by the Appellate Division.[44] The court consists of three members drawn from the public service, usually native commissioners. While the president of the court holds office continuously, the other members are appointed from time to time, and often sit only while the court is in session in one town.[45]

Native divorce courts have jurisdiction in suits for nullity, divorce, or separation between Africans married by civil rites. An appeal lies to a provincial or local division of the Supreme Court. The Supreme Court has a concurrent jurisdiction, but Africans are discouraged from bringing matrimonial proceedings before it.[46]

The inherent right of the Supreme Court to deal with suits between Africans remains unaffected by the provisions of the Native Administration Act.[47] In practice, however, the recognized rule of law that the costs awarded to the successful party are usually on the lower scale applicable in the native commissioner's court is a powerful deterrent against resort to the Supreme Court.[48] As a result, most disputes (no matter how large the amount involved, or whether customary law is applicable or not) are decided by judicial officers who, compared with judges, are inferior in qualifications, training, and experience. Furthermore, the original belief that the native commissioner's court would ensure simpler and less expensive machinery has proven to be quite unfounded. Provision for a low tariff of fees has been ineffective against agreements to pay larger amounts. Africans, for the most part, have been unwilling to conduct their cases in person, and have instructed attorneys. Frequently counsel has been briefed. Technical points are commonly taken, and hearings are often protracted.[49]

The new system of Native Administration established in 1927 rested on the assumption that native commissioners were endowed with special knowledge of customary law. They are entitled to call for evidence to establish the existence of a customary rule, but in most cases they apply customary law in the light of their own knowledge. The assumption that native commissioners constitute a depository of expert knowledge of customary law would seem to be unwarranted. Although many of them, as former officials of the Department of Native Affairs, had become acquainted with African conditions, particularly in the reserved areas, their experience and training (neither knowledge of an African language nor a course in customary law is a prescribed requirement) do not qualify them for their important duties.[50]

In the absence of evidence establishing its existence, customary law may not be applied in the Supreme Court. The court does, however, take cognizance of customary law to the extent that it has received statutory recognition, as, for example, in the Natal Native Code. The Supreme Court has not been consistent in its attitude to decisions of the native appeal courts, at times treating them as binding, at other times ignoring them.[51]

The function of the native commissioners' courts in relation to customary law was defined by the Native Administration Act:

> Notwithstanding the provisions of any other law, it shall be in the discretion of the courts of native commissioners in all suits or proceedings between natives involving questions of customs followed by natives, to decide such questions according to the native law applying to such customs except insofar as it shall have been repealed or modified: Provided that such native law shall not be opposed to the principles of public policy or natural justice: Provided further that it shall not be lawful for any court to declare that the custom of *lobolo* or *bogadi* or other similar custom is repugnant to such principles.[52]

This provision gave the native commissioners' courts an important discretionary power, to be exercised without guidance from the legislature. The Appellate Division has said that the discretion to decide which system of law to apply carries with it "a great responsibility—greater than that generally borne by courts of law." [53]

Three views may be taken in deciding the nature of the discretion conferred: (1) the court is free to make whatever choice it pleases, without being required to exercise a preference in favor of one system or the other; (2) the common law—South African law—should be regarded as the law primarily applicable, customary law being applied only if the court is satisfied that it is appropriate; (3) customary law should be applied in all cases except when the court considers it unsuitable. All three views may be found in a series of inconsistent decisions of the native appeal courts, but a preference developed for the third. In their later decisions the courts showed a marked tendency to hold that customary law should be applied by native commissioners in all cases, unless it was clearly unsuitable. In some cases this view tended to develop into the rule that the common law could apply only when customary law offered no answer at all to a question. In adopting the view that customary law should have priority, the native appeal courts were influenced by the belief that the Native Administration Act marked the abandonment of the assimilationist policy of the Cape in favor of the Shepstone policy of Natal and the Transvaal. In two cases the president of the court talked of "legal segregation."[54] The unfortunate effect of this tendency to subject African litigants to customary law at all costs is illustrated by the following two cases described by Lewin.

Plaintiff claimed damages for the loss of a stallion that had been killed by defendant's cow. According to Pondo customary law, damages are recoverable for injuries caused by bulls, but not for those caused by cows. The court gave judgment against plaintiff, holding that it was not prepared "to allow common law to oust Native law." If at a later date, as Lewin points out, a cow belonging to the plaintiff had injured a stallion belonging to a European, the owner of the stallion would have recovered damages from him under common law. In the second case, plaintiff claimed from defendant, his grandfather's brother, the price of two bags of maize, the amount of herding fees, and the refund of a sum advanced for the taxi fare of defendant's daughter-in-law, all the payments having been made at defendant's request. In dismissing plaintiff's claim the court said, *inter alia*, that "the creation of a debt in European fashion, as is alleged by the plaintiff, is a thing unknown. . . . It is foreign to Native custom in the circumstances to exact payment for board in this fashion. . . . It is so unusual as to be incredible that Natives should think in terms of recompense for hospitality, especially to relatives."[55]

The highest court in South Africa—the Appellate Division—has since rejected the view that customary law should be preferred to the common law. The court construed the discretion conferred upon native commissioners as follows:

What is intended is that wherever the case is one in which native law could be applied on the ground that the issues relate to matters in respect of which native custom exists, the discretion arises. In some cases it would doubtless be clear not only that native custom is involved, but also that the native commissioner would not be exercising his discretion judicially if he did not decide the issue by applying such custom. In other cases, on the contrary, it would be clear that no native custom could possibly have any bearing. No one would, I apprehend, suggest that an action between Natives arising out of their being members or directors of a limited liability company could ever involve such customs. But in many kinds of cases it might be an open question whether native custom could possibly or reasonably be applied. . . . I can find no support in the language [of the act] for the . . . view that native law should be treated as *prima facie* applicable in cases between natives. On the contrary the indications are rather that common law was intended to be applied unless the native commissioner in his discretion saw fit in a proper case to apply native law.[56]

But the court declined to rule affirmatively that the common law should generally be applied, with the native commissioner having the right to apply customary law in a suitable case. It was content to assume, for the purpose of the decision, that the discretion should be exercised without regarding either of the two systems as prima facie applicable. The court did, however, reject certain views expressed by the native appeal court. It was held that there would not be an improper recognition of class distinctions if a native commissioner decided to apply the common law because the litigants or either of them was "civilised, urbanised or detribalised"; that the exercise of the discretion is not decisively controlled by the fact that the parties or either of them was not exempted from the operation of customary law, the non-exemption being only one of the factors to be taken into account in deciding between the two systems; that, although the existence of a remedy under one legal system and not under the other would be a major factor in the exercise of the discretion, it must not be treated as a consideration requiring automatically the application of the system that provides a remedy. In the circumstances of a particular case, justice may best be served by applying the system that provides no remedy.[57]

The Appellate Division's guidance notwithstanding, much uncertainty remains. While the African litigant is free to invoke one system or the other in bringing a dispute before the court, the decision as to which system will apply is taken by the native commissioner in the exercise of a discretion that necessarily permits a wide diversity of views.

The decision to apply customary law often brings in its train problems arising from the fact that traditional tribal law is no longer appropriate to the social and economic realities of African life today. In the sphere of family law, particularly in regard to the legal consequences of marriage, the status of African women in general, and succession, decisions of the native appeal courts have resulted in hardship and inequity. Attempts, in some cases, to deal with the situation by legislation have met with limited success.[58]

Customary Family Law

A marriage between Africans in accordance with customary law is known in South Africa as a customary union. The term "marriage" is reserved for a monogamous union concluded in accordance with the law of the land. In Natal a customary union has received legislative definition. In the rest of the Union the task of determining the requisites of a valid customary union has been left to the courts. Native commissioners, guided by the native appeal courts, have handed down decisions whose effect, outside Natal, is that the requisites of a valid customary union are the consent of the bride and her guardian; the consent of the bridegroom and, if he is under tutelage, of his guardian; the payment of lobolo; and the handing over of the bride to her husband.[59] The decisions seem to be based on a pragmatic approach to individual cases, rather than on an analysis of tribal law in the light of its social function. Nor do they disclose adequate recognition of the wide degree of variation in adherence to tribal practice among the different sections of the African community. Simons asks: "Can it be said that Native law applies to modes of behavior current among Africans in the varied circumstances of towns, slums and locations, labour compounds, farms and reserves?" [60] He goes on to describe this juridical determination of customary law as follows:

> Imbued with a concept of "legal segregation" that has ousted earlier assimilative notions, judges of the Native Appeal courts since the enactment of the Native Administration Act have come down heavily on the side of the traditional law, and convey a desire to preserve it against a corrosive modernity. The facts of social change are too obstrusive, however, to be denied; and it is recognized, if only dimly, that the surest way to destroy the law would be to fossilize it.[61]

Proof of the existence of the essentials of a customary union gives rise to considerable difficulty in practice. The law as laid down by the courts itself leaves room for uncertainty; in addition, the frequent absence of men from the tribal area for lengthy periods, owing to the system of migrant labor, complicates the task of distinguishing between informal connubial relationships and valid customary unions. Consent of the parties is usually established by inference. Actual payment of lobolo, or agreement as to the number of cattle to be transferred, constitutes proof that the bride's guardian and the bridegroom have consented. The rule that the bride's consent is essential was unknown in traditional tribal law. The courts apply the rule as a principle of public policy, designed to prevent a woman from being compelled to marry against her wishes. In practice, however, she is at the mercy of her guardian's wishes, as his consent is essential (even when she has attained statutory majority) and his decision to withhold consent may not be challenged. The bride's consent, too, is generally inferred from her behavior. If she has moved to the bridegroom's home and has remained there, particularly if there is no evidence of any protest on her part, her consent is presumed.

Except in Natal, the amount of lobolo is determined either by custom or by agreement between the parties.[62] Guardians display a tendency to insist on the maximum, or, if no maximum is laid down, to make extravagant demands. Difficulties arise in seeking to infer the existence of a customary union from the fact that cattle have been delivered to the girl's guardian. Cattle are also delivered by way of payment of damages for seduction and pregnancy, and among some tribes the number required to be delivered does not differ widely from the number required for lobolo. This is a fruitful source of litigation.

In regard to the dissolution of a customary union, also, the law in Natal differs from that in the rest of the Union. The Natal Code, adapting tribal law to the common law, provides that a union may not be dissolved without an order from a native commissioner's court. Proceedings may be instituted by either spouse for a decree of divorce or a declaration of nullity on specified grounds, provided there has been a prior attempt at reconciliation.[63] In the rest of South Africa a customary union is usually dissolved without recourse to the courts. If one spouse has deserted the other, and satisfactory arrangements have been concluded for the refund of lobolo, the union is dissolved.[64] If the husband is prepared to forego his right to the refund of lobolo, he is entitled to terminate the union unilaterally by repudiating his wife and advising her guardian of his decision; if not, he institutes proceedings against her guardian claiming refund of lobolo unless she returns to him.[65] A wife lacks the right to terminate the union extrajudicially. Whether effect may be given to her desire to terminate the union depends upon the willingness of her guardian to refund lobolo. If he maintains that no refund is due, he may institute proceedings in his own name for an order declaring the husband to have forfeited the right to return of lobolo and for an order dissolving the union.[66] A customary union is automatically terminated if either of the spouses enters into a marriage with a third person, because the Native Administration Act defines "customary union" as "the association of a man and woman in conjugal relationship according to Native law and custom, where neither the man nor the woman is party to a subsisting marriage."[67]

According to South African law, a polygamous union is denied recognition. The female partner in such a union is not entitled to the same rights as a wife. In the absence of special statutory provision the Supreme Court takes no cognizance of a statutory union for the purpose of enforcing claims by an African woman. The native appeal courts have granted damages to the female partner in the union against the person causing her husband's death. The Supreme Court has refused to entertain such an action where the defendant is a European on the ground that, since there is no lawful marriage between the parties, there was no obligation in law upon the deceased to support the plaintiff. The result is an anomalous and unjust distinction between a white woman and an African woman as to the right in law to compensation for the loss of support which has in fact been provided by a deceased husband.[68]

Varying practices have been adopted in South Africa in regard to the right of a woman married according to customary law to the custody of her children. According to traditional law, the father's right to the custody of his children is absolute. With this practice is associated the concept of property rights in children, including the right to receive lobolo in respect to daughters. Upon dissolution of a union the wife's guardian usually restores to the husband the lobolo received by him, less a deduction for the children. In that event the husband retains the right to the children. If the whole lobolo is restored to him, the husband forfeits his rights and the children belong to his wife's guardian.[69]

Under the common law, the interests of the child are the paramount consideration in determining the right to custody. A parent held unfit may be deprived of custody, and, if parents are living apart, sole guardianship or custody may be granted to either one.[70] The Natal Code includes provisions permitting a native commissioner to exercise a discretion similar to that recognized in the common law.[71] The courts of the Cape and the Transvaal have followed a different course. In the Cape it has been held that, when proceedings are instituted for the refund of lobolo together with a claim for custody of the children of a union, the wife is not entitled to be joined as a party to the proceedings.[72] The Transvaal courts have adopted the view that the interests of the children must be taken into account when orders as to custody are made, and that the wife should, therefore, be joined as a party.[73]

Generally, however, native commissioners display a tendency to apply customary law, thus relegating the African woman to a status inferior to that of the African man. This attitude fails to recognize the extent to which African women, with their growing employment in commerce and industry, have undergone a rapid process of emancipation. There is a real need for reform of the law. It should be possible to introduce legislation calculated to remove the "prevailing obscurity and confusion" [74] by reconciling the common law with customary law. This could be done by a law providing that the principles of the common law be applied in determining questions of guardianship and custody of an African child, subject to the right of the courts to recognize any claim to lobolo which may arise.

The coexistence of the customary union and marriage in African society has created a number of problems. The two are clearly distinguished in the Native Administration Act, which defines marriage as a monogamous union entered into according to the law of the land, not including a customary union.[75] But the fact that Africans marry according to common law instead of entering into a customary union does not necessarily mean that they have abandoned all adherence to tribal practices. In many instances, for example, lobolo passes from the bridegroom to the bride's guardian as part of the arrangements for a marriage concluded according to civil or religious rites. Although accurate and reliable statistics are not available, it has been suggested that a growing number of Africans are concluding such marriages.[76]

Three kinds of marriage are recognized by the Native Administration Act. The marriage is in community of property and of profit and loss, except as to quitrent land, if the parties have made a declaration to that effect within one month prior to the celebration of the marriage, provided that the marriage did not take place during the subsistence of a customary union between the husband and another woman. On the other hand, the parties may exclude community of property and of profit and loss, and the marital power, by entering into an antenuptial contract. The third kind of marriage is one that has taken place in the absence of either a prenuptial declaration or an antenuptial contract. As the act is silent on this point, it was left to the courts to determine the property rights of the spouses in these circumstances. It has been held that each spouse retains ownership of the property that he or she brought into the marriage, but that control of the property belonging to both spouses vests in the husband by virtue of the marital power according to the common law.[77]

Most African marriages fall within the third category. The resultant exclusion of any right on the part of the wife to half of the joint estate is not advantageous to women living in urban areas. The husband is usually the main breadwinner, and it is difficult for the wife to acquire a separate estate.

The right of succession to the estate of a deceased African is governed by regulations under the Native Administration Act.[78] These regulations are a tangle of badly drafted provisions whose meaning is by no means clear. Their effect would appear to be as follows: If a deceased African executed a valid will, and if, at the date of death, he was exempted from the operation of the Natal Code and was a partner in a marriage in community or by antenuptial contract, or a widower, a widow, or a divorcee of such marriage not survived by a partner to a customary union entered into after the dissolution of such marriage, his estate devolves as if he had been a European. The estate devolves according to customary law if the deceased is survived by the partner or the issue of a marriage without community in terms of the act, or of a customary union, or of a putative marriage. If however, the minister considers it inequitable or inappropriate to apply customary law, he may direct that the whole estate or part of it shall devolve as if there had been, in each instance, a lawful marriage out of community, and as if the deceased had been a European.[79]

Clearly an African can ensure that the common law will apply to his estate by executing a will or marrying in community of property or by antenuptial contract, provided that the husband is not at the time a partner in a customary union with another woman. In fact, however, Africans seldom make wills and invariably marry without community in terms of the act, with the result that most African estates are distributed according to customary law. The wife's legal position in these circumstances, not yet clarified by the courts, remains obscure. As we have seen, if the marriage is without community, she retains ownership of both property brought into the marriage and subsequent acquisitions. During the marriage all her property is subject to the control of her husband, but upon his death full ownership of such property vests in her alone. As customary law does not recognize the right of a woman to own property other than personal possessions, serious doubt remains as to the devolution of the property after her death.

The position of the widow of such a marriage who has not acquired a separate estate, when the husband has failed to provide for her by will, is unsatisfactory. Under customary law the husband's estate is inherited by the eldest son, or another male relative of the husband. The heir is under an obligation to provide the widow and children with maintenance out of the estate, but control of the estate vests in the heir, and he may dispose of it without consulting her or without having regard to her needs and the needs of her children.[80]

The Future of Customary Law

At the root of all the problems I have discussed is the failure of the law to satisfy the needs of African society as it is today. Education has lessened adherence to tribal practice; men and women, in the process of urbanization, have broken with the extended family; the traditional authority of parents has weakened; women, in employment, earning and saving money, have developed an individualism alien to tribal ideas. Neither the court nor the legislature has shown a consistent willingness to recognize these changes and to weigh their effect on traditional institutions. When the legislature realized that the law relating to succession was unsatisfactory, it was left to the minister of native affairs to deal with the situation. The result was complex regulations which, as we have seen, created new problems. Under the Marriage Act of 1961, described as a law "to consolidate and amend the laws relating to the solemnization of marriages and matters incidental thereto,"[81] African marriages in the Cape and Transvaal provinces continued to be governed by laws passed more than sixty years earlier. In respect to certain aspects of the law relating to the status and the rights of women, notoriously out of keeping with present conditions, legislative action would be appropriate. Such aspects include the unfettered right of a husband, outside Natal, to dissolve a customary union at will, the dissolution of a customary union *ipso facto* when one of the partners marries a third person, and the denial to a woman of the right to claim dissolution of a customary union without the consent of the person who received lobolo in connection with the union. No legislative action is contemplated.

The record of the courts in adapting customary laws to modern circumstances is disappointing. In principle, judicial interpretation is preferable to legislation as a means of adaptation. When legislation is used to modify customary law operating in a changing society, there is always the risk that undesirable inflexibility will result. On the other hand, well-trained judges approaching an indigenous system with sympathetic understanding, and doing justice in a variety of cases, can formulate, over a period of years, a coherent body of consistent law corresponding to social needs and capable of further development. No such body of law has resulted from the labors of the native commissioners in the exercise of the powers conferred upon them by the Native Administration Act. Instead, with a few exceptions, the decisions handed down conform to a general pattern of anxiety to apply customary law rather than common law whenever possible, combined with marked reluctance to adapt customary law to the changed conditions of African life. The result for most Africans, particularly for those who live in the towns, is that they find themselves enmeshed in a network of uncertain laws that seem to bear no relation to the reality of their lives.

The Appellate Division has, from time to time, drawn the attention of native commissioners to the need for distinguishing between the emancipated African and the African living under tribal conditions. But there is no appeal as of right from a native appeal court, leave to appeal is not granted lightly, and few Africans can afford the expense involved; in any event, the Appellate Division is required, not to reach a decision on the facts of the case, but merely to determine whether the native commissioner has made a proper exercise of his discretion. As a result, notwithstanding the exercise by the minister of native affairs of his right to seek a ruling on controversial questions, courts of native commissioners are subject only to sporadic and fragmentary supervision by the highest court in the land.

Uncertainty in the law relating to marriage and the absence of provision for the registration of customary unions, operating within the framework of restrictions upon the right of wives to remain in urban areas, have contributed to the growth of concubinage and promiscuity in the towns. The disintegration of family life among Africans in the towns is a serious problem. While many African leaders are aware of the need for reform of the law, the general attitude of the African people toward proposals they see merely as increasing the controls imposed upon their lives by the white man is one of suspicion and distrust.

Government policy aims at the extension of tribalism. In the sphere of administration, recent legislation is designed to subject the urban African increasingly to the influence of tribal authority. During sixteen years of rule the government has turned a deaf ear to proposals for inquiry into legal disabilities suffered by the Africans. There is no indication at the present time that the Department of Bantu Administration and Development intends to deal with the question. In these circumstances there are no grounds for anticipating any change in the existing tendency of native commissioners to apply indigenous customary law, without regard to changes in African society.

In the Transkei, the government intends to use the courts as a means of entrenching tribalism. Under the Transkei Constitution Act, passed in 1963, which purports to confer "self-government" upon this area of the Cape Province,[82] the state president of the Republic of South Africa is empowered to constitute a high court of the Transkei, that is, to enjoy a status and to exercise powers and jurisdiction corresponding to those of the Supreme Court in any South African province. This court, unlike the native commissioners' courts, does not have the discretion to apply customary law, but is *obliged* to do so "in all suits and proceedings between parties involving or based on questions of Bantu custom."[83] It is thus powerless to hold that the common law should be applied, even if the circumstances (e.g., the fact that the parties are detribalized) are such that justice would best be served by applying the common law. The provision that decisions of the High Court, unlike decisions of a native appeal court, may be taken on appeal to the Appellate Division is likely to aggravate the confusion surrounding customary law in South Africa by making it possible for the same rule of customary law to receive one interpretation in the Transkei (given by the Appellate Division), and another in a different area of the Cape Province (given by the native appeal court).[84]

It is clear from the foregoing discussion of some aspects of the recognition and application of customary family law that South Africa, like all the former British territories in Africa, has faced problems resulting from the coexistence within one country of dual legal systems based on distinct bodies of law derived from different sources. In South Africa, as in the British territories, solution to the conflict between customary law and the law of the land was sought through judicial interpretation and legislative action to adapt customary law to changing conditions. In the British territories, the adaptive process took place within a framework of increasing African participation in the government of colonies moving toward independence. In South Africa, on the other hand, adaptation has been subject to an overriding bias in favor of tribalism, frequently expressing itself through the courts, as we have seen, and reinforced by laws in the making of which the Africans have no say whatsoever.

11.

THE FUTURE OF AFRICAN LAW

by Antony N. Allott

The future of African law is a subject upon which one hesitates to pontificate or prophesy. It is humbling to remember that if one had asked the question "What is the future of African law?" a hundred years ago, or fifty or ten years ago, or even four years ago, one might well have received a different answer each time from the one that might now be given. And this is to ignore the fact that persons occupying different positions—anthropologists, judges, practicing lawyers, administrators, professors of law, politicians, traditional tribal authorities, and indeed even different persons occupying comparable positions—were and are likely to respond differently to this question, according to their varying analyses of the situation, their geographical location, their race, and their political and social attitudes. In these circumstances how is one to give a general answer, valid both now and in the future, to this general question? All one can hope to do is to mention some of the undoubted facts of African legal history, show in what ways African law has already changed or been consciously altered, and, extrapolating from existing policies or trends, indicate some of the likely lines of development.

It is worth remembering, too, that the categories of persons to whom the question of the future of African law is posed have changed within the last hundred years. It is very doubtful whether a hundred years ago any colonial administrator would have bothered to question the indigenous authorities which were then administering the customary law as to the way in which that customary law should develop; the initiative, and the answers, came from the colonial governments or from the British judges, even if, to realize their objectives, they had on occasion to obtain the acceptance of these objectives by the local authorities through persuasion and agreement. Equally today, though for utterly different reasons, the present African governments do not feel it necessary to obtain the prior agreement of the traditional authorities to changes in the law; still less is the initiative to make such changes left to the traditional authorities. There are, however, apparent exceptions to this last observation; for example, the Tanganyika government's program of unification of customary law relies on persuading the local, *not* the traditional, authorities to accept an altered personal law, and no change that has not been supported by local opinion will in fact be introduced in that locality; and in several places the power to declare and, if necessary, to modify the applicable customary law is given to the appropriate traditional authorities.

I say that these exceptions are apparent rather than real because the guiding lines to which all changes must conform are laid down by the central authority; it is only the local implementation of these changes, or the proposal of changes in detail which will be in conformity with these guiding lines, which is left to local initiative or approval.

Until fairly recently, in many parts of then British Africa, African law—if by that we mean "African customary law"—was considered the peculiar and exclusive field of the administrator and the anthropologist; the legislatures, the higher judiciary, and the law officers tended to think of it as outside the strict legal field, and hence as outside their own purview. If it was a question of ascertaining the customary law, that could be left to the native court or to the district commissioner in the individual case, or to the anthropologist if a more thorough investigation was required; if it was a question of changing that law, such change was started at the grass-roots level. There was, of course, some legislative interference with the customary law—for example, one of the first acts of the colonial power often was to ban barbarous modes of trial and punishment—and there were territories where the higher judiciary had a more active part to play (e.g., in the Gold Coast Colony and in southern Nigeria). But only in recent times has there been any major participation by judges, law officers, and parliaments in the work of developing the indigenous legal institutions.

Changing Attitudes to African Customary Law

There could be no better way of marking changing attitudes to the customary law in Africa than to note the changing definitions of "African law" at different periods. There is a certain ambiguity in the term, giving rise to doubts as to the existence of an externally isolable and internally coherent body of laws describable as African law.

In earlier times "African law," if the term had been used (which it usually was not, an expression like "native law" being preferred),[1]

[1] For notes to chapter 11, see page 257.

would doubtless have been taken to mean the law of Africans, that is, of the native populations of African colonial territories. In this sense "African law" would have had a faintly derogatory implication, as if the law of the natives was not real law in the same way as the introduced English or other European law, often described as "English law" in the legislation of the time. Insofar as the colonial power had created a legal framework in a colonial territory, this framework, and the general law regulating colonies and their government, would have been referred to as "colonial law." I am aware of no attempt at this stage to distinguish terminologically the law of African possessions from the law of possessions in other parts of the world.

In more recent times the existence of indigenous legal systems in Africa, suitable for collective study on a comparative basis, has been recognized, more particularly in the universities through the creation of posts and courses in African law. What in the earlier period were thought of merely as "native law and custom," and hence assimilable to native law and custom in Asia or the Pacific, or else as a number of separate tribal laws, were now treated as constituting a family of legal systems which could be studied as a whole. The acceptance of this position did not imply the existence of any fundamental uniformity in African legal systems, still less of a single type of African law with local variations; but it did imply that the geographical contiguity and the comparable histories and backgrounds of the peoples subject to these laws, and the character of the laws themselves, were such that it had become meaningful to study them in this way.

Still more recently there have been two interesting developments. The first stems from the ending of the colonial era in Africa. With the handing over of power to, or its seizure by, the indigenous peoples, the distinction between the native or indigenous laws of the African peoples and the received laws of European origin ceases to have relevance. It is true that differences in origin, principles, and methods of European and indigenous legal institutions continue to exist until altered or removed; but the source of the laws, whether African or European, is in a fundamental political sense the same: it is the will of the people subject to the laws. Customary law had in the past been the people's law, springing directly from the African consciousness and molded to their own desires and practices by those subject to it, whereas English law had been an imposed and alien thing, corresponding imperfectly, if at all, to African structures and aspirations. This distinction is no longer valid. It is now in the power of African governments to modify or reject the legal inheritance they received at the moment of independence; if they choose to retain or to build on this inheritance they make such laws their own. All laws in independent Africa are now "African," and African law no longer means simply the indigenous customary laws deriving from antiquity, but the modern statutory laws as well; in other words, African law is the totality of African legal systems. At this point one might well ask: Does the mere fact that legal systems are to be found in the same continent give them anything in common? Is not "African law" now an empty term, like "European law"? The attempt to answer this question can help us to define all that is different, all that is "African," in modern African legal systems, and help us to appreciate the unique problems that Africa faces in the legal field.

The second development to which I have referred is that the African peoples themselves are now beginning to search for the common factor in African laws. Internally and internationally it is becoming imperative for African leaders to exploit every factor that may lead to unity. So shaky are the foundations upon which the African successor states are built that the maintenance and the enhancement of national solidarity are matters of the highest priority. The accidents of colonial history have presented African states with artificial and arbitrary boundaries, which often include peoples of different culture and divide those who share the same language or institutions. The forces of disintegration are strong; everything that divides one part of a new nation from another must therefore be eliminated or controlled. Prominent among the potentially divisive factors is the existence of a multiplicity of personal laws, whether customary, local, or religious in origin; the unification of personal laws and the progressive elimination of intertribal legal variations have already been actively pursued in many of the African states, such as Senegal, Guinea, Ghana, Northern Nigeria, Tanganyika, Malawi, and Kenya.

Yet, in an effort to stimulate national pride and self-consciousness, it is necessary for African governments to emphasize everything that is African, everything that is valuable in the African past. High on the list of such African elements are the traditional African institutions and values as expressed in their legal systems. Parallel with this feeling is the desire to break away from the overpowering influence of introduced European institutions. The aggrandizement and development of African legal institutions are an important part of the Africanizing process.

Internationally, too, African leaders are seeking ways of strengthening African unity. If it were possible to isolate or evolve a common African law, or at least to strengthen the bonds created by sharing a common attitude to life and legal problems, African unity would be substantially reinforced. A Pan-Africanist approach to African law is therefore in political vogue. Colonial laws, like colonial boundaries, stand in the way of this policy. There is no greater apparent gulf than that between the civil-law and common-law systems (although to an outsider, such as a traditional African legal expert, they look just as alike as two African legal systems do to a European), and one way of bridging this gulf may well be by a resort to African legal forms.

African Legal History and the Present Situation

It may be helpful to recall briefly the path followed by African legal history, and thereby to delimit the present situation of African legal systems. We shall then be in a better position to appreciate the nature of the problems faced by African governments today, and to understand the reasons for their answers to those problems as inspired by the attitudes I have been discussing.

THE PRECOLONIAL ERA

There are three major periods in African legal history. In the precolonial era indigenous legal institutions were evolving, more rapidly than is sometimes appreciated, on a tribal or local basis. Each legal system was autonomous, though there was some cross-cultural influence and the laws of macroethnic groups tended to keep their similarity. The laws were unwritten, except where Islam and the law of the sacred texts had intruded. There were enormous variations in the structure and the content of legal and judicial systems between societies with differing political structures (e.g., between chiefly and acephalous societies) or economic backgrounds (e.g., between pastoralists and agriculturalists). Although deriving mainly in theory from ancient custom, in practice the indigenous laws relied on the contributions of legislation by state, tribal, or local authorities and on judicial formulation by adjudicators or arbitrators for many of their detailed rules and for the modification of rules to suit changing circumstances.

THE COLONIAL ERA

The arrival of European colonial powers wrought a fundamental revolution in African legal arrangements, the results of which are with us to this day. The nature of the revolution varied somewhat with different colonial powers, but in general each power first introduced its own legal system or some variant of it as the fundamental and general law of its territories, and, second, permitted the regulated continuance of traditional African law and judicial institutions except where they ran counter to the demands of colonial administration or were thought repugnant to "civilized" ideas of justice and humanity. Although the introduction of Western legal systems into Africa may seem the most conspicuous and significant consequence of European rule, in the long run the conscious preservation, for reasons either of high policy or of inertia, of much of African customary law may be no less important. Had it not been for this intervention, African legal history might well have taken a different turn; other conquerors, or local dynasts, might have been less hesitant in doing away with the systems of law previously in force.

The impact of colonialism on African law was not limited to the first shock; it was a continuing process of overt reform and indirect pressure for change. In the British territories the reforms tended to concentrate on the machinery of justice, that is, on the native courts and the procedure they followed, rather than on the substantive law administered in such courts. The customary law was left more or less as it was except where considerations of public order or policy obtruded.

The contribution of the legislative authorities was thus limited. One searches in vain for any comprehensive codification of customary law, excluding the Natal Native Code, or other legislation radically reforming or even consolidating the customary law. Slavery and torture disappeared, of course; but the rest of the law went on much as before. The British method favored the creation of parallel institutions rather than the replacement of existing indigenous institutions by new Western ones. Customary marriage and divorce and African family structures continued, but marriage ordinances created facilities for the conclusion of monogamous marriages by Africans, which it was hoped would lead to the formation of family units on the Western model. Similarly, in the field of land tenure, English land law was often introduced to provide an alternative means of transferring or holding property, though the customary land laws usually continued in force. (One must remember that in many areas legislation was passed to protect indigenous African holdings, such as the Land and Native Rights Ordinance in Northern Nigeria; the effect was to create legal, and often physical, reservations into which English land law did not penetrate.) It is surprising to find that the parallelism extended even to the field of criminal law; in most British territories the indigenous customary criminal laws were preserved, at least in part, coexisting with the Western-type criminal law, which was usually codified.

To summarize, colonial rule in practically all the territories produced a fundamental dualism in the legal and judicial systems, with the introduced and the indigenous laws existing side by side, often applied by different systems of courts—territorial or British courts and native courts—to different classes of persons. African law usually applied to

Africans only, subject to trifling exceptions in West Africa and Northern Rhodesia, in cases where a non-African contracted with an African and a court found that to rely strictly on English law would result in substantial injustice to either party.[2]

THE INDEPENDENT ERA

The era of independence began as recently as 1957, when Ghana attained its independence; indeed, most of the new African countries have gained independence only in the last two or three years. It is therefore still too early to recount in detail the exact terms of the definitive legal arrangements which African countries have chosen. Shortages of draftsmen and parliamentary time, if nothing else, have inhibited rapid or radical change; nevertheless, much has already been achieved to overcome the disadvantages associated with the legal systems left over from the colonial period.

In former British dependencies, the legal system at the moment of independence was practically the same as that immediately prior to it; the colonial system was carried on until altered. Some countries have been quicker than others to deal with the system they inherited (Ghana and Tanganyika, for example), but the main point of attack has usually been the judicial system. The most striking changes have been in the direction of unification of the courts systems. This trend has implied (1) the integration of the appellate structure by permitting appeals to lie from the lower, formerly native, courts to the superior courts; (2) the Anglicization or standardization of the practice and procedure of the native courts, assimilating their procedure to that of the general law courts; (3) the harmonization of the laws administered by these courts by facilitating the application of the statutory law in the local courts and the customary law in the general law courts; and in some places (4) the extension of the jurisdiction of the local courts to non-Africans. The parallel type of judicial system, as formerly existed in Kenya, Tanganyika, and Sierra Leone, is rapidly vanishing.[3]

Less has been done in the field of substantive law reform in the common-law countries, except in areas exclusively governed by statutory or English law. Patent law, company law, contracts, and labor law are examples of such areas.

It is instructive to ask if any significant difference in legislative achievement is noticeable between African countries that are independent and African territories that still remain dependent. Has the fact of independence signified any new slant in legislation? The answer, in the general field with which we are concerned, is almost certainly in the affirmative. One might compare the performance of Kenya and

Tanganyika, for instance. Both countries are committed to the integration of the local or African courts systems; but, whereas Tanganyika has already gone more than three quarters of the way in the march to total unification, Kenya is barely beyond the preliminary stage. Both countries have schemes for recording and unifying customary law; the Tanganyika scheme is far more ambitious in its aim, being nothing less than the unification of customary personal law, while Kenya is doing no more at this stage than record what is there. Both countries are endeavoring to eliminate the dualism in their land laws; but, whereas official thinking in Kenya, at least in the preindependence period, seemed to favor unification based on adoption of a simplified English law, the policy of the Tanganyika government draws inspiration from the desire to remove some of the Anglicisms from their land law and to revert to a more African conception of property rights.

The basic difference in approach to law reform, however, is to be found in the attitude of legislators. Independent governments of strongly nationalist persuasion are committed to revindicating the African social heritage, to Africanizing the laws and institutions. This urge has been entirely absent from territories that are still not self-governing; in them the projects of law reform are elaborated by expatriate legal civil servants. But in the purely technical field, as, for example, in commercial law, there is little to choose between the performance of independent governments and that of dependent governments. The logic of economics is stronger than any political ideology.

To summarize, parallelism or dualism has not yet disappeared from any of the legal systems. In some places, such as Ghana, the courts are more or less integrated, but nowhere in Africa is there yet a single national system of common law applying equally to all persons within the territory. The fundamental dualism between national or common law and local, customary, or religious laws persists.

Legislative Tasks of the New African Governments

The tasks of the new African governments constitute a heavy burden. These governments must (1) modernize their legal systems in line with current economic and social needs; (2) unify their legal systems; and (3) Africanize their legal systems.

MODERNIZATION

Even had there been no independence, no urge toward rapid economic development, no desire to build a new nation, there would still have been a serious problem of technical law reform in African countries. The lag in legal reform programs during the colonial period means that much lost ground must be regained. The modernization of company law in Ghana is one of many examples of the improvements that are needed.

To this backlog of law reform must be added the demands for radical economic and social transformation. Modernization has been piecemeal so far in ex-British territories, although in some English-speaking countries—Liberia, Ethiopia, and the Somali Republic—there has been a general revision of the laws. Whether any Commonwealth country will venture to enact a comprehensive civil code on the continental model remains to be seen; the impulse toward general law reform is present, but the machinery is lacking. The program of modernization of national institutions is the background against which the more limited legal problems must be set. It serves as a signpost indicating the direction toward which legal reform, even in the sphere of customary law, must move. Modernization may thus be an obstacle hindering the Africanization of the legal system, insofar as the latter connotes a return to the past. At the same time the demand for modernization, implying that something must be done about the legal system, provides an opportunity for achieving the other two aspects of the reform program: Why not, while modernizing the law, ensure that it is unified and more African?

UNIFICATION

Dualism has remained in the legal system, and, to a lesser extent, in the judicial system. Although often linked together, and having repercussions on each other, the integration of courts and the integration of laws may be viewed as two separate problems. Integrate the courts, at least by creating a chain of appeal, by establishing common practice and procedure, and perhaps by extending the courts' jurisdiction to all persons, and soon the question will arise: Why should different bodies of law be applied to different classes of litigants or in different types of cases? Conversely, if different bodies of law applying to different classes of persons are retained, the argument for retaining courts that are expert in those laws becomes much stronger.

Either way, the decision to retain or to abolish special courts administering special bodies of law will obviously have a significant effect on the development of customary laws. Still more profound, of course, will be the consequences of a decision to unify the laws. Unification may take place at either of two levels.

Low-level unification.—At the first level of unification, the basic dualism of the legal system is retained, but each component is internally unified and standardized. In common-law countries the process presents no difficulty for the English or Western-type component, as all that remains to be done is to assimilate the imported law with the law formulated by colonial or independent legislatures. For example, the legislature of the Western Region of Nigeria repealed the statutes of general application which were in force in England on January 1, 1900, and had previously formed part of the Western Nigerian legal system, and enacted new laws in their stead. The region has not, however, integrated the received common law and doctrines of equity into a single Western Nigerian legal system; one must still look outside the region for the source and the content of a major part of its legal system. Legal autarky is not complete.

The problem is very much more complicated for the special law component of African legal systems. Even countries that lack the additional complications caused by religious personal laws usually have a multiplicity of customary laws varying from one another in some degree. To what extent is it possible to eliminate local or tribal variations and to evolve a common customary law applicable throughout the land? In a few areas—Buganda, Basutoland, Swaziland, Bechuanaland, Somali Republic—unified customary law already exists or could easily be devised, but elsewhere the answer is not so simple. In Ghana, Nigeria, Kenya, Tanganyika, Zambia, and even tiny Gambia the problem is one not merely of differing laws (as the laws of American states might differ from one another), but of different types of society; it may be impossible to devise a unified land law for the pastoral seminomadic Masai and the settled Kikuyu, for example. Complete unification of customary laws seems practicable only in areas that already possess substantial similarity in both laws and social circumstances.

This last dictum would not be accepted unreservedly by some governments and their advisers, or by some judges and textbook writers, in contemporary Africa. A government tends to assign the goals first, and then to call for the means of attaining them; it does not first conduct a survey in order to sen the limit of practical possibilities. Usually it is not a question of whether or not there will be a unified personal law, but only of how to minimize the damage to the existing legal institutions and to win the greatest degree of popular assent to fundamental changes in institutions. Some law officers, themselves imperfectly acquainted with any customary law (or, if they are Africans, with any customary law except their own), assume the similarity of customary laws on very shaky and superficial grounds. Judges in the superior courts are not immune from a similar attitude. In the colonial days it was not unusual to hear orotund pronouncements from the bench on "native law and custom," as if there were one uniform system from one end of Africa to the other. Today the personnel of the courts has changed, and so have the motives for such pronouncements; nevertheless, judicial assertions that customary law is the same throughout a particular country or even a particular region of Africa are frequently found in contemporary law reports.

The northern half of Ghana may well serve as a typical instance of the unwitting violence that may be done to indigenous legal institutions in the pursuit of a mythical unity of laws. Until recently a case originating in the Northern Territories of the former Gold Coast (later the Northern and Upper regions of Ghana) could rarely if ever reach the Supreme Court or be written up in the law reports; one searches in vain for any Northern Territories case in the Gold Coast law reports. The judges sitting at Accra or elsewhere in southern Ghana thus had no conception—except a very garbled one based on the erroneous belief that many of the population of the north were Muslims and spoke Hausa—of the indigenous legal institutions of the north. Anthropological research in the north was either more limited than in the south, or not of a style to appeal to the uninstructed reader. There were no northern barristers or judges to give guidance to the courts.

Today the jurisdiction of the superior courts covers the whole of Ghana, and the government is making a determined effort to promote uniform legislation throughout the country; an example is the Administration of Lands Act, 1962. Projects for unification of the succession law have been discussed. The legislation, prepared by legal advisers drawn from the southern half of the country, typically employs Akan customary concepts (e.g., of the stool or of family property) which are wholly or partly inapplicable to the very different people of the north. Some unofficial writers on these subjects have advocated country-wide unification and codification of the personal laws, maintaining that they are all fundamentally similar, that is, that they all recognize the institution of the family, though perhaps with varying definitions, or that the law of intestate succession generally holds that the deceased's self-acquired property vests in his family and becomes family property. Codification of the customary laws of succession, they argue, would merely entail scheduling two patterns of succession, one patrilineal and one matrilineal. The crudeness of this analysis is staggering; far from regarding all the peoples of the north and the south as sharing common legal institutions, it is hardly appropriate even to lump together the laws of all the matrilineal peoples of southern Ghana, or to see the laws of the patrilineal peoples living in the south (such as the Ga, the

Adangme, the various branches of the Ewe, the Kyerepyong, etc.) as forming a coherent and consistent group.

Comprehensive unification.—The second level of unification is replacement of a system of laws by a single system. Such unification in the field of criminal law has already been achieved in some countries (e.g., Nigeria has eliminated unwritten criminal offenses), but progress has been much slower in other branches of the law. The demand for unification at this level is inspired, at least in part, by the desire to remove the quasi-extraterritorial privilege enjoyed by non-Africans insofar as they are exempted or excused from obligations imposed by customary laws. It rankles deeply that an act committed by an African subject to customary law may give rise to civil or criminal liability which a non-African committing the same act may escape merely by proving that he is a non-African. The feeling of some African politicians that the present dualistic legal system makes them inferior persons in their own land is especially strong when criminal and tortious liability is concerned. An African who commits adultery with a married woman or seduces a young girl will probably be liable under customary criminal or civil law, whereas a European or an Asian would not be. This specific illustration has been cited in countries as far apart as Ghana and Malawi as justification for the unification of courts and for the extension of customary law to non-Africans. Under the present legislation in Ghana,[4] a plaintiff may decide whether to sue by customary law or by the common law (both terms being specially defined in the Ghana law) if no other rule for choice of law applies and if he himself is subject to any system of customary law in Ghana.

AFRICANIZATION

In the political sphere independent African governments, especially those that are strongly influenced by nationalist thinking, are committed to finding "African" solutions to the problems facing their countries. Many African countries today reject, or say they reject, slavish copying of political institutions from either side of the iron curtain; instead, they seek to evolve a specifically African type of polity. This polity, which reflects the community-centered approach of traditional African society, may be described as "African socialism."

In the legal sphere the desire for Africanism is also present, though it is not always so forcibly expressed. Most African leaders have not yet made so thorough a study of the legal problems and needs of their countries as of their political problems. (President Nkrumah of Ghana is one of the few exceptions.) Gradually, however, African governments and those who lead them are beginning to consider how to develop their legal institutions and at the same time to make them more genuinely African.

Criminal law.—The problem of Africanization has arisen in part because the legal systems of independent African countries are fundamentally those given them by the former colonial rulers. The colonial powers made little attempt to adapt to African circumstances the institutions they imposed. A typical example is criminal law. In every Commonwealth country or territory in Africa south of the Sahara, criminal law was closely based on European models or on models ultimately derived from Europe. In the common-law areas, except for Sierra Leone, it is codified as a penal or criminal code; in the Roman-Dutch areas of southern Africa, it is mainly uncodified.

In the early days of British administration in West Africa, the criminal law administered was uncodified and was virtually the same as that contemporaneously applied in England. Only toward the end of the nineteenth century did codification begin in the Gold Coast Colony, with the introduction of a criminal code in 1892. It was based on a code originally prepared for Jamaica, and in fact adopted in St. Lucia. In Northern Nigeria a criminal code partly derived from that of Queensland, and hence from English law, was introduced in 1904. Until 1930, the predominant influence on criminal law in East Africa was Indian, and the Indian Penal Code was in force throughout the area. In 1930 a penal code based on that of Nigeria was adopted in eastern Africa. More recently (in 1959), Northern Nigeria moved away from the Nigerian Criminal Code and adopted a new code derived from that of the Sudan and ultimately from that of India.

The mere recital of these facts is enough to reveal the dearth of original thinking in the field of African penal law. Codes originally drafted for the West Indies, India, or Australia could hardly have anything African about them. Furthermore, all these codes have, in varying degree, been influenced by the language and the structure of English criminal law, though some (e.g., the Indian) made some concessions in favor of a more comparatist and eclectic approach. But unless one argues either (1) that what is good enough for a native in India is good enough for a native in East Africa (precisely this kind of muddled thinking justified the original introduction of Indian law into East Africa), or (2) that the codes are so drawn as to be of universal application, it is difficult to see how such codes could possibly express African institutions or attitudes to crime and punishment. One searches in vain, except in the Northern Nigerian Penal Code, for any but the most trivial concession in this direction; and on the whole it is true that such codes could perfectly well be applied in England or the United States, for example, without doing too much damage to social institutions and without confusing criminals as to the treatment they might expect to receive.

Insofar as an African element was preserved in African criminal law, it was done through the maintenance in force of customary criminal laws. These are now under strong and not always subtle attack, first, for being unwritten, and, second, for being out-of-date or unprogressive. The sphere of customary criminal law is being cut down by legislation that either repeals it or orders local African courts to be guided by the appropriate criminal code in their area (as in Northern Nigeria and Uganda).

The Westernization of existing legal systems explains in part why any move toward Africanization is so difficult; there is so much lost ground to be made up. But there are also positive reasons that present obstacles to such a move. The most noticeable is the sheer juristic difficulty of isolating and adapting traditional or typically African legal concepts, values, and institutions for use in modern African legal systems. How is one to find, and once found, how is one to incorporate, African elements in the new law? Kenya's recent experience with the recording of customary criminal law may be illuminating.

After the London Conference on the Future of Law in Africa (Dec., 1959–Jan., 1960), the Kenya government decided that it would, in pursuance of resolutions adopted by the conference, undertake the writing down of the customary criminal law in force in the territory. As it happened, the quantum of customary criminal law being applied in Kenya's African courts was much less than in many other British territories, less even than in adjacent Uganda and Tanganyika; the size of the problem was therefore limited.

The Restatement of African Law Project in the University of London, invited by the Kenya government to assist in the task of ascertaining the customary laws, lent the colonial government a research officer, whose work has now been completed.[5] He found a number of offenses that were generally treated as such by the customary laws in different parts of Kenya, even if their exact definition varied from area to area. Notable among these were adultery, enticing a married woman, incest, receiving a second bride-price during the subsistence of a marriage, removing boundary marks made by indigenous elders, and abusing a person of a higher age-grade. The details of the offenses as stated by local experts in each area were duly recorded. The discussion as to what use could be made of these data illustrates the difficulties facing any African government that is trying to determine the future of African law in its territory.

How genuine was the customary law that was recorded by the process of consulting recognized local experts in Kenya? It might seem that nothing more remained to be done, but unfortunately their statements could not be accepted as the most authoritative presentation of the appropriate law. Many of the so-called criminal offenses have been recognized as such only since the arrival of British rule and since the establishment of African courts and local authorities by the British. Before that time many of these offenses, such as adultery, were civil wrongs only, attracting not punishment but compensation or restitution. In any event, the source of some offenses was not custom, even modern custom, but local legislation by African district councils or paralegislation (e.g., by law panels). The local experts consulted usually were senior judges, officials or members of African courts, or African local authorities; both their positions and their seniority tended to make them representative of an older, more traditionalist generation. There were doubts, therefore, as to how far their statements corresponded with the law actually observed (or rather, not observed) by the younger, better-educated generation and by residents in urban centers. The voice of women, especially important in family and matrimonial affairs, was almost entirely silent.

With the question of genuineness of the customary law is linked another question, one that is central to the present study: To what extent does the existing customary law represent the opinions of those subject to it about the shape of their future legal arrangements? This query in turn leads to a question of public policy: Even if the statements, assuming that they genuinely record the existing law, also reveal people's desires about the future law, are their desires acceptable to the nation as a whole, or do they extend beyond the fundamental parameters of social and economic planning? In order to answer these questions, one must define the parameters, a task that in its turn raises the question of uniformity in the personal laws; although in form the law dealt with is criminal and public, yet the offenses concerned touch intimate private and personal arrangements which are differently ordered among different elements of the population. Should the unification of personal laws be attempted at a low level, by bringing together different customary laws, or at a higher level, by unifying them on a national scale?

Partial low-level unification of customary criminal law was in fact carried out during the execution of the Kenya recording scheme. Unification was achieved partly by the style and presentation of the recordings, which tended to be uniform for different laws, and partly by a conscious attempt to persuade the people concerned to reduce or remove unnecessary local variations in their laws. At provincial meetings discrepancies between the laws of different groups in a particular province were discussed and, if possible, eliminated. The opportunity was also taken to improve the recorded law so as to make it correspond more closely with current structures and necessities; for instance, the offense of "abusing a person of a higher age-grade," which in detail reflects a social structure that is now disappearing, was modified to become "abuse likely to cause a breach of the peace." Changes or proposed changes in other customary offenses were generally of a kind to make easier any future unification of customary and statutory laws. What is the next step in Kenya? There are several alternatives. (1) The customary criminal law might be consolidated with the Penal Code, either by introducing new statutory offenses or by broadening or varying the wording of existing provisions of the code. This solution seems the obvious one when a customary offense closely parallels a statutory one; examples are misappropriation of property, abuse in a public place, circumcision of a person without his consent, removing boundary marks, and taking an unmarried girl from the custody of her parents. If there is no parallel in the code, a fundamental change must be made in the law; the most obvious example would be to make adultery a statutory offense. It is worth remembering that in the Indian Penal Code, which was in force in Kenya until 1930 and applied to all races, adultery is an offense. Although the tiny non-African minority might object if this change in the law affected them, it is questionable that such an objection would be sustainable in the political situation of emerging Kenya. (2) Customary criminal offenses might be codified in one form or another, but in such a way that they would continue to apply to Africans only. Such codification could either establish a uniform definition of offenses throughout Kenya, or allow the retention of variations between the laws of different localities. (3) The situation might be left unchanged. All except the last solution would imply the disappearance of customary criminal law in Kenya, though some of its essential characteristics and features might be retained in statutory form.

Criminal law is by no means the only branch of law which calls for intensive investigation and reform in contemporary Africa; the law of adjudication and arbitration, the law of succession, family law, the law of marriage and divorce, the law of property, the law of tort or delict—all clamor for attention. In this brief presentation it is not possible to give them all the extended treatment they deserve, but a few words about the problems involved and about the future of African customary law may not be out of place.

Adjudication and arbitration.—It now seems to be taken for granted that African courts, and the African style of adjudication, are to disappear from Africa. "Improvement" of the African local, customary courts means in effect their disappearance through assimilation with the courts of European type. In the common-law countries, personnel, procedure, and jurisdiction are all to be progressively Anglicized. Although continual improvement in the lower courts is both vital and inevitable, the advantages that African courts and procedure may have had should not be overlooked. I summarize them briefly as follows:

1) Justice was popular. The people could understand the machinery and the purposes of judicial arrangements, and the law applied by the courts. Often the people had control over the courts and those presiding over them, and in many places participated directly in judicial proceedings.

2) Justice was local and speedy. The first point needs no development; the structure of African traditional judicatures reflected the needs of the local community rather than any desire for administrative efficiency or ease of supervision from the center. The argument that justice was speedy may seem to require justification, as the contrary has often been argued, especially by outsiders. It is true that traditional judicial proceedings in Africa can and could be long drawn out, especially by the wish to ensure that no person's opinion would go unregarded, or that no fact that might have a bearing on the successful conclusion of the case would be overlooked. But no one contemplating the history of modern land litigation in West Africa, with its interminable appeals dragging on from court to court, could argue that African justice was slow in comparison; modern Western-style justice is often slow precisely because it is not local or popular. Using the elaborate procedures of the English law of evidence, the courts require proof of facts that would have been well known without special proof to a traditional African tribunal.

3) Justice was simple and flexible. There were no elaborate codes of procedure or evidence, though there were procedural and evidentiary rules, of course. A confrontation in detail of African and English ideas about evidence shows the advantage to lie in many respects with the African system. One healthy consequence of the desire to Africanize the legal system might be to devise an altogether different approach to the law of evidence, which, from the English side, is bogged down in technicalities dating back to the exigencies of a quite different, and now vanished, system of trial. Flexibility is to be observed, not only in the ease with which African courts avoided the procedural snags that often give English justice a bad name, but in what may be called the "arbitral approach to justice." In many African courts the judge would try, not merely to administer the law, but to find a solution to

the dispute which would appear just to the parties and would put a stop to further litigation between them; if the law had to be stretched, or even to be ignored, in the process, this was justifiable if peace and harmony were restored. And there existed outside the courts a whole apparatus of arbitration, a system by which the parties endeavored to compose their differences peaceably with or without the assistance of an arbiter, mediator, or conciliator; even in places where arbitral proceedings were not systematized, the willingness to resort to peaceful and informal means for the settlement of disputes was omnipresent.

Modern African legal systems (i.e., the statutory systems erected by the colonial powers) have adopted different approaches to the arbitral element in judicial proceedings and to extrajudicial arbitral or conciliation proceedings. Western-type legal procedures barely recognize the paramount importance of litigation as a way of removing a social grievance through the elimination of dispute, and many English-style judgments are doomed to exacerbate, and not to terminate, ill-feeling between the litigants. Some legislatures have tried to repress extrajudicial arbitrations as a "usurpation of judicial powers" which threatens the work of the established courts; others have tolerated them; but none appear to have welcomed them as a foundation on which to build a new and more civilized judicial system.

The use of compulsory conciliation in matrimonial disputes is only just beginning in the common-law world, as the damage done to husband-wife relationships by too-speedy recourse to the courts has come to be appreciated. African law has long since known all about matrimonial conciliation proceedings; indeed, conciliation is an integral and conspicuous part of traditional African matrimonial law, though legislators in British territories had done much to sabotage it by referring matrimonial disputes to the courts. In practically all customary marriage laws, the families or guardians of the spouses have a continuing function in helping to maintain the marriage in being, or in hearing about and suggesting solutions for matrimonial problems that may arise between husband and wife; indeed, in some customary laws certain relatives on either side may be specially designated as "guardians of the marriage." Now at last there are signs of a new approach on the part of African legislatures; in Ethiopia the Civil Code, 1960, codifies the traditional African procedure of dealing with matrimonial disputes by extrajudicial familial arbitration, and in Ghana the proposed new marriage law would employ an adapted, though less satisfactory, form of arbitration by local arbitration panels, instead of judicial proceedings, when a divorce is sought.

The law of succession.—In succession law there are many problems.

First, there is the problem of dualism, or rather multiplicity, of laws. In the countries with legal systems based on English law a statutory system of succession closely based on that of England, or on that of India, exists side by side with customary systems and, in areas where Hindu and Islamic law are recognized, with Hindu and Muslim laws of succession. Conflict between customary systems is increased through movement and interchange of populations; it is especially acute where both patrilineal and matrilineal systems exist, as in Zambia or Ghana. Conflict between customary law and Islamic law in succession matters raises certain questions. To what extent should personal laws that vary with a man's religion be recognized? Is personal law a matter for the individual or for the community to which he belongs? If the latter, is the community to be constituted by his race (with different systems of succession for Africans and non-Africans, as in many areas), by the local ethnic group or community to which he belongs (with succession law determined by the local law, whether customary or not), by his class, education, or aspirations (with a different system of succession applied to those who are not living a "customary mode of life" or who have married in the Western form), or by his religion (with an individual's decision to adopt a specific religion taking precedence over the local law that would otherwise have applied to him)?[6]

Succession law, as the most exact mirror of specific social and economic structures and the principal means by which a different sort of society may be built, is, in my opinion, the most significant branch of the customary law to be considered in any examination of the future of African law as a whole. If the succession law goes, the whole fabric of customary law will go with it; if the succession law changes, there will be serious and irreversible repercussions on the way people live.

The most evident sign of reforming activity in the field of succession is concerned with testamentary law. African customary law lacked the institution of the will or testament as known in Europe, though various forms of dispositive succession, notably the nuncupative will or wish, the designation of a successor, the earmarking of property, and so on, can be found. Succession in customary law is typically under the control of the family of the deceased, however the "family" is defined; it is also generally plural, in the sense that there is a plurality of heirs or others entitled to benefit from the estate. The matrilineal systems are those that appear, to some observers, the most inconsistent with a modern economic and social structure (by which in fact they mean a Western structure), as a man's wealth goes not to his own children, but to those of his mother or his sister, or to other matrilineal relatives. These alleged deficiencies in the customary law of succession are cited in support of a radical change in the law, principally by breaking the hold of the family on succession, and by giving the individual, before he dies, greater power to determine how his property shall descend. The power of Africans to make wills is now being extended by legislation. In Kenya a recent ordinance gives Africans the same power to make wills as had already been possessed by non-Africans, while in Zambia extensive use has been made of bylaws framed by native authorities which give a limited power of testation. In Ghana and Nigeria the power to make wills in English form already existed under the received Wills Act, 1837, or analogous legislation; the fact that this power has not been extensively used, except by the educated upper classes, indicates how deep is the distrust of the will as a threat to family solidarity.

Attacks on the customary law of succession are direct attacks on the African family system. In West Africa especially the family or lineage system is sustained by the law of intestate succession, and if the law is changed so that self-acquired property of deceased members no longer goes to enrich the corporate families, then the family as an institution will quickly wither and die.

What is the reaction of African leaders to this possibility? One must be frank and say that on the whole they have not yet devoted much attention to the problem, even though it touches on many of their fundamental principles of economic and social policy. African states are interested in rapid economic growth, in the rapid spread of education, and in the multiplication of individual skills; a system of succession which inhibits individual initiative and vests an individual's wealth, when he dies, in relatives for whom he cares little is an obstacle to such expansion. Hence the massive attacks on traditional succession systems launched by the East African Royal Commission and its successors. But it is not clear that African leaders, at least those who espouse socialism, are as enthusiastic as the Royal Commission was about the expansion of unrestricted private enterprise; and so there are signs, at least in East Africa, that governments may go slow in the total implementation of the commission's suggestions.

African leaders may also be reluctant to demolish the family system for another reason, a reason of sentiment rather than of economic logic. The family system (*ujamaa* in current Tanganyikan thinking) is seen as the core of the African approach to social living. "We Africans," a typical argument runs, "are quite different from individualistic and selfish Europeans; our traditional social systems have always emphasized our obligations to our brothers, real or notional, rather than our personal rights. We do not want to lose this precious part of our African heritage."

Still other influences are at work, notably the wish to move toward national uniformity in personal laws. Religious laws, different customary laws, and even the law by which a different system of succession is applied to a person who has contracted a monogamous marriage, divide citizen from citizen. This division is a major cause of the introduction of proposals for the partial unification of succession laws in Ghana, as outlined in the Marriage, Divorce, and Inheritance Bill. How governments are to reconcile these contradictory impulses (if, indeed, they can reconcile them) which drive them in different directions is a question whose answer has not yet emerged.

Family law.—The social structures of modern Africa, around which so much of the customary law is built, are rapidly changing. What, if anything, will survive? There are many pressure points (quite apart from the law of succession). The cohesion and discipline of, and the justification for, extended family groupings are threatened; the previously unquestioned authority of the father over his child, of the uncle over his nephew, of the husband over his wife, is questioned. Not only education, religion, and new economic opportunities inspire this questioning; a mere look at the legal institutions imported from England is enough to instigate an unfavorable comparison. Examples of the challenge to existing family law are innumerable: the right of wives to sue their husbands for divorce; the enhancement of the legal status of women generally; the disallowance of traditional rules regarding the custody of children when they infringe the paramount interests of the child's welfare; marriage without parental consent; disregard of the rules of exogamy; the decline in legal importance of wider social groupings such as the clan or the lineage; and the abandonment of rules of vicarious responsibility.

The law of property.—Equally vast are the problems that face us in connection with the law of property. Does one want a thoroughgoing communist system, with all the means of production owned or controlled by the state? The answer, in every African state, seems to be negative. There is, however, an interest in using the principles of public ownership, public control, or public interest more extensively than in most Western countries, an interest that springs partly from a belief that traditional African property, and especially land-tenure, systems were communalistic or community-oriented. Here another obstacle meets the law reformer in Africa, namely, that delimitation of needs and formulation of policies are not enough; expansion of our knowledge and understanding of existing institutions is also required. Ignorance or misconceptions can be a powerful hindrance to the achievement of appropriate solutions.

The notion that African land tenure is communal is deep-rooted in the thinking of both alien and indigenous observers. No received idea has been more misleading or damaging. It is perfectly true that African property law is based on or built around groups and communities of various sorts; but at the same time most serious students of particular property regimes in Africa are prepared to admit that such regimes are far from communism or communalism in any strict sense, and that the scope for individual interests and individual initiative usually is and was large. A new African property law based on a complete misconception about the old would be a disaster.

Tort or delict.—In recent thinking or writing about African law, little attention has been paid to this branch of the law, despite the fact that the law of civil wrongs is intimately linked with the average man's ideas of right and wrong behavior toward the fellow members of his society. One has to find out what were the traditional rules regarding liability for civil wrongs, what values these rules expressed, to what extent the introduced European laws of civil wrongs embody similar values, whether a new African law of civil wrongs is needed, and, if so, how it can be constructed.

In the common-law countries of Africa the current English law of civil wrongs is an untidy mess. It has never been systematized, and it is hidden in quite different parts of the law—in the law of torts, of matrimonial offenses, of quasi contract, of trusts, of contract. Its underlying premises are often out of date; its categorization derives from antique forms of procedure of no relevance in England and still less relevance in Africa. If nothing else is done in the sphere of law reform in Africa, there is a clamant need to reform and, if possible, to codify the law of civil wrongs.

This process would at the same time provide a golden opportunity to create an African law of torts. There is no need to retain dual systems of torts; why should the law that applies to an African tort-feasor be different from the one that applies to a non-African tort-feasor? A unified law of civil wrongs could incorporate just as many traditional African values and principles as desired. The change would be less radical than might be supposed, for modern English tort law is rapidly moving in the direction of African law. The extension of strict liability and insurance principles, and the movement away from fault, bring English law closer to the African emphasis on responsibility rather than on blameworthiness.

The Shape of Future African Legal Systems

What will African legal systems look like in the future, once these movements for reform have had an opportunity to produce results? It all depends on what one means by "the future." It is as difficult to prophesy what African legal systems will look like a hundred years from now as to foretell the state of American or English law at the same time. If a mid-Victorian English lawyer had ventured to forecast the shape and content of the 1963 English legal system, how accurate would he have been? There is much that he would still recognize in our legal system. We still use his cases and he could use some of ours; the language is not dissimilar; the general structure of the law, its divisions into branches, the functions (even the dress!) of the legal profession and the bench, are not so different, even though the courts have been reformed, law and equity have fused, and completely new branches of law have evolved. But in fact there are some startling differences, to which the mid-Victorian would find it difficult to adjust: a Chancery lawyer would not be happy to find that the majestic body of doctrine called equity is now a ragbag of shredded principles loosely clinging to, or completely woven into, the fabric of the law; the common lawyer would be disturbed to find that legislation, and not the common law, is now the paramount source of law; the property lawyer would feel out of sympathy with the destruction of his ancient learning; the lay justice would be dismayed to find that there was little room for lay magistrates in the new judicial system. And the law teacher of Victorian times would discover that the continuity in institutions and language was often merely a cloak for fundamental changes, and that the resemblances were superficial and frequently less significant than the differences. And yet English law today would still proclaim its descent from the English law of yesterday, and no one could mistake it for the child of another father, say, the French Civil Code.

The ultimate fate of African law may not be so different. Lay judges, especially the indigenous judges trained in the customary law, are making way for trained men. African customary laws as self-sufficient, integrated systems will vanish just as equity has vanished. The language of African law may be retained, but the substance will be different. Legislation, and not the unwritten customary law, will become the main source to which the lawyer looks to find the rules of so-called African law. But let us remember that even the modern judges of England do not despise the learning of an earlier age, and on occasion even have to hark back to Tudor or even to Plantagenet times to uncover the origins of the common law. It may well be that future generations of judges in Africa will be obliged to do likewise with their own laws.

It is, however, more instructive to focus on the foreseeable future, rather than the distant future, for its elements are more controllable and predictable from our vantage point. What, then, will African legal systems be like in ten years' time?

The courts, as we have seen, will be unified, though special tribunals may have been retained for special types of cases, and specialist divisions may have been created in the high courts to handle customary-law cases. Customary law, as a body of unwritten rules deriving from habitual conduct, will have largely disappeared. In its place we will find either a recorded version or restatement of the customary laws, having semiofficial status but lacking the authority and finality of a code, or codes replacing the customary law, though not necessarily doing away with all of its principles and institutions. Such codes may be codes of personal law, like the Natal Code, or they may go further and establish uniform national laws instead of the existing statute, common, and local laws. Customary law will thus in practice cease to be "customary." The close connection formerly existing between a particular customary system and a particular community will also be broken in many areas through the emergence of unified laws handed down from above rather than evolved from below.

The codes will in part be African in inspiration, in that they will try consciously to express traditional African legal values. The extent to which they are African will vary according to (1) the state of research (at centers inside or outside Africa) into African customary law and into comparisons of that law with English and other laws; (2) the extent to which African governments are prepared to use and rely on such research; and (3) the relative importance assigned by African leaders to Africanism as compared with modernization. But the Africanism of the new African codes will be far removed in fact from that of the traditional law, as the principles will have been abstracted from the social situation that gave them birth. The basic structure of the codes, and the legal categories and the language they employ, will on the whole be English, though there may be new African codes drafted in African languages (e.g., in Swahili for Tanganyika or in Hausa for Northern Nigeria), which would imply a profound alteration in the style of the code and its handling by the judges. The family laws provide a good example of the possibilities; the family and relationship systems, and the physical, moral, and supernatural beliefs upon which they rested, are dying and cannot be revived. But, just as in English law the legal institutions of today are often the ghosts of the social institutions of yesterday, so it is possible that new African law will be able to retain and entrench some of the fundamental principles upon which the family law of the past was based.

The famous Fanti Bond of 1844, signed between the British governor of the British possessions on the Gold Coast and some of the chiefs under his protection, regulated the jurisdiction exercised by the British authorities in the forts over crimes committed outside them. The final clause of the bond provided that "Murders, robberies and other crimes and offences will be tried and inquired of before the Queen's judicial officers and the chiefs of the district, moulding the customs of the country to the general principles of British law." It is a startling and salutary thought that the trend of contemporary law reform in English-speaking Africa is exactly that: to mold the customs of the country to the general principles of English, or at least Western, law. What started as a hope has now become a reality. But the contrary movement, though less publicized, is no less important: the principles of English law are being molded to the general principles of African law. It may well be that English law, once it has been reformed and quickened by the transfusion of all that is best in African law, will be reexported to the country from which it came. In such an eventuality, the long legal contact between England and Africa will have been mutually enriching; and African law, no less than African sculpture or African music, may become a source of universal inspiration.

NOTES

NOTES

1. *Introduction*

[1] Among the more important are Sir Henry Maine, *Ancient Law* (Everyman ed.; New York: Dutton, 1917); Bronislaw Malinowski, *Crime and Custom in Savage Society* (London: Routledge & Kegan Paul, 1926); H. I. Hogbin, *Law and Order in Polynesia* (New York: Harcourt Brace, 1934), with an introduction by Bronislaw Malinowski; A. S. Diamond, *Primitive Law* (London: Watts, 1935), and *The Evolution of Law and Order* (London: Watts, 1951); K. N. Llewellyn and E. Adamson Hoebel, *The Cheyenne Way* (Norman: University of Oklahoma Press, 1941); R. H. Lowie, *Primitive Society* (New York: Liveright, 1947); B. ter Haar, *Adat Law in Indonesia*, ed. with introduction by E. Adamson Hoebel and A. Arthur Schiller (New York: Institute of Pacific Relations, 1948); Max Gluckman, *The Judicial Process among the Barotse of Northern Rhodesia* (Manchester: Manchester University Press, 1955), and *The Ideas in Barotse Jurisprudence* (New Haven: Yale University Press, 1965); T. O. Elias, *The Nature of African Customary Law* (Manchester: Manchester University Press, 1956); L. S. Morgan, *Ancient Society* (1877) (London: Routledge & Kegan Paul, 1959); E. Adamson Hoebel, *The Law of Primitive Man* (Cambridge: Harvard University Press, 1954). Additional references to the literature, including contributions by jurisprudents, are listed in the bibliography at the end of this volume.

[2] A. R. Radcliffe-Brown, "Primitive Law," *Encyclopedia of the Social Sciences*, IX, 202-206; and *Structure and Function* (Glencoe, Ill.: Free Press, 1952); Malinowski, *op. cit.*

[3] Max Weber, in one of the major and eclectic contributions to the sociology of law, is specially concerned with ideational elements. He distinguishes the formal-substantive and rational-irrational categories of legal thought in law finding and lawmaking, and relates these to the historical and structural contexts of the societies in which they emerged. See Max Rheinstein, ed., *Max Weber on Law in Economy and Society* (Cambridge: Harvard University Press, 1954).

[4] *Structure and Function*, p. 212.

[5] For examples of African societies see E. E. Evans-Pritchard, *The Nuer* (Oxford: Clarendon Press, 1940); Paul Bohannan, *Justice and Judgment among the Tiv* (London: Oxford University Press, 1957); Meyer Fortes, *The Dynamics of Clanship among the Tallensi* (London: Oxford University Press, 1945); P. H.

Gulliver, *Social Control in an African Society: The Arusha, Agricultural Masai of Northern Tanganyika* (Boston: Boston University Press, 1963); J. Middleton and D. Tait, eds., *Tribes without Rulers* (London: Routledge & Kegan Paul, 1958). International law is often cited as an example of law in a world society where there are no courts with compulsory jurisdiction.

[6] Bohannan, *op. cit.*; and *Social Anthropology* (New York: Holt, Rinehart & Winston, 1963), chap. 17.

[7] See S. F. Nadel, *Foundations of Social Anthropology* (London: Cohen & West, 1949), pp. 132 ff.

[8] H. L. A. Hart, *The Concept of Law* (Oxford: Clarendon Press, 1961), pp. 94-95. Hart writes, "Indeed, a system which has rules of adjudication is necessarily also committed to a rule of recognition of an elementary and imperfect sort . . . . The rule which confers jurisdiction will also be a rule of recognition, identifying the primary rules through the judgments of the courts and these judgments will become a 'source' of law." See also the critical comments made by Morris Ginsberg in his review article, "The Concept of Law," *British Journal of Sociology*, XIII (March, 1962), 64-69.

[9] See Max Gluckman, "African Jurisprudence," *Advancement of Science*, XVIII (Jan., 1962), 439-454.

[10] *Ibid.*, p. 449.

[11] See M. G. Smith, "Social and Cultural Pluralism," *Annals of the New York Academy of Sciences*, LXXXIII (Jan., 1960), 763-777; and Leo Kuper, "Sociology: Some Aspects of Urban Plural Societies in Africa," in *The African World: A Survey of Social Research*, ed. R. A. Lystad (New York: Praeger, 1965).

[12] The typological or morphological approach to "traditional societies" must not be confused with the historical or chronological approach. We use the term primarily in a historical sense, and recognize the diversity of types of traditional society.

[13] For a description of the Kuba market system see Jan Vansina, "Trade and Markets among the Kuba," in *Markets in Africa*, ed. Paul Bohannan and George Dalton (Evanston: Northwestern University Press, 1962).

[14] For descriptions of the Lozi see Max Gluckman, "The Lozi of Barotseland," in E. Colson and M. Gluckman, eds., *Seven Tribes of British Central Africa* (Manchester: Manchester University Press, 1959), and *The Judicial Process among the Barotse.*

[15] According to information given to Gluckman (see "The Lozi of Barotseland," p. 232). Also see Paul Bohannan, "Extra-Processual Events in Tiv Political Institutions," in *Cultures and Societies of Africa,* ed. Simon and Phoebe Ottenberg (New York: Random House, 1960), pp. 328-341.

[16] See the discussion of this point by Arthur Phillips, "The Legal Factor in a Changing Africa," *African Affairs,* LIV (1955), 281-282.

[17] D'Arboussier phrases the argument in terms of a policy of assimilation; the argument would be the same if phrased in terms of the French theory of law as discussed here.

[18] Robert Delavignette, *Freedom and Authority in French West Africa* (London: Oxford University Press, 1950), p. 49.

[19] Ter Haar, *op. cit.*, pp. 11-14.

[20] Michael Crowder, *Senegal* (London: Oxford University Press, 1962), chap. 2.

[21] There is difficulty in comparing an explicitly formulated theory of law with

a theory of law derived from legal apparatus and practice. An explicit theory may in fact be at variance with practice.

[22] *Justice and Judgment among the Tiv*, pp. 5-7.

[23] For comments on African reactions to imprisonment see Elias, *op. cit.*, pp. 285 ff., and Bohannan, *Justice and Judgment among the Tiv*, p. 68.

2. *The Sociological Framework of Law*

[1] Adriano Moreira, "General Report, Ethnic and Cultural Pluralism in the Inter-Tropical Societies: Legal and Political Aspects," in *Record of the XXXth Meeting*, International Institute of Differing Civilizations (Brussels, 1957), p. 496.

[2] *Ibid.*, p. 498.

[3] M. G. Smith, "Ethnic and Cultural Pluralism in the British Caribbean," in *Record of the XXXth Meeting*, International Institute of Differing Civilizations (Brussels, 1957), pp. 443-444.

[4] Ernest Barker, Introduction to Otto Gierke, *Natural Law and the Theory of Society* (Boston: Beacon Press, 1960), p. lxxxvii.

[5] W. Robertson Smith, *Kinship and Marriage in Early Arabia* (Cambridge: The University Press, 1885).

[6] Reuben Levy, *The Social Structure of Islam* (Cambridge: The University Press, 1957), p. 165. For a fundamental study of the part these elements played in the growth of Muslim law, see Joseph Schacht, *The Origins of Muhammadan Jurisprudence* (Oxford: Clarendon Press, 1950).

[7] H. Lammens, *L'Islam: croyances et institutions* (Beyrouth, 1926), p. 104. See also G. E. von Grunebaum, *Medieval Islam* (2d ed.; Chicago: University of Chicago Press, 1953), pp. 149-152; Schacht, *op. cit.*, pp. 82-97. I should like to stress that the nature and the role of *ijmā*ʿ in Muslim law are matters on which specialists may differ.

[8] Levy, *op. cit.*, pp. 259-261.

[9] Koran 4:62 (cited by von Grunebaum, *op. cit.*, p. 157).

[10] Von Grunebaum, *op. cit.*, pp. 163-164.

[11] *Ibid.*, p. 164.

[12] M. Hiskett, "*Kitāb al-farq*: A Work on the Habe Kingdoms Attributed to ʿUthmān dan Fodio," *Bulletin of the School of Oriental and African Studies* (University of London), XXIII (1960), 566-568.

[13] C. W. Cole, *Land Tenure in Zaria Province* (Kaduna, 1948), pp. 32-41, 65, 69, 74-82.

[14] Levy, *op. cit.*, pp. 243, 244, 248.

[15] Max Weber, *The City*, trans. and ed. Don Martindale and Gertrud Neuwirth (London: Heinemann, 1960), pp. 168-172.

[16] Aristotle, *Ethics* 1134^{b} 18-21; *Rhetoric* 1373^{b} 4.

[17] H. G. Hanbury, *English Courts of Law* (London: Oxford University Press, 1944), chaps. 2-4.

[18] St. Thomas Aquinas, *On the Governance of Rulers* (1259), cited in Robert Bierstedt, *The Making of Society* (New York: Modern Library, 1959), pp. 52-57.

[19] Bierstedt, *op. cit.*, pp. 60-76.

[20] Max Rheinstein, ed., *Max Weber on Law in Economy and Society* (Cambridge: Harvard University Press, 1954), pp. 274-275; Barker, *op. cit.*, pp. xxxix-xlii.

[21] Barker, *op. cit.*; Ernest Barker, Introduction to *Social Contract: Essays by Locke, Hume and Rousseau* (London: Oxford University Press, 1947).

[22] Rheinstein, *op. cit.*, p. 275.

[23] Gierke, *op. cit.*, pp. 45-47, 77-79.

[24] *Ibid.*, pp. 70-76.

[25] Thomas Hobbes, *Leviathan* (1651), chaps. 13-15, 17-30. See also Richard Peters, *Hobbes* (London: Pelican Books, 1956), pp. 190-239.

[26] John Salmond, *Jurisprudence* (10th ed.; London: Sweet and Maxwell, 1947), p. 60.

[27] Oliver Wendell Holmes, *The Path of Law* (1897), cited in C. K. Allen, *Law in the Making* (6th ed.; Oxford: Clarendon Press, 1961), p. 42.

[28] B. N. Cardozo, *The Growth of the Law* (New Haven: Yale University Press, 1924), p. 52.

[29] Sir Henry Maine, *Ancient Law* (new ed.; London: J. Murray, 1905), p. 6.

[30] Allen, *op. cit.*, pp. 66-67.

[31] A. R. Radcliffe-Brown, "Primitive Law," *Encyclopedia of the Social Sciences*, IX, 202, quoting Roscoe Pound, *Readings on the History and System of the Common Law* (Boston: Boston Book Co., 1913), p. 4; Roscoe Pound, *Jurisprudence* (St Paul, Minn.: West Publishing Co., 1959), I, 13-14. See also E. Adamson Hoebel, "Letter to Editor," *American Anthropologist*, LXIV, no. 4 (1962), 36-37.

[32] A. R. Radcliffe-Brown, "Social Sanction," *Encyclopedia of the Social Sciences*, XIII, 531-534, reprinted in his *Structure and Function in Primitive Society* (London: Cohen & West, 1952), p. 208.

[33] R. M. MacIver, *The Modern State* (Oxford: Clarendon Press, 1926), p. 22.

[34] Sidney Hartland, *Primitive Law* (London: Methuen, 1924), p. 138.

[35] *Ibid.*, pp. 8, 214.

[36] Sir Henry Maine, *Lectures on the Early History of Institutions* (London: J. Murray, 1875).

[37] Sir Paul Vinogradoff, *Common Sense in Law* (London: Oxford University Press, 1913), p. 119.

[38] *Ibid.*, chap. vi; Allen, *op. cit.*, pp. 64-152.

[39] Emile Durkheim, *The Division of Labour in Society* (1893), trans. G. Simpson (Glencoe, Ill.: Free Press, 1947).

[40] Emile Durkheim, *Professional Ethics and Civil Morals*, trans. C. Brookfield (Glencoe, Ill.: Free Press, 1958); and *Socialism and Saint-Simon*, trans. Charlotte Sattler (Yellow Springs, Ohio: Antioch Press, 1958), chap. 8.

[41] Bronislaw Malinowski, *Crime and Custom in Savage Society* (London: Routledge & Kegan Paul, 1926), p. 15.

[42] *Ibid.*, p. 46.

[43] E. Adamson Hoebel, *The Law of Primitive Man* (Cambridge: Harvard University Press, 1954), p. 28.

[44] Vinogradoff, *op. cit.*, p. 23. On the distinction between perfect and imperfect law, see p. 31. Nullity (*butlan*) exists in Muslim law; in *'urf* it exists in the sense that omission of "economical" nullifies the binding character of the act.

[45] Rheinstein, *op. cit.*, p. 5.

[46] *Ibid.*, p. 13.

[47] Moreira, *op. cit.*, p. 502.

[48] Levy, *op. cit.*, chaps. 4, 6-8.

[49] Allen, *op. cit.*, chaps. 3-7.

[50] Martin Southwold, *Bureaucracy and Chiefship in Buganda*, East African Studies no. 14 (Kampala: East African Institute of Social Research, [*ca.* 1960]); Audrey I. Richards, ed., *East African Chiefs* (London: Faber & Faber, 1960), chap. 2.

[51] Lorna Marshall, "Kung Bushmen Bands," *Africa*, XXX (1960), 225-355; and "Sharing, Talking, and Giving: Relief of Social Tensions among Kung Bushmen," *Africa*, XXXI (1961), 231-249.

[52] Georges Gurvitch, *Sociology of Law* (London: K. Paul, Trench, Trubner, 1947), p. 156.

[53] Maine, *Ancient Law*, chap. vi; Vinogradoff, *op. cit.*, pp. 54-60.

[54] Robert Delavignette, *Freedom and Authority in French West Africa* (London: Oxford University Press, 1950), pp. v-vi.

[55] *Ibid.*, pp. 91-92. See also Lord Malcolm Hailey, *An African Survey* (London: Oxford University Press, 1938), pp. 185-206, 484-491.

3. *Land Law in the Making*

[1] Cf. *Report of Kenya Land Commission, September 1933* (London: H.M.S.O., 1934). Land tenure "should be progressively guided in the direction of private tenure" (par. 1650). "Some direction by authority is necessary. . . . Government should take and use the power to make rules" (par. 1408).

[2] Gusii country was first opened up by the British in the early 1900's, about twenty years before the start of the period we are considering here.

[3] In one Gusii area, Getutu, a rudimentary chieftainship seemed on the point of emerging when the British took over; the organization of descent groups and local communities was different in this area also. In this paper we refer to conditions outside Getutu. For the peculiarities of Getutu see Phillip Mayer, *The Lineage Principle in Gusii Society*, International African Institute, Memorandum XXIV (London: Oxford University Press, 1949), esp. pp. 14 f., 28 f.

[4] The system was applied with some differences in Getutu (see *ibid.*, p. 2 n. 2).

[5] *Ibid.*

[6] See Philip Mayer, *Gusii Bridewealth Law and Custom*, Rhodes-Livingstone Papers, no. 18 (London: Oxford University Press, 1950), p. 5.

[7] Arthur Phillips, *Report on Native Tribunals, Colony and Protectorate of Kenya* (Nairobi: Government Printer, 1945). Paragraph 113 gives figures for the year 1942 as follows: Gusii (Kisii), 5,835 civil cases, Luo, 1,543; Gusii, 895 appeal cases, Luo and Bakuria, 190.

[8] Cf. Philip Mayer, "Agricultural Cooperation by Neighbourhood Groups among the Gusii," in *Two Studies in Applied Anthropology in Kenya* (London: H.M. S.O., 1951), pp. 5-19.

[9] Max Gluckman, "Kinship and Marriage among the Lozi of Northern Rhodesia and the Zulu of Natal," in *African Systems of Kinship and Marriage*, ed. A. R. Radcliffe-Brown and Daryll Forde (London: Oxford University Press, 1950).

[10] Cf. Mayer, *Gusii Bridewealth Law and Custom.*

[11] Here again there was a somewhat different pattern in one Gusii tribe, Getutu (see Mayer, *The Lineage Principle in Gusii Society*).

[12] *Ibid.*, p. 28.

[13] Cf. Philip Mayer, "Bridewealth Limitation among the Gusii," in *Two Studies in Applied Anthropology in Kenya*, pp. 19-33.

4. *Justice and Judgment among the Southern Ibo under Colonial Rule*

[1] References for this chapter include E. W. Ardener, "Lineage and Locality among the Mba-Ise Ibo," *Africa*, XXIX (1959), 113-133; G. T. Basden, *Among the Ibos of Nigeria* (Philadelphia: J. B. Lippincott Co., 1921); L. T. Chubb, *Ibo Land Tenure* (2d ed.; Ibadan: Ibadan University Press, 1961); Daryll Forde and G. I. Jones, *The Ibo and Ibibio-speaking Peoples of South-eastern Nigeria*, Ethnographic Survey of Africa (London: International African Institute, 1950); M. M. Green, *Ibo Village Affairs* (London: Sidgwick & Jackson, 1948); G. I. Jones, "Dual Organization in Ibo Social Structure," *Africa*, XIX (1949), 150-156, and *Report on the Position, Status and Influence of Chiefs and Natural Rulers of the Eastern Region of Nigeria* (Enugu: Government Printer, 1947); C. K. Meek, "Ibo Law," in *Essays Presented to C. G. Seligman*, ed. E. E. Evans-Pritchard *et al.* (London: K. Paul, Trench, Trubner, 1934), and *Law and Authority in a Nigerian Tribe (Ibo)* (London: Oxford University Press, 1937).

[2] *Op. cit.*

[3] Jones, *Report on the Position, Status and Influence of Chiefs and Natural Rulers* . . ., p. 1.

[4] *Ibid.*, p. 2.

5. *A Traditional Legal System: The Kuba*

[1] Paul Bohannan, *Social Anthropology* (New York: Holt, Rinehart & Winston, 1963), p. 283.

[2] Paul Bohannan, *Justice and Judgment among the Tiv* (London: Oxford University Press, 1957), pp. 160-161. Theoretical notions used in this chapter are derived mostly from Professor Bohannan (see his *Social Anthropology*, pp. 7-14), who views the interpretation of society and culture of another people as a problem first of translation; he assumes no a priori theoretical model. Professor Gluckman, who represents an opposite trend, holds that distinctions and categories in the field to be studied should be set up first (cf. Max Gluckman, *The Judicial Process among the Barotse of Northern Rhodesia* [Manchester: Manchester University Press, 1955]; and "African Jurisprudence," *Advancement of Science*, no. 714 [Nov., 1961]). It seems to me that the translation approach avoids preconception.

[3] There are also too few data available.

[4] Cf. Gluckman, *The Judicial Process among the Barotse*, for the Lozi. Here the court is also the council. In Rwanda the chief is judge, administrator, legislator, and lord.

[5] The cowry was the local currency before 1900.

[6] Bohannan, *Justice and Judgment among the Tiv*, pp. 96-97, elaborates this idea.

[7] Cf. Gluckman, *The Judicial Process among the Barotse*, chap. iii.

[8] Cf. *ibid.*; Bohannan, *Justice and Judgment among the Tiv*; and Pierre Gravel, "The Play for Power" (unpublished Ph.D. dissertation in anthropology, University of Michigan, 1962), who gives the best available data for the legal system in Rwanda.

[9] Cf. Bohannan, *Justice and Judgment among the Tiv*, pp. 4-5.

6. *Reasonableness and Responsibility in the Law of Segmentary Societies*

[1] Some of the analysis of liability and responsibility in this paper is given in more extended form in my Storrs Lectures, delivered at the Yale Law School in April, 1963 (published as *The Ideas in Barotse Jurisprudence* [New Haven: Yale University Press, 1965]). An excellent complement to my analysis is S. F. Nadel, "Reason and Unreason in African Law," *Africa,* XXVI (April, 1956), 160-173.

[2] This brief was sent to me by Professor Hilda Kuper in a letter dated January 25, 1963.

[3] I summarize the development of analyses stressing this point in "Les Rites de Passage," in *Essays on the Ritual of Social Relations,* ed. Max Gluckman (Manchester: Manchester University Press, 1962), and in *Politics, Law, and Ritual in Tribal Society* (Oxford: Blackwell, 1965).

[4] Paul Howell, *Manual of Nuer Law* (London: Oxford University Press, 1954).

[5] Paul Bohannan, *Justice and Judgment among the Tiv* (London: Oxford University Press, 1957).

[6] E. Adamson Hoebel, "Three Studies in African Law," *Stanford Law Review,* XII (March, 1961), 418-442. See also Max Gluckman, "Comment: The Role of the Barotse King in the Judicial Process," *Stanford Law Review,* XIV (Dec., 1961), 110-119, in which I comment on one of Hoebel's queries. J. G. Marsh was also critical of my use of the "reasonable man" in "Sociological Jurisprudence Revisited: A Review (More or Less) of Max Gluckman," *Stanford Law Review,* III (May, 1956), 499-534, to which I replied in the same journal.

[7] S. F. Nadel, in his review of Howell's and my books (*op. cit.*), expresses doubt on this point.

[8] Howell, *op. cit.,* p. 227; see also pp. 138-139.

[9] *Ibid.,* p. 140.

[10] *Ibid.,* pp. 147-148.

[11] *Ibid.,* p. 194.

[12] E. E. Evans-Pritchard, *The Nuer* (Oxford: Clarendon Press, 1940), p. 89.

[13] Gluckman, *The Ideas in Barotse Jurisprudence.*

[14] E. Adamson Hoebel, *Political Organization and Law Ways of the Comanche Indians* (Menasha, Wis.: American Anthropological Association, 1940).

[15] K. N. Llewellyn and E. Adamson Hoebel, *The Cheyenne Way* (Norman: University of Oklahoma Press, 1941). See p. 27 on "unreasonable spanking."

[16] *Ibid.,* p. 23 (referred to in Max Gluckman, *The Judicial Process among the Barotse of Northern Rhodesia* [Manchester: Manchester University Press, 1955], p. 128).

[17] Llewellyn and Hoebel, *op. cit.,* pp. 20-21.

[18] *Op. cit., passim.*

[19] S. F. Nadel, *The Nuba* (London: Oxford University Press, 1947), pp. 501 f. See also Nadel, "Reason and Unreason in African Law," *passim.*

[20] *Op. cit.,* pp. 41 f.

[21] *Ibid.,* pp. 39 f.

[22] R. F. Barton, *The Kalingas,* ed. E. Adamson Hoebel (Chicago: University of Chicago Press, 1948), pp. 222-223. Alfred L. Kroeber, *Handbook of the Indians of California,* Bureau of American Ethnology, Bulletin 78 (1925), p. 20, also speaks

of a "reasonable balance" of work by a uxorilocal Yurok husband, and of reasonable cause for divorce and due cause.

[23] J. G. Peristiany, "Pokot Sanctions and Structure," *Africa*, XXIV (Jan., 1954), 17-25.

[24] Howell, *op. cit.*, p. 17.

[25] *Ibid.*, pp. 41-42, 52, and *passim.*

[26] *Ibid.*, pp. 44 f.

[27] R. F. Barton, *Ifugao Law* (Berkeley: University of California Press, 1919), p. 74.

[28] M. J. Meggitt has a good discussion of breach of grave sacred rules in relation to the doctrine of "reasonableness" in *Desert People* (Sydney: Angus & Robertson, 1962).

[29] *Custom and Conflict in Africa* (Oxford: Blackwell, 1955), chap. i. For the position of other societies see my *Politics, Law, and Ritual in Tribal Society*, chap. iii.

[30] Howell, *op. cit.*, pp. 41-42, 45-46, 52, 59.

[31] *Ibid.*, p. 55.

[32] Evans-Pritchard, *op. cit.*, pp. 162 f.

[33] Howell, *op. cit.*, pp. 26 f.

[34] Elizabeth Colson, "Social Control and Vengeance," in *The Plateau Tonga of Northern Rhodesia* (Manchester: Manchester University Press, 1962).

[35] Nadel, *The Nuba*; and "Reason and Unreason in African Law."

[36] Bohannan, *op. cit.*, pp. 33-34.

[37] *Ibid.*, p. 21 (Case 3).

[38] *Ibid.*, pp. 79-93 (Cases 31, 36, 39, 43).

[39] *Ibid.*, p. 90.

[40] *Ibid.*, p. 92.

[41] *Ibid.*, pp. 79-80.

[42] *Ibid.*, pp. 86-87.

[43] *Ibid.*, p. 83.

[44] *Ibid.*, p. 92.

[45] *Ibid.*, p. 18.

[46] *Ibid.*, pp. 170 f.

[47] *Ibid.*, p. 58.

[48] *Ibid.*, pp. 172 f. (no. II).

[49] *Ibid.*, pp. 180 f. (no. III).

[50] *Ibid.*, p. 37.

[51] *Ibid.*, pp. 105-106.

[52] *Ibid.*, pp. 134-135.

[53] *Ibid.*, pp. 25-26.

[54] *Ibid.*, p. 60.

[55] *Ibid.*, p. 135.

[56] I discuss this situation fully in *Politics, Law, and Ritual in Tribal Society.*

[57] Bohannan, *op. cit.*, pp. 65 f.

[58] *Ibid.*, pp. 103-104.

[59] *Ibid.*, p. 64.

[60] *Ibid.*, p. 41; see also preceding pages and p. 47.

[61] *Op. cit.*, pp. 251 f.

[62] Gluckman, *The Ideas in Barotse Jurisprudence.*

[63] A. L. Epstein, *Judicial Techniques and the Judicial Process* (Manchester: Manchester University Press, 1954).
[64] Hoebel, "Three Studies in African Law," p. 436.
[65] *Ibid.*, pp. 438-439.
[66] Howell, *op. cit.*, pp. 128-135, 156.

7. *The Adaptation of Muslim Law in Sub-Saharan Africa*

[1] Joseph Schacht, *The Origins of Muhammadan Jurisprudence* (Oxford: Clarendon Press, 1950), *passim.*
[2] Cf. Joseph Schacht, *Law in the Middle East* (Washington, 1955), p. 35.
[3] Examples are *bay' al-igāla, bay' al 'uhda,* and *bay' al-khivar.* Cf J. N. D. Anderson, *Islamic Law in Africa* (London: H.M.S.O., 1954), pp. 49, 66, 109, 359-360. For this whole subject of custom in Islam, see N. J. Coulson, "Moslem Custom and Case Law," *The World of Islam,* VI, nos. 1-2 (1959), 13-24.
[4] Anderson, *op. cit.*, p. 24.
[5] *Ibid.*, pp. 26 ff. The pioneer in commenting on early Egyptian legislation of this type was Joseph Schacht, *20 Der Islam* (1932), pp. 209-236.
[6] J. N. D. Anderson, "The Sharī'a and Civil Law: The Debt Owed by the New Civil Codes of Egypt and Syria to the Sharī'a," *Islamic Quarterly*, I, no. 1 (1954).
[7] Cf. J. N. D. Anderson, "Colonial Law in Tropical Africa: The Conflict between English, Islamic and Customary Law," *Indian Law Journal*, XXXV, no. 4 (1960), pp. 436 f.
[8] Anderson, *Islamic Law in Africa,* pp. 166 ff.
[9] *Ibid.*, pp. 222 ff.
[10] *Ibid.*, pp. 111 ff.
[11] J. Spencer Trimingham, *Islam in West Africa* (Oxford: Clarendon Press, 1959), p. 204.
[12] That is, when he loses his milk teeth.
[13] The more usual age is that of weaning; here only the Ithnā' Asharī (among the Shī'ites) can be quoted in support.
[14] Anderson, *Islamic Law in Africa,* pp. 214 f., 234, 245, 262.
[15] *Ibid.*, pp. 209 ff., 240 ff.
[16] *Ibid.*, pp. 208, 233.
[17] *Ibid.*, p. 211.
[18] *Ibid.*, pp. 215 f., 235, 237, 292.
[19] *Ibid.*, pp. 47 ff.
[20] *Ibid.*, pp. 136 ff., 235 ff.
[21] That is, the system is based on the common law as previously codified in the Indian Penal Code or the Queensland Code, for example.
[22] Courts Decree (1923), Sec. 7.
[23] Courts Decree (1923), Secs. 403, 387, 388.
[24] See Anderson, *Islamic Law in Africa*, p. 35.
[25] Evidence Decree (1917), Sec. 2.
[26] Anderson, *Islamic Law in Africa*, pp. 44, 87 f., 104 f., 125, 128 f., 148 f., 164, 178, 228 f., 256, 289, 309 f.
[27] *Ibid.*, pp. 92, 129 f.
[28] *Ibid.*, pp. 44, 62, 129, 255.
[29] *Ibid.*, pp. 106 f., 175.

[30] *Ibid.*, pp. 46 f.
[31] *Ibid.*, pp. 301 f.
[32] *Ibid.*, pp. 225 f.
[33] *Ibid.*, pp. 226 f.
[34] *Ibid.*, pp. 287 ff., 148 ff., 249 ff., 84 ff., 124 ff., 162 ff., 228 ff.
[35] *Ibid.*, pp. 48, 63, 76, 90.
[36] *Ibid.*, pp. 61, 70, 151, 180, 290.
[37] *Ibid.*, pp. 302 ff., 311.
[38] *Ibid.*, pp. 123 ff.
[39] Cf. the Mohammedan Marriage, Divorce, and Succession Ordinance of Kenya, Sec. 4.
[40] Wakf Validating Ordinance (1946), as amended in 1951.
[41] Anderson, *Islamic Law in Africa*, pp. 311 ff.
[42] Frequently, however, the two or more component parts rested, in origin, on mutually contradictory foundations.
[43] See J. N. D. Anderson, "The Modernization of Islamic Law in the Sudan," *Sudan Law Journal and Reports* (1960), pp. 292-312, and "Recent Developments in Sharī'a Law in the Sudan," *Sudan Notes and Records*, Part I (1950).
[44] Civil Justice Ordinance of the Sudan, Sec. 5.
[45] Such decrees are still enforced in Egypt, but this practice, it seems, is soon to be brought to an end.
[46] *Fazalan Satardin v. Din Mahomed,* 11 K.L.R. 41 (1928).
[47] *Fazalan Bibi v. Tehran Bibi*, 8 K.L.R. 200 (1921). The doctrine of *kafā'a* decrees that a woman may not be married to a man who is not her "equal" (in a number of specified respects) unless both she herself and her agnatic guardian consent to such a union.
[48] There are usually two such witnesses, but the number varies according to the nature of the case and the sex of the witnesses.
[49] Cf. also Proclamation No. 13 of 1898 in Kenya (now, of course, repealed).
[50] J. N. D. Anderson, "Wakfs in East Africa," *Journal of African Law*, III, no. 3 (1959), 152-164.
[51] *Abul Fata v. Russomov*, 22 1 A. 76.
[52] J. N. D. Anderson, "The Religious Element in Waqf Endowments," *Journal of Royal Central Asian Society* (July, 1951).
[53] *Talibu bin Mwijaka's Case*, 2 E.A.L.R. 33 (1907).
[54] *Fatuma binti Mohamed bin Salim v. Mohamed bin Salim*, A.C.I. (1952). Cf. Anderson, *Islamic Law in Africa*, pp. 340 ff.
[55] Anderson, "Wakfs in East Africa," pp. 163 ff.
[56] J. N. D. Anderson, "Customary Law and Islamic Law in British African Territories," in *The Future of Customary Law in Africa* (Leiden: Afrika Institut, 1955).
[57] J. N. D. Anderson, "Islamic Law in Africa: Problems of Today and Tomorrow," in *Changing Law in Developing Countries* (London: Allen & Unwin, 1963), pp. 164-183.

9. *The Evolution of Law and Government in Modern Africa*

[1] *King v. Crewe,* 2 K.B. 576 (1910).
[2] *Re Bethell,* 38 Ch.D. 220 (1887). See also T. O. Elias, *British Colonial Law*

(London: Stevens, 1961), pp. 113-166.

[3] See my *Groundwork of Nigerian Law* (London: Routledge & Kegan Paul, 1954), republished as *Nigerian Legal Systems* (2d ed.; London: Routledge & Kegan Paul, 1963), for an illustration of this process.

[4] For an exhaustive analysis of this subject, see Elias, *British Colonial Law*, chap. 10.

[5] *Ibid.*, pp. 20-24.

[6] See my *The Nature of African Customary Law* (Manchester: Manchester University Press, 1956), chap. xiii, for an extended discussion of this subject.

[7] *African Political Systems* (London: Oxford University Press, 1947).

[8] See my *Government and Politics in Africa* (New York: Asia Publishing House, 1961), chap. 4.

[9] See my *Ghana and Sierra Leone: Development of Their Laws and Constitutions* (London: Stevens, 1962), pp. 82-84.

[10] Recent trends seem to favor the gradual replacement of this body by the more orthodox method followed in the United Kingdom and other democracies.

[11] When Nigeria became a republic, this procedure was abolished. Since October 1, 1963, judges can be removed only by a two-thirds majority vote in both houses of Parliament, on the ground of proved misbehavior or of infirmity in body or mind. This is the same process as is used in the United Kingdom and elsewhere.

10. *The Adaptation of Customary Family Law in South Africa*

[1] "I consider that the term 'Roman-Dutch law' is confusing, for in fact the common law of the Union or for that matter of the Cape of Good Hope is not Roman-Dutch law. It is South African common law" (J. P. Claassen in *Rex v. Goseb*, 1956 (2) 696 (S.W.A.) at 698).

"Our country has reached a stage in its national development when its existing law can better be described as South African than Roman-Dutch. . . . No doubt its roots are Roman-Dutch, and splendid roots they are. But continuous development has come through adaptation to modern conditions, through case law, through statutes, and through the adoption of certain principles and features of English law, such as procedure and the law of evidence. The original sources of the Roman-Dutch law are important, but exclusive preoccupation with them is like trying to return the oak tree to its acorn" (J. Holmes in *Ex parte de Winnaar*, 1959 (1) S.A. 837 (N.) at 839).

[2] It is not easy to devise a completely satisfactory term to describe the traditional law applicable to African communities, as modified by legislation and judicial interpretation. At the conference on the future of African law, held in London in 1960, "customary law" and "native law" were the terms used most frequently; alternatives suggested were "native law and custom," "native law," "local law," and "unwritten local law." The discussion, while indicating that all the terms were open to objection on one ground or another, did not result in a unanimous preference for any one of them (see Antony N. Allott, ed., *The Future of Law in Africa* [London: Butterworth, 1960]). I have chosen to use the term "customary law" because it is familiar, convenient, and at least not more objectionable than any of the others.

[3] D. J. Swanepoel, "Oor die Resepsie van die Romeins-Hollandse Reg in Suid-Afrika," *Acta Juridica* (1958), pp. 7-26.

[4] Eric A. Walker, *History of South Africa* (3d ed.; London: Longmans, Green, 1957).

[5] George McCall Theal, "The Report of Commissioners Bigge and Colebrooke, September 6, 1826," *Records of the Cape Colony from February 1793 to April 1831*, XVII, 333, 342; XVIII, 1.

[6] In November, 1772, Warren Hastings wrote to the directors of the East India Company: "We have endeavoured to adapt our Regulations to the Manner and Understanding of the People, and Exigencies of the Country, adhering as closely as we were able to their Ancient Usages and Institutions" (G. W. Forrest, *Selections from the State Papers of the Governors-General of India*, II [London: Constable, 1910], 277).

[7] Walker, *op. cit.*, p. 164; Ordinance No. 40 (1828); Ordinance No. 72 (1830).

[8] E.g., Ordinance No. 6 (1843); Merchant Shipping Act, No. 13 (1855); Joint Stock Companies Act, No. 23 (1861). See also Johannes Wilhelmus Wessels, *History of Roman-Dutch Law* (Grahamstown: African Book Co., 1908).

[9] Wessels, *op. cit.*, chap. 35.

[10] Article 31 of the 33 articles drawn up in 1844 and confirmed by the Transvaal Volksraad in 1849. See G. W. Eybers, *Select Constitutional Documents* (London: Routledge & Kegan Paul, 1918), p. 349; O.F.S. Ordinance No. 1 (1856); Act No. 39 (1896) (Natal), Sec. 21.

[11] Walker, *op. cit.*, p. 500.

[12] See, e.g., *Peters, Flamman & Co. v. Kokstad Municipality*, A.D. 427; *Baines Motors v. Pick*, 1 S.A. 534 A.D. at 543.

[13] Roman-Dutch law as recognized in the Cape was applied in Southern Rhodesia, Basutoland, Bechuanaland, and Swaziland. In these four countries the pattern of interrelation between Roman-Dutch and English law has been similar to that in South Africa.

[14] J. S. Marais, "The Imposition and Nature of European Control," in *The Bantu-speaking Tribes of South Africa*, ed. I. Schapera (London: Routledge, 1946).

[15] Julius Lewin, *Studies in African Native Law* (Cape Town: African Bookman, 1947), chap. 10; H. J. Simons, "The Law and Its Administration," in *Handbook of Race Relations in South Africa*, ed. Ellen Hellmann (Cape Town: Oxford University Press, 1949).

[16] Simons, *op. cit.*; Native Laws and Customs Commission, G4 (1883), par. 8. See also Max Gluckman, *The Judicial Process among the Barotse of Northern Rhodesia* (Manchester: Manchester University Press, 1955).

[17] Lewin, *op. cit.*, p. 107; see also Simons, *op. cit.*

[18] Semour Massingham Seymour, *Native Law in South Africa* (2d ed.; Cape Town: Juta, 1960), chap. 1 and the cases cited.

[19] Marais, *op. cit.*

[20] Act No. 40 (1882), Sec. 17; Act No. 35 (1884), Sec. 3; Act No. 3 (1885), Sec. 3; Act No. 37 (1886); Act No. 45 (1887); Act No. 5 (1894).

[21] Act No. 26 (1894); Act No. 32 (1898). The establishment of the Native Appeal Court resulted in the collection of reports of decided cases, which have provided a valuable systematic record of some aspects of customary law in South Africa.

[22] Royal Instructions, March 8, 1948; Ordinance No. 3 (1849).

[23] Act No. 2 (1894).

[24] Act No. 48 (1898).

[25] *Ibid.*, Sec. 80.

[26] C. J. Innes in *Mcunu v. Mcunu*, 1918 A.D. 323 at 328.

[27] A new code was drawn up in 1891 (Law 19 of 1891). It was replaced by another (G. N. 168 of 1932), which was amended in 1951 (G. N. 364 of 1951). Until 1932 the code of 1878 continued to apply in Zululand; the code of 1891, in Natal. In 1932 the new code promulgated in that year was applied to Natal and Zululand (see W. G. Stafford and E. Franklin, *Principles of Native Law and the Natal Code* [Pietermaritzburg, 1950]).

[28] H. J. Simons, "Marriage and Succession among Africans," *Acta Juridica* (1960), pp. 312-333.

[29] Act No. 22 (1868).

[30] Stafford and Franklin, *op. cit.*, pp. 71-72.

[31] Law 3 (1871).

[32] Law 3 (1897).

[33] Simons, "Marriage and Succession among Africans," comes to this conclusion after a close examination of the Volksraad debates on the bill. One of the speeches included the revealing justification for rejecting the bill: "Een kaffer moest een kaffer blywen."

[34] *Kaba v. Ntela,* 1910 T.P.D. 964; *Meesedoosa v. Links*, 1915 T.P.D. 357.

[35] (1929) 1 N.A.C. (T. & N.) 1. See also E. R. Garthorne, "Application of Native Law," in *Bantu Studies,* no. 3 (1929), pp. 245-259.

[36] Proclamation No. 28 (1902), Sec. 70.

[37] Law 26 (1899), Sec. 28.

[38] Native Administration Act, No. 38 (1927), as amended by Act No. 9 (1929).

[39] Proclamation No. 168 (1932), issued pursuant to Sec. 24 of Act No. 38 (1927).

[40] The first three are provided for by Act No. 38 (1927); the fourth is provided for by Act No. 9 (1929), Sec. 10.

[41] Act No. 38 (1927), Secs. 12, 20, as amended by Act No. 54 (1952) and Act No. 13 (1955), Sec. 1.

[42] It may not, *inter alia*, grant a decree affecting mental capacity, or make an order as to the validity of a will where the estate exceeds 300 pounds in value.

[43] Act No. 38 (1927), Sec. 18; *Ex parte Minister of Native Affairs*, 1941 A.D. 321.

[44] For an example of the exercise of this power, see *Ex parte Minister of Native Affairs in re Yako v. Beyi* (1948) (L) S.A. (A.D.).

[45] Paul Behrmann, "The Native Appeal Courts," *South African Law Journal*, LXV (1948), 413-418.

[46] Act No. 9 (1929), Sec. 10; see also Simons, "The Law and Its Administration," p. 67.

[47] *Ex parte Minister of Native Affairs in re Yako v. Beyi*, at 393.

[48] Leslie Rubin, *The Law of Costs in South Africa* (Johannesburg: Juta, 1949), pp. 163 ff. See also *Mabaso v. Mabaso*, 1946 N.P.D. 183; *Moema v. Zulu*, 1950 (3) S.A. 226 (T.).

[49] Lewin, *op. cit.*, pp. 15 ff.

[50] Simons, "The Law and Its Administration," pp. 55-57.

[51] A. J. Kerr, "The Application of Native Law in the Supreme Court," *South African Law Journal*, LXXV (1957), 313-330.

[52] Act No. 38 (1927), Sec. 11 (1).

[53] J. A. Schreiner in *Ex parte Minister of Native Affairs in re Yako v. Beyi*, at 399.

[54] P. McLoughlin in *Matsheng v. Dhlamini*, 1937 N.A.C. (T. & N.) at 91, and *Kaula v. Mtimkulu*, 1938 N.A.C. (T. & N.) at 70.

[55] Lewin, *op. cit.*, pp. 22-23.

[56] J. A. Schreiner in *Ex parte Minister of Native Affairs in re Yako v. Beyi*, at 395, 397.

[57] See also *Umvovo v. Umvovo*, 1953 (1) S.A. (A.D.) at 201.

[58] When litigants are subject to different systems of customary law, the court must decide which system to apply. Obscure and complex provisions in the Native Administration Act require the court, according to the circumstances, to apply the law of defendant's tribe, the law in force at his residence or place of business or employment, or the law of the tribe among whose members he lives.

[59] Under the Natal Code payment of lobolo is not a requisite, and the bride is required to make a public declaration of consent before the official witness, in addition to her father's consent.

[60] H. J. Simons, "Customary Unions in a Changing Society," *Acta Juridica* (1958), pp. 320-341.

[61] *Ibid.*

[62] The Natal Code lays down maximum amounts and provides for a record of lobolo promised or paid in the register of customary unions.

[63] G.N. 168 (1932), Secs. 76-84. (See n. 27, above.)

[64] *Mfazwe v. Mfikili*, 1957 N.A.C. (S.) 33.

[65] *Bobotyane v. Jack*, 1955 N.A.C. (C. & O.) 9; *Mitayane v. Mate*, 1957 N.A.C. (N.E.) 49; *Kabi v. Punge*, 1955 N.A.C. (S.) 7.

[66] *Dube v. Holden*, 1941 N.A.C. (T. & N.) 129; *Nquambi v. Nquambi*, 1939 N.A.C. (C. & O.) 57; *Mokgatle v. Mokgatle*, 1946 N.A.C. (T. & N.) 82.

[67] Act No. 9 (1929) Sec. 9.

[68] *S.A.N.T.A.M. v. Fondo*, 1960 (2) S.A. 467 (A.D.). The anomaly has since been removed by the Bantu Laws Amendment Act, No. 76 (1963).

[69] Seymour, *op. cit.*, pp. 136 ff.

[70] Matrimonial Affairs Act, No. 37 (1953); Children's Act, No. 31 (1937), as amended.

[71] G.N. 168 (1932), Secs. 53, 82, 83. (See n. 27, above.)

[72] *Mpantsha v. Ngolonkulu*, 1952 N.A.C. (S.) 40.

[73] *Ngakane v. Maalaphi*, 1955 N.A.C. (C.) 123.

[74] Simons, "Customary Unions in a Changing Society," p. 339.

[75] Act No. 9 (1929), Sec. 9. Until 1961 marriage was regulated by a number of provincial enactments. In that year the Marriage Act, No. 25 (1961), consolidated the law by repealing some of the previous laws and introducing certain amendments.

[76] Simons, "Marriage and Succession among Africans." I am indebted to this excellent study for much that is contained in this section of the paper.

[77] *Ex parte Minister of Native Affairs in re Molefe v. Molefe*, 1946 A.D. 315.

[78] G.N. 939 (May 9, 1947).

[79] Seymour, *op. cit.*, pp. 182-185.

[80] See *Duma v. Swales*, 1952 N.A.C. (N. & E.) 275.

[81] Act No. 25 (1961).

[82] The term "self-government" is grossly misleading. The limited powers in internal government which are vested in the Legislative Assembly are effectively in the hands of appointed chiefs who hold 64 of the 109 seats. Furthermore, no

law passed by the Assembly may take effect unless it receives the assent of the state president of the Republic of South Africa.

[83] Act No. 48 (1963), Sec. 50.

[84] For a detailed analysis of the effect of the act on customary law see Neville Rubin, "South Africa: Transkei Constitution Act," *Journal of African Law*, VII, no. 3 (1963), 183-187.

11. *The Future of African Law*

[1] Cf. Mary Kingsley's use of "African law" in a letter to J. M. Sarbah, dated 1898, quoted in J. M. Sarbah, *Fanti National Constitution* (1906), p. 260A.

[2] The position was not dissimilar in the French and Belgian possessions.

[3] In former French territories (e.g., the Ivory Coast), reform of the judicial systems has followed the same general path of unification, though in some instances the changes have been brought about more rapidly and more completely than in former British territories.

[4] Courts Act (1960), Sec. 66(1), rule 6.

[5] Eugene Cotran, *Report on Customary Criminal Offences in Kenya* (Nairobi, 1963).

[6] Cf. the rules regarding choice of law contained in the new Tanganyika legislation (Magistrates Courts Act, 1963, and associated amendments) which touch on, but do not entirely resolve, these problems.

BIBLIOGRAPHY

BIBLIOGRAPHY

Allen, C. K. *Law in the Making*. 6th ed. Oxford: Clarendon Press, 1961.
Allott, Antony N., ed. *The Future of Law in Africa*. London: Butterworth, 1960.
Anderson, J. N. D. "Colonial Law in Tropical Africa: The Conflict between English, Islamic and Customary Law," *Indian Law Journal*, XXXV, no. 4 (1960).
———. "Customary Law and Islamic Law in British African Territories," in *The Future of Customary Law in Africa*. Leiden: Afrika Institut, 1955.
———. *Islamic Law in Africa*. London: H.M.S.O., 1954.
———. "Islamic Law in Africa: Problems of Today and Tomorrow," in *Changing Law in Developing Countries*. Pp. 164-183. London: Allen & Unwin, 1963.
———. "The Modernization of Islamic Law in the Sudan," *Sudan Law Journal and Reports* (1960), pp. 292-312.
———. "Recent Developments in Sharī'a Law in the Sudan," *Sudan Notes and Records*, Part I (1950).
———. "The Religious Element in Waqf Endowments," *Journal of Royal Central Asian Society* (July, 1951).
———. "The Sharī'a and Civil Law: The Debt Owed by the New Civil Codes of Egypt and Syria to the Sharī'a," *Islamic Quarterly*, I, no. 1 (1954).
———. "Wakfs in East Africa," *Journal of African Law*, III, no. 3 (1959), 152-164.
Ardener, E. W. "Lineage and Locality among the Mba-Ise Ibo," *Africa*, XXIX (1959), 113-133.
Barker, Sir Ernest. Introduction to Otto Gierke, *Natural Law and the Theory of Society*. Boston: Beacon Press, 1960.
———. Introduction to *Social Contract: Essays by Locke, Hume and Rousseau*. London: Oxford University Press, 1947.
Barton, R. F. *Ifugao Law*. Berkeley: University of California Press, 1919.
———. *The Kalingas*. Ed. E. Adamson Hoebel. Chicago: University of Chicago Press, 1948.
Basden, G. T. *Among the Ibos of Nigeria*. Philadelphia: Lippincott, 1921.
Behrmann, Paul. "The Native Appeal Courts," *South African Law Journal*, LXV (1948), 413-418.
Bierstedt, Robert. *The Making of Society*. New York: Modern Library, 1959.
Bohannan, Paul. "Extra-Processual Events in Tiv Political Institutions," in *Cultures and Societies of Africa*. Ed. Simon and Phoebe Ottenberg. New York: Random House, 1960.
———. *Justice and Judgment among the Tiv*. London: Oxford University Press, 1957.

———. *Social Anthropology*. New York: Holt, Rinehart & Winston, 1963.
Cardozo, B. N. *The Growth of the Law*. New Haven: Yale University Press, 1924.
Chubb, L. T. *Ibo Land Tenure*. 2d ed. Ibadan: Ibadan University Press, 1961.
Cole, C. W. *Land Tenure in Zaria Province*. Kaduna, 1948.
Colson, Elizabeth. "Social Control and Vengeance," in *The Plateau Tonga of Northern Rhodesia*. Manchester: Manchester University Press, 1962.
Cotran, Eugene. *Report on Customary Criminal Offences in Kenya*. Nairobi, 1963.
Coulson, N. J. "Moslem Custom and Case Law," *World of Islam*, VI, nos. 1-2 (1959), 13-24.
Crowder, Michael. *Senegal*. London: Oxford University Press, 1962.
Delavignette, Robert. *Freedom and Authority in French West Africa*. London: Oxford University Press, 1950. Trans. of *Service Africain*. Paris: Gallimard, 1946.
Diamond, A. S. *The Evolution of Law and Order*. London: Watts, 1951.
———. *Primitive Law*. London: Watts, 1935.
Durkheim, Emile. *The Division of Labour in Society* (1893). Trans. G. Simpson. Glencoe, Ill.: Free Press, 1947.
———. *Professional Ethics and Civil Morals*. Trans. C. Brookfield. Glencoe, Ill.: Free Press, 1958.
———. *Socialism and Saint-Simon*. Trans. Charlotte Sattler. Yellow Springs, Ohio: Antioch Press, 1958.
Elias, T. O. *British Colonial Law*. London: Stevens, 1961.
———. *Ghana and Sierra Leone: Development of Their Laws and Constitutions*. London: Stevens, 1962.
———. *Government and Politics in Africa*. New York: Asia Publishing House, 1961.
———. *Groundwork of Nigerian Law*. London: Routledge & Kegan Paul, 1954. Republished as *Nigerian Legal Systems*. 2d ed. London: Routledge & Kegan Paul, 1963.
———. *The Nature of African Customary Law*. Manchester: Manchester University Press, 1956.
Epstein, A. L. *Judicial Techniques and the Judicial Process*. Manchester: Manchester University Press, 1954.
Evans-Pritchard, E. E. *The Nuer*. Oxford: Clarendon Press, 1940.
Eybers, G. W. *Select Constitutional Documents*. London: Routledge & Kegan Paul, 1918.
Forde, Daryll, and G. I. Jones. *The Ibo and Ibibio-speaking Peoples of South-eastern Nigeria*. Ethnographic Survey of Africa. London: International African Institute, 1950.
Forrest, G. W. *Selections from the State Papers of the Governors-General of India*. Vol. II. London: Constable, 1910.
Fortes, Meyer. *The Dynamics of Clanship among the Tallensi*. London: Oxford University Press, 1945.
Fortes, Meyer, and E. E. Evans-Pritchard. *African Political Systems*. London: Oxford University Press, 1947.
Gierke, Otto. *Natural Law and the Theory of Society*. Boston: Beacon Press, 1960.
Ginsberg, Morris. "The Concept of Law," *British Journal of Sociology*, XIII (March, 1962), 64-69.
Gluckman, Max. "African Jurisprudence," *Advancement of Science*, XVIII (Jan., 1962), 439-454.

———. "Comment: The Role of the Barotse King in the Judicial Process," *Stanford Law Review*, XIV (Dec., 1961), 110-119.
———. *Custom and Conflict in Africa.* Oxford: Blackwell, 1955.
———. *The Ideas in Barotse Jurisprudence.* New Haven: Yale University Press, 1965.
———. *The Judicial Process among the Barotse of Northern Rhodesia.* Manchester: Manchester University Press, 1955.
———. "Kinship and Marriage among the Lozi of Northern Rhodesia and the Zulu of Natal," in *African Systems of Kinship and Marriage.* Ed. A. R. Radcliffe-Brown and Daryll Forde. London: Oxford University Press, 1950.
———. "The Lozi of Barotseland," in *Seven Tribes of British Central Africa.* Ed. Elizabeth Colson and Max Gluckman. Manchester: Manchester University Press, 1959.
———. *Politics, Law, and Ritual in Tribal Society.* New York: Mentor Library, 1965.
———. "Les Rites de Passage," in *Essays on the Ritual of Social Relations.* Ed. Max Gluckman. Manchester: Manchester University Press, 1962.
Gravel, Pierre. "The Play for Power." Unpublished Ph.D. dissertation in anthropology. University of Michigan, 1962.
Green, M. M. *Ibo Village Affairs.* London: Sidgwick & Jackson, 1948.
Gulliver, P. H. *Social Control in an African Society: The Arusha, Agricultural Masai of Northern Tanganyika.* Boston: Boston University Press, 1963.
Gurvitch, Georges. *Sociology of Law.* London: K. Paul, Trench, Trubner, 1947.
Hailey, Lord Malcolm. *An African Survey.* London: Oxford University Press, 1938.
Hanbury, H. G. *English Courts of Law.* London: Oxford University Press, 1944.
Hart, H. L. A. *The Concept of Law.* Oxford: Clarendon Press, 1961.
Hartland, Sidney. *Primitive Law.* London: Methuen, 1924.
Hiskett, M. "*Kitāb al-farq*: A Work on the Habe Kingdoms Attributed to 'Uthmān dan Fodio," *Bulletin of the School of Oriental and African Studies*, XXIII (1960), 558-579.
Hoebel, E. Adamson. *The Law of Primitive Man.* Cambridge: Harvard University Press, 1954.
———. "Letter to Editor," *American Anthropologist*, LXIV, no. 4 (1962).
———. *Political Organization and Law Ways of the Comanche Indians.* Menasha, Wis.: American Anthropological Association, 1940.
———. "Three Studies in African Law," *Stanford Law Review*, XII (March, 1961), 418-442.
Hogbin, H. I. *Law and Order in Polynesia.* New York: Harcourt Brace, 1934.
Howell, Paul. *Manual of Nuer Law.* London: Oxford University Press, 1954.
Jones, G. I. "Dual Organization in Ibo Social Structure," *Africa*, XIX (1949), 150-156.
———. *Report on the Position, Status and Influence of Chiefs and Natural Rulers of the Eastern Region of Nigeria.* Enugu: Government Printer, 1947.
Kerr, A. J. "The Application of Native Law in the Supreme Court," *South African Law Journal*, LXXV (1957), 313-330.
Kroeber, Alfred L. *Handbook of the Indians of California.* Bureau of American Ethnology. Bulletin 78. 1925.
Kuper, Leo. "Some Aspects of Urban Plural Societies in Africa," in *The African*

World: A Survey of Social Research. Ed. R. Lystad. New York: Praeger, 1965.
Lammens, H. *L'Islam: croyances et institutions.* Beyrouth, 1926.
Levy, Reuben. *The Social Structure of Islam.* Cambridge: The University Press, 1957.
Lewin, Julius. *Studies in African Native Law.* Cape Town: African Bookman, 1947.
Llewellyn, K. N., and E. Adamson Hoebel. *The Cheyenne Way.* Norman: University of Oklahoma Press, 1941.
Lowie, R. H. *Primitive Society.* New York: Liveright, 1947.
MacIver, R. M. *The Modern State.* Oxford: Clarendon Press, 1926.
Maine, Sir Henry. *Ancient Law.* New ed. London: J. Murray, 1905. Also Everyman ed. New York: Dutton, 1917.
———. *Lectures on the Early History of Institutions.* London: J. Murray, 1875.
Malinowski, Bronislaw. *Crime and Custom in Savage Society.* London: Routledge & Kegan Paul, 1926.
Marais, J. S. "The Imposition and Nature of European Control," in *The Bantu-speaking Tribes of South Africa.* Ed. I. Schapera. London: Routledge & Kegan Paul, 1946.
Marsh, J. G. "Sociological Jurisprudence Revisited: A Review (More or Less) of Max Gluckman," *Stanford Law Review,* III (May, 1956), 499-534.
Marshall, Lorna. "Kung Bushmen Bands," *Africa,* XXX (1960), 225-355.
———. "Sharing, Talking, and Giving: Relief of Social Tensions among Kung Bushmen," *Africa,* XXXI (1961), 231-249.
Mayer, Philip. "Agricultural Cooperation by Neighbourhood Groups among the Gusii," in *Two Studies in Applied Anthropology in Kenya.* London: H.M.S.O., 1951.
———. "Bridewealth Limitation among the Gusii," in *Two Studies in Applied Anthropology in Kenya.* London: H.M.S.O., 1951.
———. *Gusii Bridewealth Law and Custom.* Rhodes-Livingstone Papers, no. 18. London: Oxford University Press, 1950.
———. *The Lineage Principle in Gusii Society.* International African Institute, Memorandum XXIV. London: Oxford University Press, 1949.
Meek, C. K. "Ibo Law," in *Essays Presented to C. G. Seligman.* Ed. by E. E. Evans-Pritchard *et al.* London: K. Paul, Trench, Trubner, 1934.
———. *Law and Authority in a Nigerian Tribe (Ibo).* London: Oxford University Press, 1937.
Meggitt, M. J. *Desert People.* Sydney: Angus & Robertson, 1962.
Middleton, J., and D. Tait, eds. *Tribes without Rulers.* London: Routledge & Kegan Paul, 1958.
Moreira, Adriano. "General Report, Ethnic and Cultural Pluralism in the Inter-Tropical Societies: Legal and Political Aspects," in *Record of the XXXth Meeting,* International Institute of Differing Civilizations. Brussels, 1957.
Morgan, L. S. *Ancient Society* (1877). London: Routledge & Kegan Paul, 1959.
Nadel, S. F. *Foundations of Social Anthropology.* London: Cohen & West, 1949.
———. *The Nuba.* London: Oxford University Press, 1947.
———. "Reason and Unreason in African Law," *Africa,* XXVI (April, 1956), 160-173.
Peristiany, J. G. "Pokot Sanctions and Structure," *Africa,* XXIV (Jan., 1954), 17-25.
Peters, Richard. *Hobbes.* London: Pelican Books, 1956.

Phillips, Arthur. "The Legal Factor in a Changing Africa," *African Affairs,* LIV (1955).
———. *Report on Native Tribunals, Colony and Protectorate of Kenya.* Nairobi: Government Printer, 1945.
Pound, Roscoe. *Jurisprudence.* Vol. I. St. Paul, Minn.: West Publishing Co., 1959.
———. *Readings on the History and System of the Common Law.* 2d ed. Boston: Boston Book Co., 1913.
Radcliffe-Brown, A. R. "Primitive Law," *Encyclopedia of the Social Sciences,* IX, 202-206.
———. "Social Sanction," *Encyclopedia of the Social Sciences,* XIII, 531-534.
———. *Structure and Function.* Glencoe, Ill.: Free Press, 1952.
———. *Structure and Function in Primitive Society.* London: Cohen & West, 1952.
Report of Kenya Land Commission, September 1933. London: H.M.S.O., 1934.
Rheinstein, Max, ed. *Max Weber on Law in Economy and Society.* Cambridge: Harvard University Press, 1954.
Richards, Audrey I., ed. *East African Chiefs.* London: Faber & Faber, 1960.
Rubin, Leslie. *The Law of Costs in South Africa.* Johannesburg: Juta, 1949.
Rubin, Neville. "South Africa: Transkei Constitution Act," *Journal of African Law,* VII, no. 3 (1963), 183-187.
Salmond, John. *Jurisprudence.* 10th ed. London: Sweet and Maxwell, 1947.
Sarbah, J. M. *Fanti National Constitution.* 1906.
Schacht, Joseph. *Law in the Middle East.* Washington, 1955.
———. *The Origins of Muhammadan Jurisprudence.* Oxford: Clarendon Press, 1950.
———. *20 Der Islam.* 1932.
Seymour, Semour Massingham. *Native Law in South Africa.* 2d ed. Cape Town: Juta, 1960.
Simons, H. J. "Customary Unions in a Changing Society," *Acta Juridica* (1958), pp. 320-341.
———. "The Law and Its Administration," in *Handbook of Race Relations in South Africa.* Ed. Ellen Hellmann. Cape Town: Oxford University Press, 1949.
———. "Marriage and Succession among Africans," *Acta Juridica* (1960), pp. 312-333.
Smith, M. G. "Ethnic and Cultural Pluralism in the British Caribbean," in *Record of the XXXth Meeting,* International Institute of Differing Civilizations. Brussels, 1957.
———. "Social and Cultural Pluralism," *Annals of the New York Academy of Sciences,* LXXXIII (Jan., 1960), 763-777.
Smith, W. Robertson. *Kinship and Marriage in Early Arabia.* Cambridge: The University Press, 1885.
Southwold, Martin. *Bureaucracy and Chiefship in Buganda.* East African Studies no. 14. Kampala: East African Institute of Social Research, [*ca.* 1960].
Stafford, W. G., and E. Franklin. *Principles of Native Law and the Natal Code.* Pietermaritzburg, 1950.
Swanepoel, D. J. "Oor die Resepsie van die Romeins-Hollandse Reg in Suid-Afrika," *Acta Juridica* (1958), pp. 7-26.
Ter Haar, B. *Adat Law in Indonesia.* Ed. with introduction by E. Adamson Hoebel and A. Arthur Schiller. New York: Institute of Pacific Relations, 1948.
Theal, George McCall. "The Report of Commissioners Bigge and Colebrooke,

September 6, 1826," *Records of the Cape Colony from February 1793 to April 1831*. Vols. XVII-XVIII.

Trimingham, J. Spencer. *Islam in West Africa*. Oxford: Clarendon Press, 1959.

Vansina, Jan. "Trade and Markets among the Kuba," in *Markets in Africa*. Ed. Paul Bohannan and George Dalton. Evanston: Northwestern University Press, 1962.

Vinogradoff, Sir Paul. *Common Sense in Law*. London: Oxford University Press, 1913.

Von Grunebaum, G. E. *Medieval Islam*. 2d ed. Chicago: University of Chicago Press, 1953.

Walker, Eric A. *History of South Africa*. 3d ed. London: Longmans, Green, 1957.

Weber, Max. *The City*. Trans. and ed. Don Martindale and Gertrud Neuwirth. London: Heinemann, 1960.

Wessels, Johannes Wilhelmus. *History of Roman-Dutch Law*. Grahamstown: African Book Co., 1908.

INDEX

INDEX